Aesthetics of Music

VOLUME 9

Books by David Whitwell

- The Sousa Oral History Project
- The Art of Musical Conducting
- Psychological Problems in Conducting
- The Longy Club: 1900–1917
- La Téléphonie and the Universal Musical Language
- Extraordinary Women
- A Concise History of the Wind Band
- Essays on the Modern Wind Band
- Essays on Performance Practice
- A New History of Wind Music
- The College and University Band
- The Early Symphonies of Mozart
- Band Music of the French Revolution
- Stories from the Podium

On Composers

- Wagner on Bands
- Berlioz on Bands
- Chopin: A Self-Portrait
- Liszt: A Self-Portrait
- Schumann: A Self-Portrait in His Own Words
- Mendelssohn: A Self-Portrait in His Own Words

On Education

- Philosophic Foundations of Education
- Foundations of Music Education
- Music Education of the Future

Aesthetics of Music

- Aesthetics of Music in Ancient Civilizations
- Aesthetics of Music in the Middle Ages
- Aesthetics of Music in the Early Renaissance
- Aesthetics of Music in Sixteenth-Century Italy, France and Spain
- Aesthetics of Music in Sixteenth-Century Germany, the Low Countries and England
- Aesthetics of Baroque Music in Italy, Spain, the German-Speaking Countries and the Low Countries
- Aesthetics of Baroque Music in France
- Aesthetics of Baroque Music in England

The History and Literature of the Wind Band and Wind Ensemble Series

- Volume 1 The Wind Band and Wind Ensemble Before 1500
- Volume 2 The Renaissance Wind Band and Wind Ensemble
- Volume 3 The Baroque Wind Band and Wind Ensemble
- Volume 4 The Wind Band and Wind Ensemble of the Classical Period (1750–1800)
- Volume 5 The Nineteenth-Century Wind Band and Wind Ensemble
- Volume 6 A Catalog of Multi-Part Repertoire for Wind Instruments or for Undesignated Instrumentation before 1600
- Volume 7 Baroque Wind Band and Wind Ensemble Repertoire
- Volume 8 Classical Period Wind Band and Wind Ensemble Repertoire
- Volume 9 Nineteenth-Century Wind Band and Wind Ensemble Repertoire
- Volume 10 A Supplementary Catalog of Wind Band and Wind Ensemble Repertoire
- Volume 11 A Catalog of Wind Repertoire before the Twentieth Century for One to Five Players
- Volume 12 A Second Supplementary Catalog of Early Wind Band and Wind Ensemble Repertoire
- Volume 13 Name Index, Volumes 1–12, The History and Literature of the Wind Band and Wind Ensemble

Ancient Voices

- Ancient Views on Music and Religion
- Ancient Views on the Natural World
- Ancient Views on What Is Music
- Contemporary Descriptions of Early Musicians
- Early Views of Music and Ethics
- Early Thoughts on Performance Practice
- Music Performance in Ancient Societies

Renaissance Voices

- Essays on Renaissance Philosophies of Music
- Renaissance Men on Music

Baroque Music

- Essays on Italian and Spanish Music of the Baroque
- Essays on Music of the French Baroque
- Essays on Music of the German Baroque
- Philosophy and Performance Practice of Music during Jacobean England
- Music during the English Restoration: Philosophy and Performance Practice

www.whitwellbooks.com

David Whitwell

Aesthetics of Music

VOLUME 9
ANNOTATED INDEX, VOLUMES 1–8

EDITED BY CRAIG DABELSTEIN

WHITWELL PUBLISHING • AUSTIN, TEXAS, USA

Whitwell Publishing, Austin 78701
www.whitwellbooks.com

Printed in the United States of America

Paperback
ISBN-13: 978-1-936512-88-1
ISBN-10: 1-936512-88-2

Composed in Minion Pro

CONTENTS

	Foreword	ix
	Acknowledgements	xiii
1	*Aaron to Avison*	1
2	*Baberini to Byrd*	23
3	*Cabestanh to Czepko*	31
4	*Dalla Casa to Dynamics*	43
5	*Ea to Eyselin*	49
6	*Faidit to Fux*	57
7	*Gabrieli to Gwynn*	61
8	*Hades to Hypodorian*	69
9	*Iamblichus to Ivanovich*	73
10	*Jacopo to Juvenal*	75
11	*Karl II to Kytson*	79
12	*La Barre to Lysippas*	81
13	*Maarten to Myron*	87
14	*Nagel to Nymphs*	99
15	*Obrecht to Ovid*	103
16	*Paculla to Pythodlides*	105
17	*Quadrivium to Quirini*	115
18	*Rabanus to Rymer*	117
19	*Sacadas toi Symposium*	121
20	*Tacitus to Tyrrhenian*	129
21	*Uberti to Utrecht*	137
22	*Vulckenborch to Vondel*	139
23	*Wace to Wycherley*	143
24	*Xenacles to Zwingli*	145
	About the Author	147
	About the Editor	149

FOREWORD

WE DEFINE MUSIC to be that form of music performed live before listeners. We define Aesthetics in Music to be a study of the nature of the perception of music by the listener.

We believe the performance of music in actual practice falls naturally into four classes. These are Art Music, Educational Music, Functional Music and Entertainment Music.

I. ART MUSIC

Art Music we believe is defined by four conditions, *all* of which *must always be present*. These are:

1. *Art music is inspired.* Art music is music in which it seems evident that the composer has made an honest attempt to communicate genuine feelings. Feelings, which may range from lofty and noble to superficial and vulgar, must be presumed to be generally recognizable in music, as they are in any other art form, including painting, sculpture, dance, and architecture. In Art Music, lofty and noble feelings are paramount.

    Due to the common genetically understood nature of emotions, it must also be understood that in music emotions or feelings cannot be 'faked.' They will always be recognized as such by any contemplative listener.

2. *Art Music has no purpose other than the communication of its own aesthetic content.* Art Music is free of any purpose or function, save the spiritual communication of pure beauty.

3. *Art Music is that which enjoys a performance faithful to the intent of the composer.*

4. *Art Music must have a listener capable of contemplation.*

If any of these conditions are missing, the performance must result in a lesser aesthetic experience. For example, the *Ninth Symphony* of Beethoven played in a stadium, during the half-time of a professional football game, would fail for the lack of the presence

of Condition Number Four. The same Symphony heard in a concert hall, but in a poor performance, not faithful to the intent of the composer, would fail for the lack of the presence of Condition Number Three.

II. Educational Music

Educational Music may or may not have the same conditions as Art Music, excepting Condition Number Two; it may or may not occur within an educational institution. Educational Music is didactic music, music which has the specific and *additional* aim to educate. In the strictest sense, if the *primary purpose* of Music is to educate, it cannot be Art Music—for Art Music has no purpose.

III. Functional Music

Functional Music is music put at the service of something else. We include here, for example, all kinds of religious music, music for weddings, music for the military, and occupational music. Functional Music may share the same conditions as Art Music, excepting Condition Number Two.

One may ask, How can a Mozart Mass be called Functional Music, and not Art Music? If the observer were not contemplatively listening to the music, but were rather contemplating religious thoughts, then the Mozart Mass becomes merely a very high level of Functional Music. If, on the other hand, the observer is a contemplative listener of music, forgetting about religion, then the Mozart Mass is Art Music, but has failed in its purpose as church music.

Military and wedding music are examples of music in which the contemplative listener is missing entirely. How about airport, supermarket and elevator music where there is no listener at all? According to the definition we have given above, recorded music without listeners is not to be considered music at all.

IV. ENTERTAINMENT MUSIC

Entertainment Music is music with no object other than to please. It will always be missing Condition Four, the contemplative listener. For this reason, Entertainment Music may be inspired music, but the composer is unlikely to be inspired by lofty and noble emotions, knowing there will be no contemplative listener. Entertainment Music and Art Music can never be the same thing because of Condition Number Two: Art Music has no purpose other than the communication of its own aesthetic content. It is inconsistent with the nature of great art to have any extrinsic purpose, including the purpose to entertain.

The first philosopher to address the impact which Art has on an observer was Aristotle, in his *Poetics*, as part of a discussion of Tragedy, which like music has both a material, written form and a live performance form. In this treatise, Aristotle first considers the nature and contribution of each of the specific components of the written form of the Tragedy in his typically methodical style. His great contribution, however, comes when he has completed this discussion, for he then goes beyond the material form of the play itself to discuss the observer. He makes it clear that not only is the end purpose of the elements of the play to produce a specific experience in the observer, but that the nature of this experience is what distinguishes Tragedy from other dramatic forms, such as Spectacle. It was in this moment that he created a new branch of Philosophy which we call 'Aesthetics.'

Our purpose is to provide source books of representative descriptions of actual performances, observations by philosophers, poets and other commentators which contribute insights to our understanding of what music meant to listeners during the early Renaissance. It is for this reason that when discussing contemporary treatises on music that we concentrate on those passages which offer insights relative to the aesthetics of music and musical performance rather than the usual technical subjects such as scales, modes and counterpoint which fill most books on Renaissance music.

Since traditional musicology has focused almost exclusively on sacred and secular vocal music of the Renaissance, we have also included numerous references which we hope will reveal a much wider world of music during this period.

We are also interested in contemporary views on the physiology of knowing, especially with regard to the relationship of the senses and Reason, and related psychological ideas, such as Pleasure and Pain and the Emotions, which might offer a frame of reference for their perspective on the perception of music.

This final volume is an index of the earlier eight volumes which discuss the music of the ancient civilizations through the Baroque Period.

David Whitwell
Austin, Texas

ACKNOWLEDGMENTS

This new edition would not have been possible without the encouragement and help of Craig Dabelstein. His experience as a musician and educator himself has contributed greatly to his expertise as editor of this volume.

David Whitwell
Austin, 2016

Aesthetics of Music Series

by

David Whitwell

Annotated Index for Eight Volumes

I. Aesthetics of Music in Ancient Civilizations

II. Aesthetics of Music in the Middle Ages

III. Aesthetics of Music in the Early Renaissance

IV. Aesthetics of Music in Sixteenth-Century Italy, France and Spain

V. Aesthetics of Music in Sixteenth-Century Germany, the Low Countries and England

VI. Aesthetics of Baroque Music in Italy, Spain, the German-Speaking Countries and the Low Countries

VII. Aesthetics of Baroque Music in France

VIII. Aesthetics of Baroque Music in England

Aaron, Old Testament person, **I:** 92

Abbatini, Antonio, 1595–1679, Italian poet, **VI:** 78ff

Abblasen (tower music), **V:** 141ff, sixteenth century Germany, Leipzig, Lübeck, Zürich; **VI:** 137ff; praise by Kuhnau; 138, poem in praise of by Jacob Lottich (1679)

Abyngdon, the Singer, V: 277, poem on his death by Sir Thomas More

Academies, IV: 199ff, the *Pléiade* in sixteenth century Paris, a group of humanist poets led by Pierre de Ronsard with members Jean Dorat, Ronsard, Du Bellay, Baïf, Belleau, Tyard and Jodelle, with sung poetry as their primary vehicle; 202ff Baïf's Academy; 205, the Palace Academy, centered more in philosophy than music; **VI:** 8, seventeenth century academies of Bologna and Rome; 22, closely related were the religious fraternities in Venice, one performance by the *Scuole San Rocco* is reported by the visitor Thomas Coryat; 23ff, also the *ospedali,* charitable instutions for orphans which featured the study of music, one of which in Venice employed Vivaldi; 25, reports of visitors hearing concerts by these young ladies include K. L. von Poellnitz and Charles de Brosses; 78, autobiographical of an seventeenth century one by Abbatini; **VII:** 8ff, Louis XIV creates a royal academy of music after the Italian model; 10ff, the *Académie Française* and formal French academies of all the arts founded in the seventeenth century; 78, on the Baïf Academy in Paris; 83, the French academies

Acoustics, I: 316; **VIII:** 21, Avison: placement of is important; 48, North: listener distance is important; 233, Locke, one of the first philosophers to correctly understand the physics of sound; education, **VIII:** 233, Locke believed in a severe experience in all aspects. For example, if you can not stop children crying by command, "then blows must!"

Adam von Fulda, sixteenth century composer, **V:** 143, leads Mass with instruments in 1500

Adam, first man, **III:** 269; **VIII:** 149

Addison, Joseph, 1672–1719, Restoration poet, journalist and Secretary of State, **VI:** 11, visits Venice in 1701; **VIII:** 10; 354ff; 355, a poem set to music by Daniel Purcell; 360; 364; 371; 445, with Steele created the *Spectator* in 1711; 446; 447; 450; 451

Adelinda, female jongleur, eleventh century, **II:** 237

Adjudicators, I: 239ff, 319, Plutarch: men trained only in details of music may not be capable of judging music.

Adolphus, Gustavus of Sweden, VI: 6, father to Christina of Sweden; 121

Adomnan, seventh century Church writer, **II:** 210, on hymns

Adonis, I: 300, in a dirge by Bion

Adrian VI, Pope, **V:** 8, 1522 letter to Erasmus against Luther; 11, 1522 letter by Erasmus describes the pope as "a scholastic, not wholly well disposed to the humanities."; 39

Aelianus, Claudius, 175–235 AD, Greek writer on animals living in Rome, **I:** 345, fn., 16

Aeolian, a Greek mode, **I:** 104

Aeolians, I: 147

Aeschines, 389–314 BC, Greek statesman and orator, **I:** 397, reference by Cicero on the musical qualities of the orator.

Aeschylus, 525–456 BC, Greek playwright, **I:** 105; 169ff; 175ff; 185; 188; 189, "one of the greatest musicians of history"; 343; **II:** 12

Aesculalpius, mythical son of Apollo, **V:** 16

Aesop, 620–560 BC, fable writer, **I:** 142; 169

Aesthetics, I: 204, Plato, major discussion; 218; 228, Plato; 214, Plato, quality of performance in decay; 249, Aristotle; 259, Aristotle; 260, Plutarch; 273ff, Pherecrates, fifth century BC decay of music and decay of music culture in 323–146 BC; 286, Arcesilaus, Epicurus, Diogenes, Zeno, Pyrrho; 314, Roman period of ancient Greece; 316, decay in practice of modes; 317, fn., 30, Strabo: gods prefer panpipe and aulos to voices; 318, Athenaeus on philosophic reflection and educational purpose; 318, Eupolis: music is deep and intricate; 320, last period of Greek music being made by slaves; 320, on performance; 324ff, Plutarch on the decay in music education; 345, musicians in social order of early Roman society; 354, Cicero on the decline of music; 385, Cicero on Imitation; 388; 396, Roscius: the chief thing is taste, which cannot be taught; 392ff, major Cicero aesthetics and music discussion; 402ff, Horace on; 423, fn., 6, Horace on Roman vs Greek lyric poetry; 487, Roman Imperial Period; 499, fn., 8, costs of actor vs eunuch in Roman Imperial Period; **II:** 4, Honestus on the first century decay of lyre music, has become entertainment music; 21, only experts can judge art, Sextus Empiricus, Anacharsis; 29ff, Sextus Empiricus against contemporary music; 43, as reflected in *Daphnis and Chloe*; 73ff, church's hostility toward Art; 74, on the divine connection: St. Justin Martyr, Origen, Clement of Alexandria; 75ff; 81, distinct and indistinct sounds; 83, sounds without meaning; 87, Dark Ages decay; 101ff, Truth; music cannot be seen; 109, 110, decay of music; 110, Julian: music invented for pleasure; 111, Martianus Capella: purpose of music is to delight the mind; 127, fourth and fifth centuries: a Christian cannot love Art; 127, fourth and fifth centuries: Art must follow Nature; 128, St. Ambrose: nothing remains when music stops, aesthetics; 149ff, St. Augustine, art is in the mind, not the object; 155, St. Augustine on music; 156, St. Augustine classifies music as a form of communication, not an art; 157ff, St. Augustine, Reason not senses; 166ff, St. Augustine's book *On Music*; 170, St. Augustine: value of music, "to see God"; 175ff, sixth to eighth centuries; 186ff, on aesthetics in sixth to eighth centuries; 188, Alcuin; 189ff, the famous letter of Cassiodorus to Boethius; 194, on decline, sixth to eighth centuries; 219, Boethius on the decay of music; 221, Isidore of Seville: when music stops it is gone; 229, ninth-eleventh centuries, Dark Ages begin to end; 241ff, ninth - eleventh centuries; 248ff, *Musica Disciplina,* first treatise after the Dark Ages to argue for the power and importance of music; music unites Reason and body, rational and irrational; unless imprinted in the memory music is not retained; "There is as much difference between a musician and a singer as there is between a grammarian and a mere reader";

aesthetic qualities in 15 different kinds of voices [based on Isidore of Seville]; still emphasizes relationship of music and mathematics; on music and emotions; 253, Hucbald believed reading music was the key to "the inner regions of this discipline"; 254, Al-Farabi the science of practical music and the science of theoretical music; 257, Guido, if a singer cannot sing at sight he is neither a musician nor a singer; Guido will omit those things which cannot be understood; 260, Guido: taste must rule; 261ff, c. 1100 AD, ability to judge music is most important, not performance; knowledge distinguishes a musician from a mere singer [the latter is a beast]; problems in changes in the modes; correspondence of singers personality and sharp or flat; relationship of modes and character; 271, twelfth and thirteenth centuries, the Pre-Renaissance and the beginning of Humanism; universities founded; 295, Roger Bacon on two kinds of music: that which you can hear and that which you can see (dance); 303, general observations by Grosseteste and Duns Scotus; 306, Anglicus, "to bring joy" and for music therapy and madness; 310, the important contributions of Bacon on the nature of music and grammar, ie "accent" comes from "accino," "I sing;" 311ff, aesthetics of music in twelfth and thirteen century philosophers; 319ff; 322, Bernard of Clairvaux: emphasis is on the artist, not what he does; 323, aesthetics of music, twelfth and thirteenth centuries: no making changes in the music, no improvisation (by chance and not Reason), no dancing in cemeteries, only the organ allowed (except for papal processions), problems with the jongleurs (Abelard: the aulos is for the delectation of the sense, not for the understanding of the mind), Old testament metaphors (but Hildegard accepts as face value), ensemble precision as an analogy for government, prejudice tied to how an instrument is held; 345, major discussion by Thomas Acquinas: artist must have knowledge and technique, questions the importance of church music, vocal music must be accepted because Jesus, in one report, sang [Matthew 26:30]; 360, purpose of music in late medieval French literature; 357ff philosophy of aesthetics as described in the twelfth and thirteenth century French Romances, here the *Romance of the Rose,* Reason vs love; 382ff, on the purpose and process of composition among the troubadours; 401ff, in Italian literature in the twelfth and thirteenth centuries; 409ff, in German literature in the twelfth and thirteenth centuries; 417ff, Minnesinger art song; 409ff, in German literature in the twelfth and thirteenth centuries; 417ff, Minnesinger art songs; 436, Grocheo, in 1300, on why music is important; 437, Grocheo: performance is more important than the numbers; **III:** 8, Marchetto of Padua: Music surpasses the other arts in Beauty; 8ff, aesthetics of music, organization by harmonic, organic (breath, but not vocal) and rhythmic, altered tones: *chroma* is from color in Greek; 27ff, Petrarch on universality, imitation vs originality, the public, on the other arts; 32ff, on the aesthetics of Music, purposes and virtues of Music; 52ff, Boccaccio on treating character, Beauty and Nature; 54ff, on poetry; 57, on the purposes of music; 80, Machaut, purposes of music, importance of feeling in music, feeling is inseparable from inspiration; 87ff, Jacques de Liège, author of *Speculum Musicae* of 1313 (*ars antiqua*); 117, Rolle; 117ff, fourteenth century English philosophers, purposes

of music; 138ff, Chaucer, poor state of philosophy; 143ff, Chaucer, art or craft?; 146 Chaucer: music is something beyond the sound; 169ff, fifteenth century Italy, Alberti: art combines man and body; 170 Valgulio, on the importance of music; 170, Cortese: one of the virtues of music is that, unlike the other arts, the technique is hidden from the listener; 171, Gaffurio: we like things well put together; 171, Valla on the aesthetic qualities of individual tones; Valgulio: music in decay; 187, Gaffurio on the ethical potential of music and Poliziano finds same purpose in solo singing in ancient Greece; 198ff, Leonardo da Vinci, on Beauty; 199, Art is found in the mind, not in the hands; 202, on painting; 204, on painting vs poetry; 206, on painting vs sculpture; 207ff, on the aesthetics of music; music disappears; 217ff, in fifteenth century France the environment of war reduced philosophic thought; aesthetics of music; 218, polyphony beginning to disappear, new respect for the artist; Jean de Gerson with subjective descriptions of instrument sounds; 240, Tinctoris believed the emotional aspect of performance had more to do with the emotional makeup of the listener; 264ff, Nicholas of Cusa: Art is in the artist, not the object and God made the artist; 265, Art is in the soul first; 265, on Beauty, only in the eye; 266, on the purpose of art—humanity; 268ff, aesthetics of music: Nicholas understands that the purpose of music is to express feelings; 269, but error: you cannot know music but by conceptual data, which distinguishes man from beast; 270, art is merely a craft; 271, Nicholas: but the enjoyment of music is due to the senses; 271, Brant on the social rank of various instruments; 294ff, fourteen and fifteenth century Spain; purpose of music; 297ff, aesthetic descriptions of instruments; 314ff, on beauty, Nature; 315ff, aesthetics of Music; purposes of music; **IV:** 13ff; 14, Bruno worship of Art is almost a sin; Art is in the object, credit goes to Nature; 15ff, on Beauty; 17ff, on imitation, art vs nature; 20, born or learned?; 20, role of genetics; 23, opposed to public who know nothing; 24, aesthetics of music, 24, Girolamo Mei on moving away from the old Scholastic toward an art of feeling; 25, theory vs practice; away from mathematics; 26, purpose is not entertainment; catharsis; 27, Bruno, in music art is in the player, not the instrument; 33, decay of polyphony; 51, on sixteenth century moving from mathematics to feeling; 65, Vicenzo Giustiniani in his book of 1623 considered Arcadelt, Orlando Lassus, Striggio, Cipriano de Rore and Filippo di Monte the best composers of the 16th century, with Palestrina, Soriano and Giovanni Maria Nanino composing church music with good melody and decent ornamentation; 68ff, sixteenth century Italians, increased tuning problems; 70ff, quality of singing and improvisation; 73, Galilei, on instrumental performance, including avoiding repeated notes; 74, Galilei on aesthetic goals of improvisation, purely aesthetic goals, Beauty, grace and delight of the ear, not instilling moral virtues; 79, decline of music in the Italian courts in France and Flanders; 94ff, sixteenth century Italian poets; 110ff, Giraldi on the definition of art in poetry; 113, Tasso on the definition of poetry [and music]; 129, Scaliger, Julius, 1484–1558, in his *Poetics* (1561) adds to Aristotle's purpose of Tragedy, that it must also be educational; compares Minturno vs Machiavelli in definition of Comedy; Castelvetro (1570), Tragedy cannot

affect it's purpose by reading, with no performance; 143, Castiglione: universality; 144ff, the effect of Nature on art; 147, the orator and the listener; the gentleman must be a musician; 150, must have nonchalance and grace; 153, Castiglione: on the aesthetics of music; 164ff, Cardano, the value of music must be in the present, not the past; 165, what the ear cannot hear (fast notes) cannot bring pleasure; construction and emotions; 169ff, on the aesthetic qualities of various instruments, ranks in similarity to voice; 175, why musicians rarely become rich; 177ff, Michelangelo on the value of art; it takes a lifetime to learn an art; 181ff, Art is found in the mind of the artist, not his hands; 187, Michelangelo's caveat on artist or sculptor?; 188ff, on the aesthetic difference between painting and sculpture; 198ff, sixteenth century France, concerned with the emotions of the text; Tyard on the impact of music; 221ff, on the aesthetics in poetry; 226ff, aesthetics in music; 229, Rabelais on the decline of life in general; 236, Bodin affect of numbers and ratios on life; 237 on the affect of harmony on life; 238, Rabelais: is music an art or skill?; 260ff, Montaigne; 261ff, art is difficult to talk about; 263, on "chance" in works of art; 267, intrigued how music affects the listener; 284ff, sixteenth century Spanish philosophers, Vives: Art was evolved for delight; 285, experience is uncertain unless ruled by Reason; Art is more in the artist than the art object; 286, on the art observer; some art is injurious to man (books not in Latin, popular music); 286, on imitation in art education; on the aesthetics of Music, the other liberal arts seek Truth, music only for relaxation; he classifies all poetry under heading of music; 287, music is "arithmetic applied to sounds"; 287, Francisco de Salinas, 1513–1590, Spanish philosopher, author of *De musica,* rejects the old classification of *mundana, humana* and *instrumentalis* and instead classifies music as either for the senses or the intellect or both; 298, Cervantes on the similarity of the arts; 334, Lope de Vega and Cervantes on art vs entertainment in theater; **V:** 27, Erasmus: Art is in the art object, purpose of art is simply to please; 28, Art is not worthy of being considered a profession; 29, the environment in which Art is found is inseparable from the art work; no artist can copy Nature; 32, on painting; 35, Erasmus on the aesthetics of music seems to misunderstand early writings on this subject; Zeno, Greek philosopher quoted by Erasmus, 36, the soul is a "self-moving harmony, and for this reason can be caught up and carried away by harmonious things"; 37, poem in Ockeghem's honor by Erasmus—Music is something divine; 45, views on early music; 57, environment for the arts in sixteenth century Germany; 67ff, destruction during the sixteenth century civil strife; 70, on aesthetics in music; 70, Agrippa on the power of music; 88ff, Luther on the divine in music; 89, on Luther's compositions; 90, on the purposes of music; 92, Luther's poem on the ability of music to soothe and comfort; 93, Luther on the ability of music to express feelings; 94, to affect the character of the listener; 104, in 1511 Germany polyphony is almost "entirely neglected"; 105, "four categories of musicians" include poets and mimes (Cochlaeus, 1511); 108, Ornithoparchus admits theory is understood not by the ears but "wit and reason"; 109 and he cannot explain why he has heard some good music written by composers who do not know the theory of music; 110, precepts

for singers; 112, Listenius (1537) on the importance of music as a "serious art"; 112ff, divides music into theory, practical and poetic—which results in *total* performance; 116, Glarean on the subjective character of various modes; 125, Glarean on the aesthetics of church music; 125ff, Coclico, *Compendium musices* (1552), the first treatise to emphasize performance over theory; 184ff, change at end of sixteenth century where the upper class no longer are expected to be musicians, for example: Ascham, 185, the "quickest wit" may have other problems; on the ill effects of too much study of music; quotes Galen (second century, AD), "Much music marreth men's manners"; 186, in his *Toxophilus* he again questions the value of music education, in particular popular music, and whether Aristotle and Plato knew what they were talking about; 187, on secondary values of music education; 188ff, similar views by Peacham, Greee and Lyly; 189ff, very strong attacks on music and dance by the religious right, Puritans, including the minister, Northbrooke; 192ff, Gosson; 195ff, and Stubbs. Writing in support of music and the arts were 196ff, Lodge and 198ff, Sidney; 212, on the aesthetics of music by Richard Hooker; 213, Sir Thomas More, *Utopia* (1515), value of music is to cheer the spirits, affects the senses, raises the passions; wants more emotional church hymns; 214, Lodowick Bryskett, *A Discourse of Civil Life,* many examples of corruption are caused by the music we listen to; young men must be more selective as listeners; 215, Thomas Morley, *A Plain and Easy Introduction to Practical Music* (1597), music must please the ears as well as being capable of being defended by reason; music must match the emotions of the words; discuss the aesthetic values of various forms; 217, Henry Peacham, *The Complete Gentleman,* "whom God loves not, that man loves not music"; on music therapy; on the purposes of music; 218, Peacham's list of important composers: Byrd (whom no one can equal), Lassus, Marenzio, Ferrabosco (the father of many others); 218, John Case, in *The Praise of Musicke* (1586), on how specifically music soothes the listener; 263ff, some sixteenth century English poetry still intended to be sung; 266, the arts value is questioned by the poets; 267, poetry and music are only for recreation; 268, Greville: the arts must be learned from practice, never from books; 268, Daniel on the decline in the appreciation of music; 281, a poem by Lyly says the music will not sound well unless the bass line can be heard; 287, Greene, Robert, 1560–1592, on the decay of letters and lack of honor for art; 296ff, among Elizabethan fiction writers; Greene, a poet, actor and musician compare their value to society; 296, fn., 32, a list of professions according to social status; 297, Nashe on Poetry; 298, Nashe on the theater; 300ff, aesthetics of music, no serious discussion in Elizabethan England; 304ff, consorts of dogs; 315; noble complaints that sons have been reared in dance and lute playing; courtiers do not need higher education, because they can learn in court through practice what they need; 316, Lyly, *The Maydes Metamorphosis,* "I can tune her with my hounds" (dog consort); 316, stage performances based on real Elizabethan practice; trumpet fanfare to begin the play and concerts after the production (see Hentzner) or before (see Philip of Stettin-Pomerania); 318ff, music in the stage directions of the plays containing music description; 324, Marlowe's *The*

Massacre at Paris comments on the secularization of the universities; 335ff art songs in the Elizabethan plays; 341, Shakespeare on the decay of the arts; 344, consort of dogs (Shakespeare); 345ff, Shakespeare never praised formal education and in *The Taming of the Shrew* (I, iii, 25ff) a character warns not to let philosophy and the liberal arts get in the way of happiness; 346ff, Shakespeare's emphasis on melancholy; 348ff, Shakespeare on Poetry; 350ff, Shakespeare on the Theater; 352ff, on Painting; 353ff, Shakespeare on the aesthetics of music; 353, music was still associated with mathematics; 353, on the mysterious impact of the string instrument; 354, in praise of harmony; 365, Shakespeare's music references in his stage directions (see "Theater"); 367, specific forms of trumpet fanfares given by Shakespeare (see "Trumpet Signals" for *Flourish, Sennet, Tucket, Alaru, Retreat, Parley*); 376ff, stage direction references for woodwind music and hunting music; **VI:** 1ff, extensive examples of seventeenth court entertainment music; 4, Monteverdi outlines the duties of the court wind band in 1611; papal wind bands; 9ff, early opera and other entertainments in Venice in the seventeenth century; 10, on the cost of opera; 12, Pier Jacopo Martello in praise of the new Italian opera form; Metastasio, 13, discusses the direction toward entertainment in Italian opera in 1750; 14, on the political advantges of public performance in seventeenth century Venice, but difficult in Rome due to Church opposition; 15, the audience role in Naples; a 1630 account of concert activity throughout Rome; 17, church music in seventeenth century Rome, lots of instruments begin to participate, with original compositions for voices and instruments; 18, Giustiniani reports improvisation over chant; 29–36, historical (and many modern) musicologists misunderstand the relationship of words and music in seventeenth century music, especially opera and thus misunderstood the *Camerata* and the birth of opera; 40 on the remarkable emotional singing in the first operas; 46, Agazzari, Agnostino, in 1607, reports polyphony is no longer in use, preference is moving from wind to string instruments; 47, Gasparini notes, the noble class no longer has time to become musicians; 48, following the new interest in emotions, music is now classified as being church, theater or chamber; 51, Berardi: music is the ruler of the passions of the soul; 53, first-hand description of Corelli's playing; 53, to move the emotions of the audience the player must first feel the emotions himself; 53, Frescobaldi: the player must find the emotions in the music; Giovanni Bonachelli (1642): even tempi is adjusted according to the emotions of the words; 54, Tossi, on singing from the heart; 71, Marino (1623) writes the ear is the only door to the soul; 76, in Tommaso Campanella's utopia, *The City of the Sun* (1602), music is reserved for women and children; 97ff, Gracián: Art changes beasts into people; it is good to appreciate Art, but not practice it; 102, Spanish literature of the seventeenth century treats music in only symbolic references; 106, Valdivielso's *The Bandit Queen* and Calderón's *The Great Theater of the World* cast Beauty in a dark tone, perhaps reflecting the decay of Spanish society in the seventeenth century; 108, Calderón gives the purpose of poetry to please everyone; 108ff, on the use of music as a metaphor for ordinary language; 123ff, on the Italian influence on the German Baroque; 126ff, German

and Austrian court entertainments; 135ff, growth of civic music; 142ff, development of instrumental church music; 151ff, Heinichen against paper nonsense and old rules and music is for the ear, not the eye; 154, Marpurg thought Bach's music found left and right hemisphere, "the heart and the understanding are set into gentle motion together with the ear." But Mattheson added that Bach "did not teach the supposed mathematical basis of composition. This I can guarantee"; 156ff, on the differences between seventeenth century German and French music; 157, Scheibe on Germans learning Taste from the Italians; 159, Germany felt pre-eminent in the seventeenth century; 160, Bach: the old style of music no longer sounds good to our ear; 161, catharsis represented by the German Baroque phrase "refresh the spirits"; 167, emotions become the foundation of music; 177, continued criticism of polyphony; 182, Mattheson made a strong case for ending the ancient association of music and mathematics and instead associating music with feelings and the soul; He was attacked in publications by Johann Buttstedt and Johann Fux, but supported by Handel and Johann Kuhnau; 183ff, Mattheson continues with discussion of mathematics and measurement resulting with an attack on polyphony; 186ff, on the "Art of Gesticulation" or *Hypocritica,* the communication of emotions through movement and face (central to conducting); 188 and 191, Mattheson on national differences in singing; 189, in the decay of music in society; 192, in the classification of music in which the singer is the highest aesthetically because melody is the primary element in music which communicates feeling; 193ff a lengthy discussion of writing good melodies; 198, "Movement" is associated with emotions; 200ff, on the purposes of music (Mattheson), all tied to feelings; 206ff, Mattheson on the range of emotions in music; 215, Mattheson on the requirements and education needed for the conductor; 222, a poem in honor of Schütz and the dismal environment during the war; 244ff, Leibniz: understanding of arts is experiential, not the product of Reason; 245, because of this, Wolff says this is why there is no philosophy of the arts or law or medicine; 248ff, Leibniz: music is still a branch of mathematics, but comes to understand this is too limited; 250, Leibniz: Music is a form of Truth; 251, Leibniz on the perception of music; 252, Leibniz on the genetic aspects of music; 298, Spinoza: good and bad do not exist in the arts, only the opinion of the observer; 299, Spinoza: art is in the mind of the artist, not the art object; 300, Huygens, in arguing there must be music among the people on other planets, provides a few of his ideas on perception and aesthetics of music; **VII:** 2ff, the extensive organization of court music under Louis XIV; 10ff, the *Académie Française* and formal French academies of all the arts founded in the seventeenth century; 14, clergy of Paris in 1662 forbids any instruments except the organ; 19ff, seventeenth century definition of music, by Charpentier and by Rameau; 22ff, seventeenth century French views on Taste by Rousseau, Couperin, Rameau, Saint-Lambert, Brossard; 25ff, on the comunication of emotions; 26ff, on movement vs time; 28ff, examples of strong emotions expressed in performance; 29, Rameau: don't listen to the rules, be swept away; 31, improvisation, including Couperin, Bénigne de Bacilly, Mermet; 33, seventeenth century French vews on music education;

44, Mersenne on the aesthetics of the voice and singing; 45ff, Mersenne on the classification of music and forms; 45ff, Mersenne on the various Baroque dance forms; 49, Mersenne: music has to do with the expression of emotions, therefore a single line of music must be the most striking; 50, assuming that the center of the emotions is in the words, not the music, great emphasis must be placed on how a song is performed, etc.; 51, but the composer must be inspired also and Nature is also involved, the artist is born, not made by art; 53, the notational system is inadequate regarding the expression of emotions; 54, the rules of harmony are not like those of geometry, which force the mind of all those who have common sense to adopt them; 54ff, you can only judge music by hearing; 55ff, on the relationship of emotions and humors; 56, on the origin of emotional speech in man and animals; 57–68, major discussion of music, humors and emotions; 70, Mersenne: the heart of improvisation is nature, not rules of division; 84, Renaissance French philosophers have renewed interest in catharsis, 89, in bicameral theory and 90, in genetic musical information; 102ff, French philosophers find the emotions as variations in self-love and central to communication; the idea of educating women is questioned; 107, Truth is perfection and beauty; 107, intention and performance must be all of the one pattern (La Rouchefoucauld); 107, Boileau on Truth and the sublime in performance; 115, 117 on the historical development of poetry; 117, on the development of poetry from music; 118, Chaulieu, 1631–1720, believed that poetry in aiming at eloquence lost the art of singing; 118, Gresset found music superior to poetry for intimate communication; 119ff, French Baroque philosophers consider the aesthetics of music vs the other arts; 120, Batteux on the requirements of expressive music; 120ff, beauty in music exists on three levels; 121, André on some form of innate rational understanding in the listener; 123–126, debate on French vs Italian music by Le Cerf de La Viélle and Raguenet; 128, on the affect of music on man; 129, Raguenet on praise for the emotions in Italian music; 134, on the role of music in ancient and modern societies; 138–147, On French vs Italian music, vocal and instrumental, major discussion; 147, Maugars, on improvisation; 148, Bonnet-Bourdelot, on improvisation; 149–159, major discussion on opera performance; 160, De Bosses, "not every sort of music is fit to praise God"; 178, Descartes discredits "speculative music"; 179, Descartes: purpose of music is to communicate emotions to the soul of the listener; 181, Descartes: neither beauty nor pleasure can be defined as everything is a matter of individual preference; 185, Chapelain (1637), art must not only pleasse but follow the rules of experts; 188ff, Corneille on the nature of Tragedy and its emotions; 193, Fénelon on tragedy vs comedy; 201ff, Molière on the music making in the home of the wealthy businessman; 263, Voltaire discussion on the perception of art; 266, Voltaire: music communicates passion, not ideas, 271, Voltaire on the decay of opera; **VIII:** 7, the musical tastes of Charles II of England; 7, fn., 32, North suggests it was the new violin which retired the multi-part polyphony; 21, Avison: the foundation of harmony and expression; aesthetics of music, views in Baroque England; Christopher Simpson, d. 1669, complains most people prefer "light and airy" music; Charles Butler,

d. 1647, English theorist at Oxford classifies music as mathematical, practical and performers; by late seventeenth century mention of mathematics was replaced by discussion of music and emotions; 25ff, Playford (1674), Mace and Avison lament the loss of aesthetic music, replaced by popular music and see the loss of serious music because music had become a performer's art and not a composer's art; 27, Avison on the affect of hearing the emotions in music, pointing out it never produces bad emotions; 32ff, major discussion by English writers; 41, North: children must learn from physical experience, not from the rules of the grammarians; 42, what makes a good melody cannot be expressed in words; 43ff, North's classification of music: solitary (made for ones self), social (natural emotions), ecclesiastical, and theatrical; 44, the primary purposes of music are to please and to communicate emotions; 45, on the universality of emotions; 46, North: Music is the representation of Humanity in all its states; 68, Harvey on Art vs Science; James I, "Art is better learned by practice than speculation"; 68, Bunyan classifies dramatic plays with "… fools, apes, knaves and rogues"; 72, Donne: listeners and players prefer improvised music rather than written music; 72, Donne on the value of music as a tool for memory 73, Bunyan suggests that to be a contemplative listener one must have some education in music first; 77, Bacon classified the mind as consisting of Memory, taught through history, Imagination, taught through poetry, and Reason, taught through philosophy; 80, for Bacon the foundation for the professions; softens manners; 84, Bacon divides music into divine contribution and man's reason; 85, Bacon provides seven parts of music which can be discussed, one of which is "exterior, interior"; 90, Bacon: melodic quarter-tones are possible; vibrato is like light playing on water; 93, Donne on kinds of poets beneath respect; 97, a Phineas Fletcher poem which describes dog consorts; 97ff, examples of poetry describing various aspects of our twin brain hemispheres; 103, Herbert: "Honor and profit lie not in one bed"; 104, a poem by Marvell which is a virtual history of music; 108ff, purposes of music as viewed by the Jacobean poets; 112, a poem by Withers implores London to turn to music to improve the behavior of the citizens and in his "Hymn for a Musician" he suggests some musicians have manners which might be improved by changing their reperoire; 116ff, on performance practice; 119, art music described by Jacobean poets; 133, Milton's tribute to Arts for their contribution to society; 134, skill in Art depends in practice alone; 137, Milton's tribute to music; 157, Marston notes, like music, it is the performance version of the play that is important, not the written version; 157 improvisation in the Jacobean plays; 158, Ben Jonson against playwrights who pander to public taste; Jonson gives the purpose of plays as aesthetic delight and to teach; 162, Chapman: Fortune, not Reason, rules the state of things; 163, Jonson: Art must be based on Reason; 164, in Beaumont and Fletcher: the consequece of writing for the lowest level is that their level is never raised; 164, "and choice music's sound"; 165–173, on music and society, in the Jacobean plays, its reflection of society, its use as metaphor, etc; 172, in Chapman's play, *All Fools,* there is a lengthy exchange on the cultural training of the young courtier, including ability in music;

173–179, views on the purpose of music among the Jacobean playwrights; 179–189, incidental music in the Jacobean plays, reflecting English life; 189–193, art music described in the Jacobean plays; 195ff, descriptions of instrumental performances in the Jacobean plays; 197, descriptions of educational music in Jacobean plays; 198ff, church music described in Jacobean plays; 209–222, Jacobean Prose writers; 209, Brown: As reason is a rebel to faith, so passion is to reason; 209, Brown: the multitude; that numerous piece of monstrosity; 211, Puritan prejudice toward education: "Rhetoric," the mother of lies"; "A mere scholar is an intelligible Ass"; 212, Browne: nature is not at variance with art... Nature is the art of God; 214, Browne on music's connection with divinity; 215, Walton: what man hears is conditioned by his perspective as a listener; a number of metaphors which reflect on music's relationship with the public; 220, Dekker on the beer fiddler; 223–301, views of English Restoration philosophers; Thomas Hobbes: 224, all thoughts have their origin in the senses, [but] the senses are located in the heart; 229, Hobbes: the study of sounds is music; the study of passions is Ethics; 230, Hobbes is the first to fully understand that music is in the mind, not the instrument. His proof: the echo; John Locke: 235, considering his left-hemisphere view of the world, Locke failed to appreciate music—a waste of time—seldom is anyone commended for excellency in music—last place in any list of accomplishments; Isaac Newton, 237ff, his ideal curriculum for university studies, in which music is still taught by the mathematics professor; William Penn, 243, Penn discounts too much education, for example, "The first thing obvious to children is what is sensible; and that we make no part of their rudiments"; 244, Penn finds concerts [music-meetings] among a long list of activities inappropriate for a Christian; 245, Penn describes apparent religious activities of American Indians; 248, Hume assigns emotions a much higher level of importance than earlier philosophers; George Berkeley, 258ff; 266, Temple finds the climate in England makes the people, "unequal in our humors, inconstant in our passions ..."; 267, Temple: The powers of music are either felt or known by all men; Thomas Rymer; 267, concerned mostly with the theater; 269, a harsh critic of opera; 269, Wotton argues that Nature has nothing to do with prominence: Why are there no eminent poets in Peru?; 271 Wotton finds epic poetry too complete, "Men should rise from the table with some appetite remaining..."; 271, Wotton finds it curious that while mathematicians are conversant with earlier writers, musicians are not; 272, there are certain qualities in music which are universally understood regardless of the education of the listener; 275, Charles Gildon, 1665–1724, writing about actors and the bicameral nature of our brain makes a point rarely mentioned in conducting clinics: When practicing before a mirror, to the confusion of the player/viewer, everything is seen as reversed. That is, the conductor would, in common time say, "my second beat goes left," but for the entire orchestra it in fact is seen as going right!; 276, Gildon on the power of music—it has nothing to do with Reason; Cooper, Anthony, Earl of Shaftesbury, 1671–1713, known as Shaftesbury; 279 Durant called him the most important writer on aesthetics in modern philosophy; 281, Shaftesbury believed emotions

are genetic, which in general is true; 282ff, Shaftesbury gives a lengthy and valuable discussion on Art and the character of the artist; 285, Shaftesbury on the development of taste; 286, Shaftesbury on an interesting discussion on the development of poetry (and theater) in England; 287, Shaftesbury finds the laws of music are found in Nature; 288, Shaftesbury on universality in music; 288, Shaftesbury on the nature of adjudication; 289, Shaftesbury on the importance of the contemplative listener, an art of hearing; 290ff, Hutcheson, 1694–1746, author of "An Essay on the Nature and Conduct of the Passions and Affections" (1742) helped bring England up to modern thinking on the emotions; 290ff, Hutcheson in an important discussion, classifies and connects the senses with emotions; 296ff, Hutcheson, author of "An Inquiry into the Original of our Ideas of Beauty and Virtue" (1729) provides a very important discussion of the subject of beauty and art and music; 296, the pleasure of a fine composition is incomparably greater than any single part; 300, James Harris, 1709–1780, the power of music is to raise the emotions; 303, Hawkins, in his general history of music (1776) provides interesting comments on the Restoration theater and its tendency toward low entertainment and the development of popular music; 304, Sedley, Sir Charles, Restoration playwright, finds more enthusiasm for sermons than for plays; 304, Betterton, a leading seventeenth century actor in England, assigns part of the failure of contemporary theater to the training of the actors themselves; 306, William Congreve, 1670–1729, perhaps the best of the Restoration writers, on the definition of comedy, "Humor shows us as *we* are"; 306, on drama's universality and being too close to human experience; 306ff, on the educational purpose of drama; 309ff, views of Restoration composers on the purpose of music; 310, on idioms of French singing; 314ff, concerts in the home described by Restoration playwrights; 327, Dryden: Time is the surest Judge of Truth; 322, Dryden dismisses traditional universities; 329, Dryden: both the best and worst of the modern poets will equally instruct you to admire the ancients; 330, Dryden: [The French] do out of gaiey that which would be an imposition upon us; 332ff, Dryden's tribute to the arts; 333, Dryden on the purposes of music; 336 Dryden's discussion of opera; 347–375, comments by Restoration poets; 348, Young, on the poor reputation of poets; 350, more and more intellectuals are becoming aware, by introspection, of our bicameral nature; Sheridan, here, could not be more accurate; 351–354, Restoration poets on music and society; 354–362, Restoration poets in honor of St. Cecilia; 359–362, Resoration poets on the purposes of music; 363–367, Restoration poets on opera; 377, Restoration philosophers on Reason and emotion; 378, Restoration philosophers on education and its limits; 385, Defoe on the meaning and purposes of music; 386, Daniel Defoe on music education; 388, Swift, as dean of St. Patrick's cathedral in Dublin, forbids church musicians from appearing in public performances—notwithstanding this ban, the premiere performance of Handel's *Messiah* was given in the cathedral a few weeks later; 391ff, contemporary descriptions of a gentleman of high taste in London; 393ff, views on music by the English upper class; 395, descriptions of music in the home in Restoration novels; 401ff, opera described in

Restoration fiction; 409, Restoration writers on emotion and its importance; 412ff, views of Restoration writers; 414, views on Beauty by Restoration writers on manners; 416, Restoration writers on manners on the aesthetics and perception of music; 420 Restoration art music in the home; 422ff, Restoration writers on manners view opera; 427, a reference to a consort of dogs in Restoration England; 427ff, description of the dance fiddler; 428, on the broadside ballads and their singers; 448, Addison on program music; 453–462, discussion of opera in Restoration England

Aesthetics, Physiology of, I: 252, Aristotle; 480ff; **II:** 22ff; 62, early Church; 124ff, fourth and fifth century church; 141, St. Augustine; 183, (sixth to eighth centuries; 296ff, thirteenth century philosophers; 313; 397, Italian literature in the twelfth and thirteenth centuries; **III:** 18ff, Petrarch disassociates with general public; 28ff, the public; 47ff, Boccaccio on Reason, on senses, experience; 70ff, Machaut: Reason must rule, 73, Reason must rule emotions, except when Love is present; 164ff, fifteenth century Italy; 171, Cicero believed in internal tuning; 192ff, Leonardo da Vinci on experience, 194, on the senses; 213ff, French pessimism: Christine de Pizan old fashioned views: senses not important, Reason must rule; pessimistic views of Philippe de Commynes: neither Reason nor common sense curb his instincts, it is probable that knowledge does more good than harm; 254ff, on Reason and Wisdom; 287ff, fourteenth and fifteenth century Spain; 288, Ruiz: fear of God is the beginning of wisdom, hence the importance of memory—painting, writing and sculpture were invented for the purpose of keeping things in the memory; 304ff, English fifteenth century, 306, Lydgate, fifteenth century England, Lydgate, *Reson and Sensuallyte,* and Henry Medwall, *Nature,* on *Reason and Sensuality*; **IV:** 5ff, sixteenth century Italian; 47ff, views of the sixteenth century Italian theorists; Zarlino: music must not be judged by the senses alone, still thinking of mathematics; 48ff on whether theory is necessary to performance; 49, Giustiniani says both are needed; 67, Zarlino, all theory must be directed toward performance or else if vain and useless; 67, Mei: purpose of theory is to find Truth, but it is found in performance; 68, Benedetti, you cannot understand theory without performance; 92ff, sixteenth century Italian poets; 124, sixteenth century Italian playwrights; 132, Machiavelli, singers never listen to you; 135, in Castiglione; 136, senses vs Reason; 137, the education needed by a gentleman; 161, Cardano on experience, the senses; 195ff, Pontus de Tyard: role of arts to help man climb back toward the divine; four kinds of *fureur divine,* two of which include music, which in particular helps the soul rise, man ignorant of music is lame in soul; 216ff, sixteenth century French poets; 216 on the bitter life of the courtier in Rome; 229ff, sixteenth century prose, on the influence of climate and geography; **V:** 14ff, Erasmus: Reason must rule; 15. senses distort the truth; 16, doubts the value of experience; 61 in sixteenth century Germany: Agrippa on the senses, Melanchthon on man and beast; 63, Zwingli on university ethics; 82ff, Luther struggles with Reason vs Faith; 200, Bryskett, sixteenth century, the senses are responsible for all evil things; 254ff, sixteenth century poets discount the senses and education; 289, on the importance of Reason to ward off

bad behavior, but Sir Philip Sidney confesses that Reason is defenseless against feminine beauty; 290, Greene on four things which dull the senses; 72, Marino (1623) writes the ear is the only door to the soul; **VI:** 152ff, music is for the ear, not the eye; 182ff, The old debate, music as mathematics or feeling, continued and in his book *Das Neu-Eröffnete Orchestre* (1713) Mattheson argues the case for feeling, saying music communicates with the inner soul. He was attacked in publications by Johann Buttstedt and Johann Fux, but supported by Handel and Johann Kuhnau; 183ff, Mattheson continues with discussion of mathematics and measurement resulting with an attack on polyphony; 186ff, Mattheson on the "Art of Gesticulation" or *Hypocritica,* the communication of emotions through movement and face (central to conducting); 206ff, Mattheson on the range of emotions in music; **VII:** 101 views of Baroque French philosophers on emotions; **VIII:** 379, Prior on how aging follows passions;

Aesthetics, Psychology of, I: 256, Aristotle; **II:** 27; 69, Tertullian on "pleasure" vs Church; 126, fourth and fifth centuries; 146ff, St. Augustine; 185, Boethius; 260, Guido on stress and pitch; on the needs of ritardando; 300ff, thirteenth century philosophers on emotion; 318; 400ff, Italian literature in the twelfth and thirteenth centuries; **III:** 22, Petrarch on emotions; 49ff, Boccaccio on emotions, pleasure; 76ff, Machaut on the emotions, pleasure and pain; 114ff, fourteenth century English philosophers, emotions; Chaucer, psychology, 147ff, 167ff, fifteenth century Italy; 197ff, Leonardo da Vinci, on emotions; **III:** 216ff; 263, Brant on Love; 288ff, fourteen and fifteenth century Spain; 290, all emotions interfere with Reason; 311, English fifteenth century; pleasure and Nature; **IV:** 10ff, sixteenth century Italy, Tosso: church: distrust of emotions; 11, Aretino: advice to writers: express feelings, not words; 11, Machiavelli on Love; Aretino on Love; 94 Ariosto, in love follow the senses, not Reason; 138ff, emotions in Castiglione; 143, the artist's work should correlate with his own character; pleasure and pain, 141, in Castiglione; 197, sixteenth century France; 219ff, emotions, Love and Reason; 282, Vives and St. John of the Cross on the emotions; **V:** 257, sixteenth century poets discount emotions; 258, on the conflict between Reason and Love; 262ff, the pain of Love; 292, in Elizabethan England, Greene, Sidney; 293, bicameral: Greene, Lodge; 325, Lyly's *Loves Metamorphosis* uses music as a metaphor to express a lady's emotional state; Lyly's *The Maydes Metamorphosis* notes Reason and Love disagree; **VI:** 73, Marino (1623) writes that it was Love who first taught man music; 83, Kircher (1650) classifies music first by individual styles (based on the "humors", then by national styles and third by by function, which deals mostly with subjective qualities; 96, Gracián follows the Church teaching that the emotions are the first step toward sin and must be overcome. "The emotions are the breaches in the defenses of the mind."; **VII,** 15, Mersenne, on the psychological value of the military trumpet; 17, Saxe on the psychological relationships with the drum cadence

Agathias Scholasticus, poet, sixth to eighth century, **II:** 197ff

Agatho, ancient playwright, **VII:** 284

Agathon, 448–400 BC, ancient Greek poet, **I:** 170; 259;

Agazzari, Agnostino, 1578–1640, Italian composer, **V:** 168; **VI:** 46ff, in 1607, polyphony is no longer in use, preference is moving from wind to string instruments; 51; 59; 67

Aglais of Megacles, ancient Olympic winner of the trumpet contest, **I:** 110

Aglaophon, ancient Greek painter, **I:** 373, Cicero on;

Agricola, Martin, 1486–1556, **V:** 75; 104, author of *Musica Instrumentalis Deutsch* (1528)

Agrippa, Henry, 1486–1535, **V:** 60ff, anti-university and humanism; 67 on the emotions; 69ff, on lies in poetry; 70 on the power of music; 74 on geographical influences on man and music

Aimeric de Belenoi, troubadour, **II:** 385

Aimeric de Peguilhan, fl. c. 1195–1230, troubadour, **II:** 370; 380; 389

Ainard, twelfth century German abbot, **II:** 330

Akenside, Mark, 1721–1779, Restoration poet, **VIII:** 347; 351; 381

Al, musical instrument in Mesopotamia, **I:** 62

Alasco, Albertus, Palatine of Siradia (Poland) welcomed at court of Elizabeth I, **V:** 230

Albert de Rippa, sixteenth century French lutenist, **IV:** 210, more prized than Orpheus

Albert of Brandenburg, V: 9, letter of 1519 from Erasmus

Albert v of Munich, sixteenth century German noble, **V:** 74; 133, hunting practice; 147, diary of Massimo Troiano

Albert, Duke of Prussia, second-half, sixteenth century German noble, **V:** 9; 136ff, extensive knowledge of music

Alberti, Domenico, 1710–1740, Baroque composer, **VIII:** 26, fn., 16, judged by Avison as being a composer defective of in harmony and invention, music "fit for children"

Alberti, Leon Battista, b. 1404, Florentine philosopher, **III:** 161; 164, Reason must rule; 166, humanist viewpoints; 167, on the power of Love; 169, on beauty; 172ff

Alberto, Florentine artist, **III:** 8

Albmeyer, Giorgio Christoforo, VI: 27, German band leader in Italy in 1720

Albrecht of Brandenburg, 1440–1486, **III:** 282

Alcaeus, c. 640–550 BC, lyric poet, **I:** 124ff; 170; 298; 424

Alcibiades, 450–404 BC, Greek general, nephew to Pericles, **I:** 109; 111; 274, Pronomus of Thebes, his aulos teacher; **III:** 36

Alcuin, eighth century English teacher, **II:** 184

Aldorise, Prosper, VII: 59, cited by Mersenne on the subject of emotions and laughter

Alexander the Great, 356–323 BC, **I:** 104ff; 109; 111; 249; 273; **III:** 9; **V:** 40 (Erasmus); **V:** 40; 194; **VIII:** 460

Alexander VI, 1431–1503, pope, **IV:** 88

Alexander VII, 1599–1667, pope, **VI:** 7, welcomes Christina of Sweden in Rome

Al-Farabi, *Ihsa Al-Ulum,* c. 900 AD, an early treatise centering on the conceptual aspects of music, **II:** 254ff, "The Science of Music [includes] the science of practical music and, second, the science of theoretical music."; 255ff, *De Ortu Scientiarum,* c. 900 AD, discusses the educational value of music, the influence on character and dance ('visible music');

Alfonso II, 1533–1597, duke of Ferrara, **IV:** 78

Alfonso V of Aragon, 1416–1458, **III:** 295, imported a wind band of Philip the Good

Alfred, King of England, 849–899 AD, **VIII:** 139, sang and played lute

Alkman, c. 640–600 BC, lyric poet, **I:** 123ff; 175; **II:** 39; 188

Allegorical productions with music, **IV:** 214, the arrival of Charles IX in Bayonne; Henry II water pageant in 1548; **VI:** 2ff, extensive description of entertainments given for Madame of France in 1620; 127, for the duke of Saxony, 1621; a Danish wedding in 1634, music by Schütz; for Friedrich August I of Dresden

Allegre, Lorenzo, seventeenth century composer whose song "Coseferite" was set to poetry, **VIII:** 95

Allman, William F., twentieth century writer on the bicameral brain, **I:** 51

Altenburg, Johann Ernst, 1734–1801, court trumpeter, **VI:** 133, on the importance of the trumpet choir (1795); 146ff

Ambrose, jongleur to Richard I of England, **II:** 282ff

Amenemhab, a musician of the 18th dynasty, Egypt, **I:** 79

Amenophis IV, ruler in ancient Egypt 1570 BC, **I:** 76

Ammianus Marcellinus, fourth century AD Roman writer, **I:** 470

Amphion, ancient singer, **I:** 426, **VIII:** 267; 272

Amsdorf, bishop of Naumberg, **V:** 142

Amunoph III, fifteenth century BC, Egyptian leader, **I:** 103

Anacharsis, the Scythian, philosopher, sixth century BC, **II:** 21; **V:** 207

Anacreon of Teos, c. 550–500 BC, lyric poet, **I:** 124ff; 170; 298; 423; 466; **II:** 34

Anaxenor, I: 323, famous rhapsodist

Anaxeron, kitharode player, **I:** 467, given tax income from four cities by Mark Anthony

Anderson, Hans Christian, 1805–1876, Danish writer, **I:** 45

Andrè, Yves-Marie, 1675–1764, author of *Essay on Beauty* (1741), **VII:** 108; 119; 120, beauty in music exists on three levels

Andrea, Giovanni, IV: 65, sang bass with a variety of improvisation new and pleasing to the ear of all: (1575)

Andron of Alexandria, period of Alexander the Great, **I:** 273, on the decay of music culture

Andronius, music teacher to Marcus Aurelius, 121–180 AD, **I:** 463

Anerio, Felice, 1560–1614, Italian composer, **IV:** 67

Angels, II: 211, bishop could hear choirs of angels

Anghiera, Pietro d', **III:** 287, Italian moves to Spain in late fifteenth century to help introduce humanism.

Anglicus, Bartholomew, thirteenth century philosopher, **II:** 302, on emotions

Animals and music, I: 478, dolphin; 478ff, Pliny the Elder on birds; **II:** 147, St. Augustine; 307, Albertus Magnus on similarities with human listeners; 308, dolphin story by Magnus and the tale of the Sirens; 308ff, Magnus on birds; **IV:** 269, Montaigne; **VII:** 56, Mersenne on the development of speech in man and animals

Anna d'Orléans, niece to Louis IV, **VI:** 5

Anna van Borssele, Princess of Veere, **V:** 14, Erasmus requests an honorary doctorate.

Annarus, Viceroy under Cyrus the Great, sixth century BC, **I:** 69

Anne of Austria, 1601–1666, visits Louis XIV in 1664, **VII:** 5

Anonymous, *De Musica Mensusrata*, c. 1279, **II:** 434ff

Anonymous, *Scholia Enchiriadis*, c. 900 AD, **II:** 254, a mathematics based treatise dealing with improvisation over a given chant.

Antef, Egyptian king of the 18th dynasty, **I:** 75

Anthony of Dornstätt, flutist under Maximilian I, **III:** 280

Antigonus, teacher of Alexander the Great, **III:** 9

Antipater of Thessalonica, early Christian writer, **II:** 39

Antiphon, fifth century BC orator, **I:** 157

Antoniano, Silvio, sixteenth century Italian singer, **IV:** 116

Antonio de Salazar, 1650–1715, **VI:** 92, composer of the seventeenth century cathedral in Mexico

Antwerp civic band, III: 231, regular concerts in fifteenth century; **V:** 2; 3; 4

Apollo, Greek god, also known as **Phoebus, I:** 103; 106; 111; 117; 119; 125; 128; 143; 146; 171; 208; 245; 295, as harp player; 426, Tibullus, Ovid; 428ff; 432; 434; 442; 448; 451; 460; 500; 507; **II:** 39; 49; 197ff; 430; **V:** 328; **VIII:** 95; 96; 121; 144; 190; 265; 366

Apolonius, VIII: 271, ancient writer mentioned by Wotton

Aquilanus, Seraphinus, fifteenth century singer, **III:** 184

Aquinas, Thomas, 1224–1274, important Church writer, **II:** 312, life's work was in trying to reconcile Reason and Faith; **VII:** 80

Arbeau, Thoinot, 1519–1595, French author of fifteenth century dance manual, *Orchesography* (1588); **IV:** 194; 206ff, found there was still some dancing in the church; knowledge of ancient Greek dances has been lost; dance is a kind of mute rhetoric; when mime is added to dance it has the power to stir the emotions; musicians accompanying dance are free to improvise; *basse danse* has been out of date for 40 -50 years

Arcadelt, Jacques, 1507–1568, Franco-French composer **IV:** 65, Giustiniani considered him among the best composers of the 16th century; 201

Arcesilaus, 318–242 BC, Skeptic School, **I:** 286; 292;

Archias, first century poet, **II:** 44

Archilei, Vittoria, 1582–1620, Italian singer, **IV:** 66, "famous lady musician," Giustiniani (1623)

Archilochus, 680–645 BC, lyric poet, **I:** 124ff; 406; 424; 499;

Archimedes, II: 4ff, second century builder of water organs; 213; 271

Archpoet of Cologne, twelfth century poet, **II:** 276; 321; 428; 431

Archytas, Pythagorean School, musician and philosopher before Plato, **I:** 153; 165

Arcimboldo, Antonello, sixteenth century composer, **IV:** 38

Ardalus the Troezenian, I: 130, said to have invented Prosodia

Aretino, Pietro, 1492–1556, Italian writer; **IV:** 1, fn., 1; 2ff; 9, ashamed of Michelangelo; 11, advice to writers: express feelings, not words; on Love, and on the torment of Love; 18ff; 20ff; 33ff, on art music; 40ff, on entertainment, including pornography; 92ff, too many people are writing poetry; 94; 96; 123; 127; 128; 132; 133

Aribert, eleventh century Archbishop of Milan, **II:** 238, the *carroccio*

Arion, fable of being saved by a dolphin, **I:** 141, fn., 1; 308; **V:** 40; 280; **VIII:** 142

Ariosto, Ludovico, 1474–1533, Italian poet, **IV:** 94; 106; 114ff; 119ff; 121; 126; 127; 132; 133; 135; **VII:** 276

Aristhenes, nobleman mentioned by Plutarch, **I:** 260

Aristides Quintilianus, late third and early fourth century AD, **I:** 326, major discussion on music education, 472ff

Aristippus of Cyrene, Greek philosopher said by Plutarch to be fond of single-pipe girls, **I:** 337

Aristippus, I: early Greek teacher, **I:** 299

Aristodemus, late Greek writer on music, **I:** 276

Ariston, 320–250 BC, Greek philosopher, student of Zeno, **I:** 284

Aristonicus, ancient Greek musician, **V:** 194

Aristophanes, 448–380 BC, Greek playwright, **I:** 126; 129; 169ff; 174ff; 180; 185; 187; 189

Aristotle, ancient Greek philosopher, 384–322 BC, **I:** 7; 43; 49; 95; 104ff; 145; 163ff; 172; 224; 249ff, major discussion; 273; 284; 285; 317, impact of *Poetics*; 511; **II:** 12; 16; 72; 107; 154, St. Augustine on catharsis; 213; 216; 249; 296ff, rediscovered in the thirteenth century; 303; 311ff, modern translations begin c. 1150; 312, in 1210 church council in Paris bans two of his books; 333; 338; 341ff; 345; 349; 353; 403; **III:** 5, "things spoken are symbols of the passions of the soul; 27; 105; 239; 241; 289; **IV:** 8; 26; 93; 105; 114; 128; 130; 166ff; 231; 252; 260; 279 (Vives); 287; **V:** 17, Erasmus: the Christians made Aristotle famous; 82ff, misunderstood by Luther; 26; 80ff; 117, fn., 44; 120; 186; 209; 324; **VI:** 237; 299; **VII:** 58; 84; 138; 188ff; 273; 284; **VIII:** 65; 134; 136; 267; 327; 394; 429

Aristoxenus, 355 BC, writer, student of Aristotle, **I:** 104; 173; 274ff ; 282ff; 289; **II:** 68; 114; 200; **III:** 90, 171, on internal tuning; **VIII:** 271

Arnald, Antoine, Jansenist theologian, **VII:** 165

Arnaut Daniel, fl. 1180–1200, troubadour, **II:** 375, born a noble but too poor to own a horse

Arnobius, celebrated teacher of rhetoric, **V:** 39, reference by Erasmus

Art Music, I: 62; 65; 75, Egypt; 87, Hebrew; 114, Greek Epic poets; 13, (Greek Lyric poets; 141, Xenophon; 143, Thucydides; 174ff, Sophocles, Aristophanes; 214, Plato; 258, Aristotle; 274 and 287, Alexandrian Period of Greece; 296, Alexandrian poets; 344, Etruscans; 346, early Rome; 351, general scene in Roman Republic, 240–27 BC; 353ff, Roman Republic; 412ff, Horace; 435ff, Ovid, Tibullus, Propertius; 463ff, Roman Empire Period, 14–476 AD; 502ff, Roman Imperial Period; **II:** 47ff; 89, fourth and fifth centuries; 116ff, views of fourth and fifth century Church philosophers; 136, St. Augustine; 193ff, sixth to eighth centuries; 237, ninth-eleventh centuries; 241, ninth - eleventh centuries; 275, twelfth and thirteenth

centuries; 362ff, in the twelfth and thirteenth century French Romances; 412ff, in German literature in the twelfth and thirteenth centuries; **III:** 10ff; 38ff, Petrarch on decline; 60ff, Boccaccio; 94ff; 126ff, fourteenth century English philosophers; 154ff, Chaucer, songs of the troubadour tradition; 178ff, Gaffurio: civic bands and ensembles of nobles flourish; 219, in fifteenth century France; 230ff in fifteenth century Burgundy, concerts by civic bands; 276ff, *Limburger Chronik* of 1360 on the improvement of the shawm; civic bands growing larger in fifteenth century Germany; 295, fourteen and fifteenth century Spain; 318ff, fifteenth century English, growth of concerts by wind bands; **IV:** 33ff, examples of aesthetic sixteenth century performances of art music; 75, sixteenth century Italians; aristocratic music; 114ff, sixteenth century Italian poets; 133, sixteenth century Italian playwrights; 152, Castiglione; 190, Michelangelo; 209ff, sixteenth century France; consort principle, including dogs; aristocratic weddings and arrivals; 320, Spanish art songs; 341, art songs in Spanish sixteenth century theater; **V:** 3, sixteenth century low countries; civic wind band activity in Ghent, Antwerp, Mechelen; 4, Mons; 138, sixteenth century German nobles court music; Ludwig Senfl in Munich; the Innsbruck court; royal weddings; 139ff, music by civic ensembles; 279ff, described in sixteenth century English poetry; 305ff, in Elizabethan England, consort of cornetts; 306ff, on the feelings of singers; 310, dancers playing a pipe while dancing; 312, contemplative listeners; 335ff, art songs in the Elizabethan plays; 377ff, Shakespeare stage directions which include genuine art music; **VI:** 116ff in seventeenth century Spanish theater; 173, Heinichen: one must play for the honor and perfection of the performance; **VII:** 134ff, on the role of music in society: Le Bruyère is disappointed in level of society; 135 Fénelon on the role of music in ancient and modern societies; 137, Montesquieu; 236ff, of the seventeenth century French court; 256, Voltaire on Art and Society; 268, music in the context of the debate between modern and ancient music; 310ff, examples of performances from Voltaire; **VIII:** 73, Bunyan describes some seventh century music in the home; 119ff, described by Jacobean poets; 164, "and choice music's sound"; 189–193, art music described in the Jacobean plays; 195ff, descriptions of instrumental performances in the Jacobean plays; 314ff, concerts in the home by Restoration playwrights; 341ff, descriptions of art music in Dryden's plays; 362, Restoration poets; 395, describing mainly music in the home; 420ff; 433, Pepys describes music in the home; 439, music in the home of Lord Brouncker

Artemis, Greek goddess of childbirth, according to Socrates, **I:** 196

Artemon, fl. 230 AD, painter, **I:** 129

Arthur, mythical king of England, **V:** 21

Artist: Born or Learned?, II: 19; **IV:** 20, Aretino, the gift of art is genetics, not instruction; 110, Giraldi: Nature produces the poets, but art makes the orators; 301, Cervantes; **VI:** 218 (Mattheson); **VII:** 51 (Mersenne); 260, Voltaire discussion; **VIII:** 103, Ben Jonson on Shakespeare; Herrick: man is born of both Naure and Art

Asaph, Hebrew singer in Old Testament, **I:** 129

Ascham, Roger, 1515–1568, tutor to young Elisabeth I, **V:** 76, impressed with German Lutheran singing in 1551; 185, the "quickest wit" may have other problems; on the ill effects of too much study of music; quotes Galen (second century AD), "Much music marreth men's manners"; 186, in his Toxophilus he again questions the value of music education in particular popular music, and whether Aristotle and Plato knew what they were talking about; 187. on secondary values of music education; 202ff; 207; 212; 229, personal description of Elizabeth I

Asclepiades, third century BC, philosopher, **I:** 27; 96, music therapy

Ashur-Idanni-Pal, 668–626 BC, king of Assyria, **I:** 67

Asopodorus of Phlius, ancient competitor on the aulos, **I:** 274

Aspendus, V: 45, fable of early lyre player mentioned by Erasmus

Assyrian Empire, I: 67

Aston, Anthony, Restoration writer, **VIII:** 35

Ateas, king of the Scythians, **I:** 135

Athanasius Bishop of Alexandria, in 367 AD headed a committee which created the New Testament, **II:** 82, fn., 8

Athenaeus, late second or early third century AD historian, **I:** 69; 81; 103ff; 112; 118ff; 171ff; 273ff, on the decay of music culture; 276ff; 291; 293ff; 309ff; 315ff, on the development of the modes; 317ff, Strabo on delight vs artistic beauty; 320ff; 323ff; 336ff; **III:** 35; **V:** 44

Attaingnant, Pierre, publisher in Paris, 1528–1555 of wind *basse danse* music, **IV:** 195

Attila the Hun, II: 94, on his funeral

Atys, servant of mythical goddess Cybele, **II:** 6

Aubade, an early morning song warning lovers to return home, **II:** 421ff

Audefroy le Bastard, troubadour, **II:** 383

Audience (see also **Listener** and **Public**), **I:** 489, Roman Imperial Period; **II:** 112, Julian on audience; 163, St. Augustine; 189, Gregory the Great; **IV:** 85, sixteenth century Italy; 225, Jean de la Taille; **VI:** 12, audience behavior in Venice in 1715 and in London in 1727; 66, Tosi on not begging for applause; **VII:** 107 and art, Pascal and La Bruyère; 118, Gresset found music superior to poetry for intimate communication; 118, Fénelon, a writer should not get too far ahead of his audinece; 186ff, on the emotions of the viewers of drama; 199, Molière and Racine on the audience; 227, on the debauched youth of the seventeenth century in Paris; 229 and no genuine emotions among the artistocrats; **VIII:** 21, Avison: placement of is important; Christopher Simpson, d. 1669, complains most people prefer "light and airy" music; 146, Milton and the contemplative listener; 164, in Beaumont and Fletcher: the consequece of writing for the lowest level is that their level is never raised; 325, Dryden: a poet must live by the many, but please the few; 384, Pope: For what I have published I can only hope to be pardoned; but for what I have burned I deserve to be praised

August, sixteenth century elector of Saxony, **V:** 136

Augustanus, Jacobus, d. 1577, merchant in Krakow, **V:** 140, personal consort

Augustin, leader of the cornetts in Maximilian I's church band, **III:** 278

Augustine of Augsburg, fifteenth century civic musician in Florence, **III:** 178

Augustus, Caesar, Roman emperor, 27 BC – 14 AD, **I:** 412; 416; 450ff

Aulos, I: 63; 64; 67; 76; 78; 81; 106; 108; 109, Ismenias, fourth century BC player; 69; 81; 111ff, use of aulos in battle; 126, Midas of Acragas, Greek players, Olympus and Pratinas; 146; 149; 169; 171ff; 174; 183ff; 186; 214, in concert; 228, repertoire; 250; 263; 269, Aristotle; 274, Asopodorus of Phlius, contest player; 274, on Pronomous of Themes, first to play all modes on one aulos; 276, Dorion, ancient Greek player; 282, lost books on aulos by Aristoxenus; 288, Ismenias; 292, Caphisius, early Greek teacher; 298, Philoxenus; 317, fn., 30, Strabo: God played the aulos; 321, fn., 42, Athenaeus on types of aulos and its repertoire; 344, Roman changes; 344, Ovid; 345, famous Etruscan hunting story; 347, fourth century BC aulos players go on strike; 353, original compositions in Roman Republic; 354, Thedorus of Boeotia, Theopompus, Hermippus, Lysimachus, Roman aulos players; 479, Pliny the Elder on aulos made from the lotus tree and details on reed; **II:** 7, military use; **V:** 46, Erasmus mentions a Greek myth unknown to us today

Aulus, Gellius, 117–180 AD, Roman grammarian, **I:** 466

Aurelian of Réome, ninth century theorist, **II:** 248ff, *Musica Disciplina,* c. 843 AD;

Ausonius, fourth century AD Greek poet, **II:** 93; 99ff; 101; 103, listener;

Avison, Charles, 1709–1770, English organist and composer, **VIII:** 21; 23; 26 sees the loss of serious music because music had become a performer's art and not a composer's art; in a footnote he groups a number of contemporary composers in categories from the lowest to the highest; 27, on the effect of hearing great music; 27, on the affect of hearing the emotions in music, pointing out it never produces bad emotions; 36; 37, on music education; 39

Baberini, Cardinal, mentioned by Milton, **VIII:** 139

Babst, publisher of an hymnal of 1545, **V:** 95

Bacchus, Festival of, I: 453ff.

Bacchylides, c. 518 BC, lyric poet, **I:** 123ff; **II:** 17

Bach, Johann Sebastian, 1685–1750, German composer, **I:** 15; 37; **IV:** 71; **VI:** 130, letter wishing he were a court musician; 133; 136; 139; 140; 142; 145, loses an audition to Heimann, who bribed the jury; 154, Marpurg found Bach's music both left and right hemisphere, "the heart and the understanding are set into gentle motion together with the ear." But Mattheson added that Bach "did not teach the supposed mathematical basis of composition. This I can guarantee"; 154; 159; 160, Bach, the old style no longer sounds good; 161; 166; 168, on choice of instrument; 170ff on his improvisation; 172, begins writing out the music; 173, as conductor; 177, as a teacher; 179 on the ethics of church music; 192

Bach, K. P. E., 1714–1788, German composer, **VI:** 171, on his father's improvisation

Bacon, Francis, 1561–1626, English philosopher, **VIII:** 77, major discussion

Bacon, Roger, b. c. 1214, thirteenth century Scholastic philosopher, **II:** 291ff, disrespects the public and the universities; 297ff, on the senses; 301, on emotions; 305, music for prophesy; 310

Baïf, Jean-Antoine de, 1532–1589, French poet, humanist, **IV:** 19ff; Baïf's Academy, **IV:** 202ff, begun under Charles IX in 1570, included composers, performers and listeners; Baïf's aim to bring back the Greek union of music and text and attempts to do so; 203 description by Marin Mersenne; 205; **VII:** 49; 65; 78ff; 117

Baldhead, trumpet player slave of Cicero, **I:** 351

Baldwin, King of Jerusalem, eleventh century, **II:** 281

Banchieri, Adriano, 1567–1634, Italian priest near Bologna, composer, **VI:** 67

Bandello, Matteo, 1480–1562, Italian secular writer, **IV:** 13; 33ff

Bannister, John, 1625–1679, violinist, privately sponsored concerts in seventeenth century London **VIII:** 9; 434; 435

Banquet music I: 466, Persius, 35–62 AD; **II:** 55ff, transition from Greek to Christian; 97, a king is killed; 196, sixth to eighth centuries; 278, banquet music for Earl Richard of England in 1243; traveling with a noble; 326, Hereward the Wake kills 14 during a banquet; **III:** 133ff, fourteenth century English; 225ff, fifteenth century France; 284, Maximilian I dining alone; **IV:** 115, Ariosto on the musical pleasures; 214, music for banquet of François I and Henry VIII in 1520; 228, described by Marguerite de Navarre; **V:** 55, Erasmus objects to banuet music; **VIII:** 3, seventeenth century description of use of music; 119

Baptist, John, VIII: 422, an harpsichordist heard by Evelyn in 1684, "A stupendous artist"

Baptista, Seignor, Italian opera composer mentioned by Pepys in 1667, **VIII:** 436

Baratti, seventeenth century soprano, **VI:** 15

Barbarini, Mme, Italian singer, **VII:** 279

Barberini, Cardinal, **VIII:** 139, correspondent with Milton

Barbers and popular music, **VIII:** 12

Bardi, Giovanni de', 1534–1612, Florentine nobleman, host of the Camerata, **IV:** 44, on the failure of polyphony; 60; 71, improvisation; **VI:** 34, clear Plato was thinking of song, not speech

Bargagli, Elfinspell, 1540–1612, Italian poet, **IV:** 85

Barnfield, Richard, 1574–1627, English poet, **V:** 264

Baroni, Leonora, famous Italian singer, heard in 1639, **VII:** 128

Basile, Giambattista, 1575–1632, **VI:** 79, Italian poet

Bathyllus, man in lyric poem by Anacreon, **I:** 424

Batteux, Charles, 1713–1780, French philosopher, **VII:** 83; 109, on the perception of art; 110, on art vs nature; 120, on the requirements of expressive music; 126ff, on the perception of music; 131, on man's forms of communication; 159, on opera

Bayer, Conrad, German seventeenth century poet, **VI:** 225, a poem composed for the marriage of Schütz

Beaumont, Francis, 1584–1616, and **Fletcher, John,** 1579–1625, university educated Jacobean playwrights, **VIII:** 158, *The Knight of the Burning Pestle,* 158; 160; 165; 178; 187; *The Little French Lawyer,* 160; 193, fn., 55; *The Two Noble Kinsmen,* 160, fn., 16; 184 and 184, fn., 44; 186, fn., 47; 199; 201; *Wit at Several Weapons,* 161; 175; 194; 201; *The Chances,* 161, fn., 17; 186, fn., 45; 193, fn., 55; 207; *The Little Thief,* 163; 168; *The Martial Maid,* 164; 201; *The Fair Maid of the Inn,* 164; *The Noble Gentleman,* 165; *The Prophetess,* 165, fn., 19; 180, fn., 34; 184; 187; *The Loyal Subject,* 168; 170; *The Coronation,* 168; 175; 204, fn., 66; *The Womans Prize,* 170; *The Elder Brother,* 171; *The Lovers Progress,* 173; 193, fn., 55; *The Spanish Curate,* 174; 193, fn., 55; 194; *Thierry and Theodoret,* 174; 184, fn., 44; 206, fn., 72; *The Queen of Corinth,* 175; 204, fn., 66; *The Faithful Shepherdess,* 176; 189; *The Tragedy of Valentinian,* 176; 193, fn., 55; 206; *The Mad Lover,* 177; 181, fn., 35; 185; 186, fn., 47; 204, fn., 66; *The Captain,* 177; 195; *The Humourous Lieutenant,* 178; 183, fn., 43; 201; *Cupid's Revenge,* 180; *A King and No King,* 181; *The Double Marriage,* 181, fn., 35; 182; 183; 188; *Four Moral Representations,* 183; *The False One,* 184; 204, fn., 66; *The Sea-Voyage,* 184; 188; *The Bloody Brother,* 185; 193, fn., 55; *The Maids Tragedy,* 185; 204, fn., 66; 207; *The Loyal Subject,* 186; *Bonduca,* 186; 187; 198, fn., 58; *The Pilgrim,* 186, fn., 47; 187; 199; 199, fn., 59; *Monsieur Thomas,* 187; *The Elder Brother,* 193; *The Knight of Malta,* 193, fn., 55; 198; *The Maid in the Mill,* 200; *A Wife for a Month,* 204, fn., 66; *The Coxcomb,* 204, fn., 66; *Women Pleased,* 204, fn., 66; *The Passionate Mad-man,* 204, fn., 66; [Masque] *Masque of the Gentlemen,* 204, fn., 66; *The Honest Man's Fortune,* 207

Beauregard, François, seventeenth century oboist in Germany, **VI:** 131

Beauty, I: 200ff; 305; 310ff, Plotinus; **II:** 108; 153ff, St. Augustine; 186, Pseudo-Dionysius Areopagite; 319, Bonaventure; 345 Thomas Acquinas: has to do with God; **III:** 25, Petrarch; 144ff, Chaucer; 169. Alberti, fifteenth century; 200ff, Leonardo da Vinci; 217, poem by Charles d'Orléans discusses beauty; **IV:** 15ff, sixteenth century Italy; 181ff, Michelangelo; 260, Montaigne; 299, Cervantes; 333, Lope de Vega; **VI:** 245, Leibniz: is simply pleasure; **VII:** 48 (Mersenne); 106ff, French Baroque philosophers views, including 108, art is not found in its externals (Fénelon); 108, Andrè's *Essay on Beauty*; 109, art can be perceived only through feelings which words cannot express (Batteux); 120, on beauty in music; **VIII:** 82, (Bacon); 103; 135, Milton, Beauty is Nature's coin; 251, (Hume); 296ff, Hutcheson, author of "An Inquiry into the Original of our Ideas of Beauty and Virtue" (1729) provides a very important discussion of the subject of beauty and art and music; 414, views on Beauty by Restoration writers on manners

Bede, Venerable, 672–735, monk and historian, **II:** 177; 196; 211, the myth of St. Cuthbert; dates Roman church music in England from 635 AD

Beer, Johann, 1655–1700, court musician in Weissenfels, **VI:** 130

Beethoven, Ludwig van, 1770–1827, German composer, **I:** 4; 16; 21; 28; 29; 32; 43; 200; **VI:** 126; 148, influence of Turkish Music in his Ninth Symphony

Begabredus, VIII: 139, ancient Anglo minstrel, said by Milton to have excelled in music all before him

Behn, Aphra, 1640–1689, first English woman to make a living writing, **VIII:** 312; as playwright: *The Forced Marriage,* 312; 313; *The Emperor of the Moon,* 313; 315, fn., 32; 319; 320; *The Lucky Chance,* 314, fn., 29; *Abdelazer, The Young King,* 315; *Sir Patient Fancy,* 316; 317; *The Amorous Prince,* 316; *The Widow Ranter,* 317, includes an Indian religious ceremony set in Virginia; 319

Bentley, Richard, 1662–1742, English writer, **VIII:** 246, fn., 85

Beldgabred, medieval minstrel of fame, **II:** 355, fn., 2

Belisarius, 500–565, Byzantine general, **II:** 195

Bellay, Joachim du, b. 1525, French poet, **IV:** 200; 215ff, in awe of Rome; 217, on education; 220; 222ff; 226; 228

Bembo, Pietro, 1470–1547, Cardinal, poet, papal secretary to Leo X; **III:** 18; also appears as a character in Castiglione; **IV:** 17; 136ff; **VI:** 6

Benedeti, Giovanni, IV: 68, you cannot understand theory without performance

Benelli, Alemanno, a character in Bottrigari, **IV:** 48; 68ff

Bénigne de Bacilly, 1621–1690, French composer and theorist, **VII:** 32

Benivienti, Girollamo, 1453–1542, Florentine poet, **IV:** 88

Beowulf, **II:** 206ff, sixth to eighth century music in

Berardi, Angelo, 1636–1694, Italian music theorist, **VI:** 30; 51

Berdic, eleventh century English jongleur, **II:** 237

Bergerac, Cyrano de, 1619–1655, French writer, **VII:** 219; 221

Bergerotti, Anna, seventeenth century singer, a favorite of Louis XIV, **VII:** 4

Berkeley, George, 1685–1753, Irish philosopher, follower of Locke, **VIII:** 258

Bernard of Chartres, fl. 1115–1124, neoplatonist philosopher, **II:** 321

Bernard of Clairvaux (St. Bernard), 1090–1153, **II:** 248; 281; 311ff, ends career of Abelard for teaching Reason instead of Faith; 315; 318; 322ff; 327ff; 330; **III:** 6

Bernard of Cluny, fl. 1122–1156, Church writer, **II:** 320ff

Bernardino de Padova, first cornett in the Lucca civic band, **IV:** 83

Bernart de Sayssac, troubadour, **II:** 372

Bernasconi, Italian composer, **VII:** 144

Bernhard, Christoph, 1627–1692, German writer, **VI:** 40, remarkable list of emotions used in singing; 163, fn., 36; 167; 178

Berni, Francesco, subject of a poem by Michelangelo, **IV:** 187

Berselius, Paschasius, letter to Erasmus, **V:** 3

Bertran de Born, b. c. 1140, troubadour, **II:** 382; 384

Bertrand, Anthoine de, 1530–1581, **IV:** 193; 198ff, French composer of quarter-tone harpsichord music

Bes, Egyptian god of childbirth with music, **I:** 74

Betterton, Thomas, 1635–1710, leading English actor of the seventeenth century, and one of few who failed to appreciate Shakespeare, **VIII:** 274; 304, an interesting discussion of contemporary theater; 306ff, on the educational purpose of drama

Bianchi, Angioletta, singer and wife of a wealthy seventeenth century merchant in Venice, **VI:** 16

Bible, II: 82, fn., 8, creation of the New Testament in 367 AD; 82ff, pagan myths;

Bicameral Man, I: 8; 45, Liszt, music relieves us from the left hemisphere; 153; 194ff, Plato; 252ff; 258, fn., 40, Aristotle; 283ff; 284, Ariston, 320–250 BC; 284, Epicurus; 284, Theophrastus, 372–287 BC, student of Aristotle; 285; 305, Epictetus; 306, Plutarch, "emotions give meaning to Reason"; **II:** 125, St. Basil, left brain even fails in speech; 141, St. Augustine; 192, Boethius; 260ff, Guido, 1026–1028, early man could not have understood music on a rational level; 310, Roger Bacon one of the first to clearly understand "two modes of knowledge, reason and experience; 334, Thomas Acquinas: Man is a fusion of two natures, intellective and sensitive; 359, the experiential side gives meaning to Reason 359, fn., 16, the shepherd's pipe as a metaphor for communication; 436, Grocheo, in 1300 "music is the principal means of the intellect explaining itself"; **III:** 7, emotions vs Reason in the fourteenth century; 19ff, Petrarch on experience; 22ff; 106ff, William of Ockham on intellect vs senses; 139, Chaucer; 306, Medwall, *Nature,* on Reason and Sensuality; **IV:** 7, Mirandola on role of left brain; 124, Guarini; 296ff, Cervantes on whether we communicate words or feelings?; **V:** 293, separate sides for Reason and Love, Greene, Lodge; 347, Shakespeare on the separation of Reason and Love; **VI:** 154, Marpurg found Bach's music in both left and right hemisphere, "the heart and the understanding are set into gentle motion together with the ear." But Mattheson added that Bach "did not teach the supposed mathematical basis of composition. This I can guarantee"; 221, a poem by

Angelus Slesius; 234ff, Leipniz; 237, Wolff; **VII:** 41, (Mersenne); 86, major discussion by Pascal and Rochefoucauld; 164ff, (Descartes); 229, Mareschal de Créqui as an older man, "How unhappy is my condition! I have lost everything on the side of Reason and I see nothing for me to pretend to on the side of Passion"; 248ff, Voltaire; 294, Voltaire; 304, Voltaire: "Though I distrust my head, I am always sure of my heart"; **VIII:** 23, Avison makes a complete break between musical communication and Reason; 41, Roger North on the rational vs the experiential; the rules are very few and children must learn without an explanation of them; 42, what makes a good melody cannot be expressed in words; 78, Bacon had a modern understanding of the organization of the mind, except for his failure to give emotion its due; 79, for Bacon the greatest pleasure was that associated with the left hemisphere, surpassing any pleasures of the senses; 97ff, examples of poetry describing various aspects of our twin brain hemispheres; 224, Hobbs had a good basic understanding; 247, interesting thoughts by Hume, but not all accurate; 265, (Temple); 270, (Wotton); 274ff, Gildon, much concerned wth actors notes that a mirror creates confusion for the viewer sees everything reversed; 279, (Shaftesbury); 300, (Harris); 337ff, (Dryden); 348ff, (Pope); 350ff, Sheridan, Pope, Thomson, Akenside and Gay; 377, Swift on the emotional impact on speech; 378, Wycherley on Reason and emotions; 385, Swift; 407ff; 417, (Shenstone); 446, (Steele)

Bichi, Cardinal, Italian host for Baroque concerts, **VII:** 147

Biedermann, Rector of the Freyberg Gymnasium in 1748, **VI:** 141

Bigaglia, Diogenio, seventeenth century Italian Benedictine monk and composer, **VI:** 17

Binchois, c. 1400–1460, Franco-Flemish composer, **III:** 211, already old-fashioned in the fifteenth century; 221; 228; 241

Bion, fl. 105 BC, **I:** Alexandrian poet, **I:** 293ff

Birnbaum, Johann, 1702–1748, **VI:** 155, German music critic; 172, defends Bach

Bishop of Numana, II: 229

Blas de Castro, sixteenth century Spanish composer, friend of Lope de Vega, **IV:** 327

Blind musicians, I: 76; 115, Demodocus; 121; **III:** 10, Landini; **IV:** 316, Francisco Salinas, 1513–1590, blind professor at Salamanca

Blondel de Nesle, late twelfth century, English noble and trouvére, **II:** 275, finds Richard I in captivity; 377ff; 386; 389

Blow, John, Dr., 1649–1708, English composer, organist Westminster Abbey, **VIII:** 340; 356

Boccaccio, Giovanni, 1313–1375, Italian humanistic poet; **III:** 1, begins humanism in literature; 2, on *The Decameron*; 8; 18; 32; 45ff; 144; **IV:** 142ff; 265

Bodin, Jean, 1530–1596, French writer, **IV:** 229ff on the influence of climate and geography; 232, on history and Truth, on right hand preference; 233, on emotions; 235ff; 240, questioning the instruments use in church

Boësset, Antoine, intendant of the music for Louis XIV, **VII:** 139

Boethius, 475–524 AD, mathematician and philosopher **II:** 183ff; 213ff, *De Institutione Musica*; 214, Reason music judge music, not the senses; 216, senses perceive music, not

the mind; 217, pleasure is found in the materials [grammar] themselves; 217, emotions; 218, music develops character; 224; 247ff; 261; 353; 403; 434; 437ff; **III:** 147; 238ff; 255; **V:** 36; reference by Erasmus

Böhme, Jacob, 1575–1634, German philosopher, **VI:** 247ff

Boiardo, Matteo Maria, Count of Scandiano, 1434–1494, philosopher, poet and author of *Orlando Innamoratio,* **III:** 165, wrote in the style of fourteenth romances; 168

Boileau, (Nicolas Boileau-Despréaux), 1636–1711, **VII:** 107ff, on Truth and the sublime in performance; 112ff, *L'Art Poétique* (1674); 307; 313

Boldrani, Pietro, trumpeter in Treviso, **III:** 11

Boleyn, Anne, second wife to Henry VIII, **V:** 226, arrival procession music

Bolingbroke, Lord, English noble, **VII:** 294

Bologna Civic Wind Band, IV: 82, sixteenth century; **VI:** 16, described in procession in 1602

Bologna, II: 287, thirteenth century university;

Bombasi, Gabriele, 1531–1571, Italian philosopher, **IV:** 27

Bona, seventeenth century composer of canzoni, **VI:** 21

Bonachelli, Giovanni, seventeenth century Italian, **VI:** 53ff, even tempo is adjusted according to the emotions of the words

Bonagiunta Orbicciani da Lucca, d. 1296, Italian poet, **II:** 396

Bonandrea, Giovanni, fourteenth century lecturer in rhetoric at Bologna, **III:** 13

Bonaventure, thirteenth century Church writer, **II:** 316ff; 319ff

Bonelli, Aurelio, 1569–1620, Italian composer of canzoni, **VI:** 21

Bonini, Severo, seventeenth century Italian writer, **VI:** 40, on Peri's emotional singing; 43

Bonnet-Bourdelot, Jacques, 1644–1724, French philosopher, **VII:** 140; 148; 155, on opera

Bono, Pietro of Ferrara, lutanist, **III:** 250

Bononcini, Italian singer, **VIII:** 367

Bononcini, seventeenth century Italian composer, **VI:** 13; **VIII:** 386

Bontempi, Giovanni, famous seventeenth century castrato, **VI:** 14, on singing schools

Bordoni, Faustina, 1700–1781, first generation opera diva, **VI:** 13; married the German composer Johann Adolf Hasse

Borromeo, Cardinal, sixteenth century, **IV:** 38

Borso d'Este of Ferrara, 1450–1471, **III:** 179

Bottrigari, Hercole, 1531–1612, Italian scholar, **IV:** 48ff; 56; 59ff, on the meaning of the word *Concerto*; 68ff; 72, improvisation by singers, also in church; 78ff; 83ff

Bouchart, Abbey (see Gillotot, François)

Bowzybeus, itinerant musician in a Gay poem, **VIII:** 374, includes some titles of actual popular songs of the Restoration

Brahe, Tycho, 1546–1601, Danish astronomer in Prague, **VI:** 261

Brancaccio, Giulio Cesare, IV: 65, sang bass with a variety of improvisation new and pleasing to the ear of all (1575)

Brant, Sebastian, 1457–1521, German humanist, **III:** 256ff, *The Ship of Fools,* 1494; wisdom and common sense; 260ff; 271; 275, satire on the local church service; 284ff

Brantôme, Pierre, 1540–1614, French hisorian, **VII:** 225

Brathwaite, Richard, 1588–1673, author of a treatise on how to organize an English noble house, **VIII:** 3

Brécourt, 1638–1685, French playwright, **VII:** 195

Brendel, Alfred, Austrian pianist, **I:** 37

Britain, II: 202, sixth to eighth century; 205, instruments known in Britain in eighth century;

Britton, Thomas, poor citizen who sponsored early concerts in London, **VIII:** 9

Brive, the Limousin, a poor jongleur, **II:** 371

Brooke, Arthur, sixteenth century English poet, **V:** 270

Brossard, Sebastien, de, 1654–1730, author of an early *Dictionnaie de Musique* (1703), **VII:** 23, on Taste; 27, on Time vs Movement; 122, on early styles

Brosses, Charles, 1709–1777, French scholar traveling in Italy in 1739, **VI:** 15 description of opera in Naples and audience's role; 25, visitor to Venice in 1739

Brounckerk, Lord, Pepys hears music in his home, **VIII:** 439

Browne, Edward, son to Thomas Browne, **VIII:** 220

Browne, Sir Thomas, 1605–1682, physician, theological philosopher, **VIII:** 209ff; 214; 217

Browne, William, 1591–1643, Jacobean poet in the ancient pastoral style, **VIII:** 96

Bruges civic band in 1499, **III:** 231, plays town fair under Obrecht; **V:** 4, band guild, sixteenth century

Brulé, Gace, fl. 1180–1213, trouvére, **II:** 379; 388

Brumel, Antoine, 1460–1512, French composer, **III:** 162; **V:** 138

Bruno, Giordano, 1548–1600, Italian friar, philosopher, representative of the Church's Counter-Revolution; **IV:** 8ff, opposed to Aristotle; 9, distrust of the senses; 10, cautious attitude on traditional education; 12, on pleasure and pain; 14, worship of Art is almost a sin; 27, in music art is in the player, not the instrument; 30; 34; 92

Brussels civic band, 1495, **III:** 230

Bryskett, Lodowick, 1546–1612, English writer, **V:** 200, the senses are responsible for all evil things; 203; 214ff, *A Discourse of Civil Life,* many examples of corruption are caused by the music we listen to; young men must be more selective as listeners; 218

Buaval, Mme, seventeenth century French actress, **VII:** 273

Bubastis, site of ancient Egyptian festival, **I:** 80

Bucholczer, Noe, sixteenth century poet, **V:** 131, on the purposes of music

Buck, Craig, twentieth century writer on the bicameral brain, **I:** 48

Bugenhagen, Johann, 1485–1558, **V:** 64, his 1528 school plan for Brunswick

Bukofzer, Manfred, VI: 165, misses the point on emotions and music

Bull, John, 1562–1628, Baroque English composer living in Antwerp, **VI:** 278

Bunyan, John, 1628–1688, English Puritan preacher, **VIII:** 57; 59; 60; 65; 68; 69; 73; 74; 75

Burgkmair, Hans, fifteenth century German woodcut artist, **III:** 277

Burney, Charles, 1726–1814, English diarist, **VI:** 13; 47; **VIII:** 35; 36, recalled Handel as a teacher

Burton, Robert, 1577–1640, author of *The Anatomy of Melancholy* (1621), **VIII:** 57; 61; 66; 70

Busino, Horatio, seventeenth century Venetian ambassador in London, **VIII:** 2

Butler, Charles, d. 1647, English theorist at Oxford, **VIII:** 22; classifies music as mathematical, practical and performers; 27, composers need divine frenzy; 32; 35

Butler, Samuel, 1612–1680, Restoration poet, **VIII:** 368; 372; 419; 429

Buttstedt, Johann, 1666–1727, organist at Erfurt, **VI:** 182

Buxtehude, Dieterich, 1637–1707, German–Danish composer, **VI:** 175

Byrd, William, 1540–1623, English composer, **V:** 216, fn., 103; 218; 245; 271, a madrigal begging music for solice; **VIII:** 28, there is emotional power in the words of church music which inspire the composer

Cabestanh, troubadour, **II:** 370, made love to patron's wife; wife forced to eat his heart

Caccini, Giulio, 1551–1618, Italian composer; **IV:** 85; **VI:** 9; 30; 34; 36; 38; 41ff

Caedmon, d. 670, Anglo-Saxon monk, poet, **II:** 196

Caesar, Julius, 100–44 BC, Roman emperor, **I:** 368, bored with functional music

Caius Gracchus, pipe player for oratorical support, **I:** 365

Caldara, VIII: 26, fn., 16, judged by Avison as a composer of the highest regard, being "sublime"

Caldenbach, Chr., Baroque writer on the Doctrine of the Affections, **VI:** 163, fn., 36

Calderón, Don Pedro, 1600–1681, Spanish playwright, **VI:** 105ff, as playright, *Life is a Dream; Mornings of April and May, Belshazzar's Feast; The Surgeon of Honor; The Great Theater of the World; The Painter of his Dishonor; The Devotion of the Cross; The Constant Prince; The Fake Astrologer; The Moyor of Zalamea; Love after Death; The Wonder-Working Magician*

Caligula, 12–41 AD, Roman emperor, **I:** 459; **III:** 36

Calius Calpurnius Piso, Roman senator, **I:** 459

Callimachus, third century Roman poet, **II:** 6, on accompanied choral music; 8

Calliope, one of the Greek Muses, **I:** 210; 426ff, Horace; 449; 442; 447ff; 451

Calmeta, Vincenzo, 1460–1508, secretary to Beatrice d'Este, **III:** 172; **VI:** 31, on words vs emotions

Calpurnius Piso, Roman poet, **I:** 499, on his poems

Calpurnius Siculus, c. 50 AD, **I:** 499, on singing poetry; 502ff

Calvin, Jean, 1509–1564, French Protestant church leader, **IV:** 212ff; **V:** 75; **VII:** 253

Calvisius, S., Baroque writer on the Doctrine of the Affections, **VI:** 163, fn., 36

Camerata, seventeenth century group of Italian nobles who founded opera, **VI:** 9; 29, major discussion; historical musicology's misunderstanding of the context of the birth of opera

Camöes, Luis de, 1524–1580, Spanish poet, **IV:** 311ff; 322

Campanella, Tommaso, 1568–1626, Italian poet, **VI:** 76ff

Campion, Thomas, 1567–1620, sixteenth century English poet, **V:** 272; 279

Canale, seventeenth century canzoni composer, **VI:** 21

Canossa, Lodovico, 1476–1532, Veronese noble; **IV:** 146ff

Canterbury Tales, **III:** 137ff, musical skills of the Squire

Canus, most famous first century aulos player, **I:** 467

Canzoni, VI: 21ff, the early composers of instrumental church canzoni in Venice

Capella, Martianus, fifth century AD writer, **II:** 95; 104ff, *Marriage of Mercury and Philology;* 109ff, aesthetics of music; 112ff, a 'pagan' early history of music

Caphisius, fourth century BC Greek aulos teacher, **I:** 292

Capone, Neri, sixteenth century noble, **IV:** 77

Caporale, Signor, Italian cellist living in London during the late Baroque, **VII:** 11

Caracalla, 188–217 AD, Roman emperor, **I:** 459; 463

Cardaillac, troubadour, **II:** 375, had bad breath

Cardano, Girolamo, 1501–1576, Italian physician, mathematician, philosopher and author of a treatise, *On Music*; **IV:** 43; 148; 159ff; 161 self-description; **VI:** 33, on words vs emotions, "A song is related to music," i.e. music is emotions; **VII:** 42

Cardenal, Peire, 1180–1278, troubadour, **II:** 370; 390

Carestini, VIII: 462, famous singer mentioned by Lord Chesterfield

Carew, Thomas, 1594–1639, English poet, **VIII:** 107; 109

Carinus, 284 AD, Roman theater producer, **I:** 466, mass horns and trumpets on stage; **II:** 8

Carissimi, Giacomo, 1605–1674, Italian composer, **VI:** 86; **VII:** 23; 122; 160; **VIII:** 433

Carl Albrecht, 1726–1745, son to Maximilian II, patron of Italian opera, **VI:** 125

Carmina Burana, manuscript book of the monastery of the Benediktbeuren, **II:** 428, fn., 7

Carus, Roman emperor, **II:** 8

Case, John, d. 1600 English Aristotelian writer, **V:** 218, *The Praise of Musicke* (1586)

Casimir, Margrave of Brandenburg, d. 1527; **V:** 143

Cassiodorus, 480–573 AD, Roman statesman and philosopher, **II:** 175ff; 187ff; 189ff; 193ff; 195ff; 213; 219ff, *Institutiones Divinarum et Humanarum Lectionum;* 220, on the relationship of music with philosophy and mathematics, thinks of music as "speculative" not practical; music is innate to man related to the organization of the heavens and fundamental to religion; 248; **VI:** 186ff

Cassius, Roman poet mentioned by Horace, **I:** 408

Castel, Louis, 1688–1757, French mahematician and inventor of the *clavecin oculaire,* **VII:** 271

Castelvetro, Ludovico, 1505–1571, author of *Poetics* (1570); **IV:** 131; **VIII:** 136

Castiglione, Baldassare, 1478–1529, Italian diplomat and author of *Il Cortigiano* (The Courtier); **IV:** 1; 61ff; 135ff; 178; **V:** 184ff; 188, a gentleman only plays among friends; Peacham adds, but never sight-read; prepare privately; **VI:** 43; 125; **VIII:** 3

Castiglione, Cristofano di, fifteenth century subject of a painting admired by Leonardo, **I:** 5

Caterina, Infanta of Savoy, 1620, **VI:** 2

Catharsis, I: 262 (Aristotle); **II:** 113; 154, St. Augustine; 330, Hildegard von Bingen; **III:** 239, Tinctoris; **IV:** 26, Mei; 114, Tasso; 130, Minturno (1563), compares to physician's role; 166, Cardano; 185, Michelangelo, in a letter to Niccolò Franco; 305, Cervantes; **VI:** 161, represented by the German Baroque phrase "refresh the spirits"; **VII:** 84; **VIII:** 112 (Donne); 267, Rymer accepts Aristotle's definition but adds, "still Reason must rule"

Catherine de Medici, 1519–1589, **IV:** 212ff

Catherine the Great, 1729–1796, Empress of Russia, **VII:** 244; 277; 296

Cato, 95–46 BC, Roman writer, **I:** 355

Catullus, Gaius Valerius, 84–54 BC, Latin poet, **I:** 124; 355; 358ff; 363ff

Cavalieri, Emilio, 1550–1602, Italian composer, **IV:** 35; **VI:** 9; 40, on the purpose of the first operas, to express emotions; 50; 163

Cavalieri, Tommaso, recipient of sonnets from Michelangelo, **IV:** 180; 183

Cavendish, Margaret, 1624–1673, English writer on manners, **VIII:** 410; 416; 420

Cavendish, William, Duke of Newcastle, **VIII:** 3

Caxton, William, 1422–1491, English writer, **III:** 310; 317

Caylus, Count, 1692–1765, archaeologist, **VII:** 84

Cazzati, Don Maurito, head of music, St. Petronio in 1657, **VI:** 45ff

Cecchi, Giovanni, 1518–1587, Italian playwright, **IV:** 127

Celibadache, Sergiu, 1912–1996, great twentieth century Romanian conductor, **I:** 7; 46; 217; **VII:** 108, on beauty in music

Cellini, Benvenuto, 1500–1571, goldsmith and writer, **IV:** 14; 28, on his early life as a musician; 33 on art music; 39; 75ff, his account of the papal wind band performance

Celtes, Conradus, 1459–1508, German humanist, **III:** 253; 279

Cerone, Domenico, VI: 89ff, Italian, author of the first important book on Spanish music, *El Melopeo y Maestro* (1613)

Cerone, Pietro, 1566–1625, Italian writer living in Spain on church choir singing, **IV:** 288ff

Cervantes, Miguel de, 1547–1616, great Spanish prose writer, **IV:** 294, fn., 8; 294ff; 325; 342ff, **VI:** 93

Cerveri de Girona, fl. 1250–1280, leader of minstrels under Pedro III of Aragon, **II:** 274; 375

Cesti, Antonio, 1623–1669, Italian composer, **VI:** 129

Chabanon, Michel-Paul Gui de, 1730–1792, violinist and theorist, **VII:** 277

Chambonnières, Jacques, 1601–1672, French keyboard player, **VII:** 237, description of his playing

Chandos, John, singer under Edward III, **III:** 132

Chanut, Pierre, seventeenth century French ambassador to Sweden, **VII:** 176; 178

Chapelain, Jean, 1595–1674 French poet, **VII:** 185, on pleasure

Chapman, George, 1559–1634, Jacobean playwright, **V:** 279; **VIII:** 162, *Bussy D'Ambois,* 162; 167; 172; *The Gentleman,* 164; *The Blind Beggar,* 165, fn., 19; 181, fn., 37; 166; 182; 186, fn., 47; *All Fools,* 167; 172; 202; *Alphonsus Emperor of Germany,* 181, fn., 37; *The Tragedy of Cesar and Pompey,* 181, fn., 37; *Revenge for Honor,* 182; 201; [Masque] *The Maske of the Genlemen of the two combin'd houses, or Inns of Court, the Middle-Temple, and Lincolns Inne,* 203; *Byron's Tragedy,* 204, fn., 66

Character development, I: 253; 256, Aristotle; 288, Eratosthenes, attacked by Strabo; 289, Aristoxenus; **II:** 32, 35ff, Sextus Empiricus, music has no effect on; 218, Boethius; 255, Al-Farabi, c. 900 AD; 259, Guido, 1026–1028 AD; 265 (c. 1100 AD); 438, Grocheo emphasizes influence on character; **III:** 9, anonymous author finds music is harmful to character; 240, Tinctoris rejects this idea; **IV:** 21, on expression of modesty in Michelangelo, anecdote; 55, Giustiniani; 213, Calvin on music; 335, Cervantes in theater; 339 Lope de Vega on music affecting manners; **V:** 41, Erasmus is mostly negative; 94, Luther on the ability of music to affect the character of the listener; 106, Ornithoparchus emphasizes this value in music (gives Nero as an example!); 185, Galen (second century, AD), "Much music marreth men's manners"; 189, Lyly, music education may not be 'unfit,' but has nothing to

do with virtue; 354, Shakespeare on the characteristics needed in a woman to marry: Rich, good-looking, noble and an excellent musician; **VII:** 67ff, (Mersenne); 96, (La Bruyère); **VIII:** 80, Bacon: liberal arts softens and humanizes manners; 89, major discussion; 112, a poem implores London to turn to music to improve the behavior of the citizens and in his "Hymn for a Musician" he suggests some musicians have manners which might be improved by changing their reperoire; 386, (Prior)

Character of a Man vs his Music, I: 181, (Euripides), 320, (Strabo); **III:** 298, Rojas, fifteenth century Spanish poet; **IV:** 55, Galilei, Bardi; 268, Montaigne; 301, Cervantes; 342ff, the player is out of tune; **VI:** 66, (Tosi); **VIII:** 146, (Milton); 156, (Ben Jonson); 213, Dekker on a musician's bad behavior: there is no music without frets; 282, Shaftesbury gives a lengthy and valuable discussion on Art and the character of the artist

Charlemagne, 742–814, emperor of the Holy Roman Empire, **II:** 180ff; 188; 235; 237; 252; 357; 366

Charles d'Orléans, 1394–1465, **III:** 213, 217, a poem on beauty

Charles I, King of England, 1600–1649, **VIII:** 4, physical description; 5; 6; 138; 353

Charles II of Spain, 1665–1700, a lame half-wit, **VI:** 90, turned government over to Philip, Duke of Anjoy of France

Charles II, King of England, 1630–1685, **VIII:** 6, restoration and physical description; 7 musical tastes of Charles II; 8; 11; 212, fn., 13; 337

Charles IV of France, III: 14

Charles IX of France, 1560–1574, **IV:** 194; 202; 209ff, arrival music at Fontainebleau (1564); 211, welcoming procession for his queen in Paris; 214

Charles the Bold, last Duke of Burgundy, 1433–1477; **III:** 214; 216; 223; 229ff; 250

Charles V of France, III: 69, fn., 1; 95; 212, an idiot, insane by 1392

Charles V, 1500–1558, Emperor, Holy Roman Empire, **IV:** 178, fn., 7; 211, welcoming procession in Valenciennes in 1539; 252; 291; **V:** 68; 226, arrives in London in 1522

Charles VI of France, 1368–1422; **III:** 212, in 1401 founded a Court of Love in which members wrote love sings in the trouvère style; 212, weak and overwhelmed by war; 320

Charles VI, 1685–1740, Emperor, Holy Roman Empire, **VI:** 130, fn., 33, accidently shoots Prince Schwaisemberg; 146

Charles VII of France, 1403–1461; **III:** 212, weak and could not prevent the tragedy of Joan of Arc; 224

Charles VIII of France, 1483–1498, **III:** 213, led a failed Crusade but brought the Renaissance back to France from Italy.

Charles, Thomas, Jacobean composer who set poetry to music, **VIII:** 95

Charpentier, Marc-Antoine, 1634–1704, French composer, **VII:** 14; 19, definition of music; 24ff, on communicating emotions

Chartres Cathedral, in France, **I:** 8

Chastellain, George, fifteenth century chronicler of Burgundy, **III:** 228

Chaucer, Geoffrey, 1340–1400, English poet and composer, **III:** 137ff; 319; 324; **VII:** 301

Chaulieu (Guillaume Amfrye, abbé de Chaulieu), 1631–1720, poet and friend of Lully, **VII:** 118

Chaumont, Lambert, c. 1630–1712, Dutch composer of instrumental church music, **VI:** 280, fn., 13

Cheek, Mr., composer of a song in Behm's *The Lucky Chance;* **VIII:** 314, fn., 29

Chenaniah, Old Testament conductor, **I:** 88

Chesterfield, Earl of, 1694–1773, **I:** 108; **VIII:** 459ff, on opera

Chinelli, seventeenth century Italian composer for voices and winds, **VI:** 17

Choral conductors, I: 74, Egyptian Old Kingdom, 2686–2181 BC; 75; 77; 79; 80; 292

Choral movements, II: 6

Chrétien de Troyes, twelfth century writer, **II:** 359ff; 368

Christian I of Saxony, sixteenth century German noble, **V:** 134; 137, instrument collection; 146

Christian IV, 1577–1648, King of Denmark, **VIII:** 1

Christian, Duke of Weissenfels, 1712–1736. **VI:** 127, birthday celebration with trumpet choir, Hautboisten and horn ensemble as well as civic trombones

Christina of Sweden, 1626–1689, **VI:** 6ff, lengthy discussion of one of the great women of the seventeenth century; 7, hired Alessandro Scarlatti; **VII:** 169. **VIII:** 421; 421, fn., 62, Evelyn mentions a murder committed by Queen Christina of which we have not read elsewhere

Christine de Pizan, 1364–1430, **III:** 95; 212ff, writes from an older Church perspective with little interest in music 225ff

Christmas, Mr., best trumpeter in England in 1673, **VIII:** 220

Christopher, Bishop of Basel, sixteenth century hostile to clergy, **V:** 58

Christopher, sixteenth century duke of Württemberg, **V:** 134

Chronicle of St-Denis, II: 239

Chrysogonos, Roman noble, strong supporter of music, **I:** 352, Cicero;

Church music, see also Aesthetics, **II:** 116, instruments no longer wanted; 127ff, aesthetics of in 4th and 5th centuries; 129, purpose; 129ff, general ban on music except for vocal music—angels sang a birth of Jesus; 130, some instrumental music still defended; 130, fifth century: anti-Semitic explanation of Jews use of instruments in the service; 131ff, origin of Church music, on hymns and psalms; 133ff, it is the words which are important, not the music; St. John Chrysostom: even if you don't understand the words!; 144, St. Augustine: it is the words which matter; 164ff, St. Augustine, the words most important; Old Testament instruments were metaphors; 181ff, under Charlemagne; 209ff, on hymns in the sixth century, St. Columba, on punishment for one coughing while singing; 238, ninth century emperor killed during service; 252, Aurelian on the new Church modes; on singing chant and modeling the cadence after the waves of the ocean; "sweet music" promotes contemplation of Communion; 256, Odo of Cluny, c. 935 AD on use of modes; 254, a 900 AD treatise dealing with improvisation of a given chant; 266, John, 1100 AD recommends music other than singing; 306, Grosseteste in thirteenth century recommends all the instruments for worship; 365, in the twelfth and thirteenth century

French Romances, including use of organ and strings; **III:** 13, instruments in the 14th century fresco in the church of San Leonardo al Lago near Sienna; 66, Boccaccio; 90ff, fourteenth century *ars antiqua* objections of John XXII; 124ff, fourteenth century English philosophers; 130; 157, Chaucer; 173, Alberti on the power of church music; 188, fifteenth century Italy; 222, evidence of instruments returning to the service; Gerson mentions the pagan New Moon service, quality of church singers; 231, using winds in fifteenth century Burgundy; 248 Tinctoris on aspects of performance of church music, including *cantus regalis,* the improvisation on chant; 272ff, *De modo bene cantandi* (1474) by Conrad von Zabern, on singing with refinement, on vocal production, on correct Latin and intonation; 274, major discussion on the "pyramid" system of balance (less highs and more lower tones); 275, singer must inspire, not detract; 275, Brant satire on the local church service; 282, ensembles at the Council of Constance, 1414–1418; 321, England fifteenth century; **IV,** 37, Machiavelli on church ceremonies; 67, reference to as many as twelve choirs by Giustiniani (1623); 72ff, improvisation in church, including above the chant; 86ff, sixteenth century Italy, appearances of winds; 117, Crusaders organize outdoor Mass; 211, winds used in a Mass in 1520; winds in a *Te Deum* in Bayonne for visit of Charles IX; ceremonial church winds when Charles IX visited Paris; 212, criticisms of church music; 213, Calvin on affect of music on character; Calvin found the music more dangerous than the words; 227, delight by Marguerite de Navarre; 240; 270, Montaigne finds choral responses boring by repetition; singers in Rome were magnificent; 288ff, Pietro Cerone on improvements needed in choir singing; 290, some dance still found in Spanish churches in sixteenth century; instruments used in the Seville cathedral; spread of church music styles to New World in Mexico; **V:** 48ff, psalms, the center of Erasmus's interest in music; 49, opposed to a variety of instruments; against polyphony; improvisation in the service; 51, in favor of instruments in the church; on speech and music; 75, Calvin, Zwingli and Frederick the Wise; 95, Luther on the spirit of the singer; 96ff, long discussion; 119, Glarean prefers the old chant; 125, on the aesthetics of church music; 142ff, sixteenth century court church services; 144ff, instruments in civic church services (Lutheran and Catholic); 145, convents and monasteries, minstrels; 380, (Shakespeare); **VI:** 17, in seventeenth century Rome, lots of instruments begin to participate, with original compositions for voices and instruments; 17ff, André Maugars visits Rome in 1639 and left a description of performances in the new Church Concerti style, as described in Praetorius; 18, Giustiniani reports improvisation over chant; 19, Maugars reports on *Stile recitativo,* original church composition modeled after the new opera medium; 20, papal edicts aiming to prevent secular influence; 37, Northbrook on style of church singing; 67ff, subjective character of instruments; styles of music used in the service; including the influence from opera; 91ff, examples of the frequent use of wind instruments in the Spanish cathedrals, as well as in Spanish Mexico during the seventeenth century and in Puebla; 92, in Portugal in the seventeenth century, winds accompanied singers in the Badajoz Cathedral; 118, references in the text and stage

directions in seventeenth century Spanish theater; 142ff, German Baroque church music, both Catholic and Protestant; 146, the conservative style in Vienna under Fux; 177, views of German Baroque composers, especially against influence from the theater; 280, anti-instruments in Baroque Low Countries; **VII:** 80, Mersenne confirms improvisation over chant; 160, views of De Brosses; 238ff, descriptions of seventeenth century Catholic and Lutheran church music; 280, Voltaire's famous desciption of the *Te Deum;* **VIII:** 36ff, discussion on the performance of church music by Playford, Mace; 123, in praise of instruments used in the church; 124; 125, importance of sincerity; 147, Milton's comments; 198ff, in Jacobean plays; 218, Puritan views on the common man in church; 404ff, humorous descriptions in Restoration fiction; 426, Evelyn documents the first appearance of strings in English churches; 463ff, comments on Restoration church music

Church, early philosophy, **II:** 11ff; 88ff, Gibbon: success of early Church; 115, St. Basil describes the early Christian; 176, sixth to eighth centuries, "don't ask, just do what we say"; 232ff, milieu of the Church in ninth-eleventh centuries; 236, church schools in tenth century; **III:** 100, fourteenth century flagellants; **IV:** 244, Montaigne doubts the ability of man to understand God; **V:** 220, on the destruction of organs by the Puritans under Henry VIII; 221, the restoration of instruments and subsequent comparison with Rome; **VII:** 14, clergy of Paris in 1662 forbids any instruments except the organ; **VIII:** 16, Jacobean and Puritan practice

Cicada story, II: 4, with Eunomus, the lyre player; 4, fn, 4; 197;

Cicero, 106–43 BC, Roman philosopher, **I:** 351ff; 354ff, on music of the theatre; 356ff, music education; 358ff; 363ff; 365; 367; 369ff; 371ff, emotions and soul; 384, pleasure and pain; 389, on music in plays; 392ff, aesthetics and music; **II:** 139; **III:** 17; 26; 36; 56; 171, Cicero believed in internal tuning; 245; **IV:** 250; 262; 266; **V:** 19; 30; 86; **VI:** 211; 261; **VII:** 296

Ciconia, Johannes, 1335–1411, Italian composer; **III:** 11

Cini, Giovanbattista, 1525–1586, Italian playwright, **IV:** 30

Cinthio, Giraldi, 1504–1573, Italian novelist and poet, **IV:** 106ff

Ciruelo, Pedro, 1470–1548, important Spanish mathematician, who still believed music was part of mathematics, **IV:** 273

Cithara, harp-like instrument, **I:** 177

Civic music, I: 349, Livy on Rome; 364, Roman Republic; 467, public musicians who compose for plays; **II:** 273, begins to expand in the pre-Renaissance in size and duties; 276, twelfth century trumpet player described; 364, to announce an execution in the twelfth and thirteenth century French Romances; 421, German tower singing in thirteenth century; **III:** 11ff, growth in the 14th century; 101, civic duties in fourteenth century France; 159, Chaucer, watchman; 178, Gaffurio: civic bands flourish in fifteenth century; 179ff, music under the fifteenth century Italian courts; 221, new statues for the *Confrérie de St. Juliaen;* 223 political singing; policing the streets; 230, concerts in Burgundy, the *Ommegang,* civic band contract; 231 welcoming music; 276, civic bands growing larger in fifteenth century Germany, regular concerts with a extant collection of their literature in

Germany, the *Lochamer Liederbuch* of 1490; edicts regarding weddings; a torture device; 319ff, fifteenth century English, growth of concerts by wind bands; **IV:** 82, in sixteenth century Italy, Bologna, Florence, rehearsal contract of the *Musica di Palazzo of Lucca* in 1557; 83, Venetian Civic wind band with Dalla Casa; 212, music for the executions of the Huguenots; **V:** 139ff, Rothenburg an der Tauber; Memmingen; Nürnberg; 141, Raimund Fugger of Augsburg in 1566; 141ff, tower music; 144ff, civic church services; 149, performing for universities, civic banquets, weddings; 240ff; the Waits of England; 242, Lord Mayor's Parade; 242ff, use in the theater; 245ff, amateur civic music, wealthy merchants and lawyers; **VI:** 14ff, seventeenth century Italy; **VI:** 135ff, civic music in Baroque Germany; 278ff, Dutch civic music, *Collegia musica;* **VIII:** 9ff. civic music of the Restoration in England; 12ff, the Wait Bands; 438, Pepys finds the contemporary Waits to be very poor

Clairon, Mme, French actress, **VII:** 278; 287

Clarke, Edward, correspondent with Lock in 1686, **VII:** 247; **VIII:** 235

Claudius, Tiberius Caesar, 10 BC – 54 AD, Roman emperor, **I:** 363; 475; 490

Clayton, Thomas, 1673–1725, **VIII:** 450, 453, involved in the development of opera in England

Cleisthenes, Athens leader in 508 BC, **I:** 141; 148

Cleland, James, author of *The Institution of a Young Nobleman* (1607), **VIII:** 4

Clemens, Jacobus ('Clemens non Papa'), 1510–1556, Flemish composer, **IV:** 75; **V:** 144

Clement of Alexandria, 150–215, Church philosopher, **II:** 6, on the choral dance; 46ff, his version of "Know thyself"; 52, against poetry; 53, attack on cult-rituals, including Egyptians; 53ff; 59ff; 66, on the senses; 70; 75; 77ff, on Church music

Clement VII, 1523–1534, **IV:** 75, description of his wind bands, 96; 135

Clement VIII, pope, **VI:** 1

Clonas, ancient Greek composer of Prosodia, **I:** 130

Clovis, Christian king of the Franks, 482–611, **II:** 189

Clytosthenes, second century AD percussionist, **II:** 40

Cochlaeus, Johannes, 1479–1552, German theorist and professor at Köln, author of *Tetrachordum Musices* (1511), **V:** 104ff, hired to see that polyphony is not entirely neglected; 106; 114

Coclico, Adrian, 1499–1562, Flemish theorist who taught in Wittenberg in 1545, author of *Compendium musices* (1552), **V:** 103; 125ff, the first treatise to emphasize performance over theory repeatedly criticizing rules-based learning

Colet, John, friend of Erasmus, **V:** 16

Coliseum entertainment, II: 56ff; 196, sixth to eighth centuries; Cassidorus recommends tuning the howls of the audience;

Collingwood, Robert, twentieth century writer, **I:** 45

Collins, John, correspondent with Newton in 1670, **VIII:** 238ff

Colonia, Johannes, fifteenth century Italian composer, **IV:** 64

Colonna, fourteenth century cardinal; **III:** 17

Colonna, Francesco, 1433–1527, Italian monk, humanist poet, **III:** 161

Comanini, sixteenth century writer, **IV:** 23

Commodianus, third century Church poet, **II:** 46, fn., 6; 50, against theater; 52, against poetry

Compère, Loyset, 1445–1518, French composer; **III:** 162

Competition, I: 118, Hesiod, 850 BC, on competition; 142, Xenophon, Hiero; **VI:** 74ff, Marino, in *Adonis* gives the most memorable of all examples of pasoral competitions, here a lover and a nightingale; **VIII:** 52, North opposed; 288, Shaftesbury on the nature of adjudication

Compositional process, III: 83ff, Machaut, 85, emotions; **IV:** 165, Cardano on how technique produces emotions; 168ff, Cardano on the affect of the elements of music on emotions; **VIII:** 29, Simpson: advice to composers on making music reflect words; 30, Avison on same and on choice of instruments

Comtessa de Dia, fl. c. 1160, female troubadour, **II:** 377

Concert hall, I: 145ff; 214; 251, Aristotle; 462ff, built by emperors Domitian, 81–96 AD on the Campus Martius; Trajan, 52–117 AD on the Forum; and Maximian, 286–526; **II:** 116, still existed in fifth century;

Concert, when tables cleared, III: 127, fourteenth century English harp player; 156, Chaucer; **V:** 3, letter of Berselius to Erasmus in 1518; 379 (Shakespeare)

Condivi, Ascanio, student of Michelangelo who published his biography in 1553, **IV:** 180, fn., 17; 183

Conducting, I: 38; 98, Chenaniah, of the Old Testament; 146; 231ff, qualifications; 250, God; 251, 251 (Aristotle), 283, conductor in ancient Greece, 292 (choral conductors), 297, Damomenes, fine conductor of a male choir; **II:** 167, St. Augustine; **VI:** 173 (Bach); 215, Mattheson on the requirements and education needed for the conductor, **VIII:** 275, Charles Gildon, 1665–1724, writing about actors and the bicameral nature of our brain makes a point rarely mentioned in conducting clinics: When practicing before a mirror, to the confusion of the player/viewer, everything is seen as reversed. That is, the conductor would, in common time say, "my second beat goes left," but for the entire orchestra it in fact is seen as going right!; 368, Pope, the poet, proposes Raphael as the conductor of the heavenly choir; 452, Addison suggests having someone conduct the audience

Confrérie de St. Julien, fourteenth century guild in Paris, **III:** 101; 221

Congreve, William, 1670–1729, perhaps the best of the Restoration writers, **VIII:** 305ff, on the definition of comedy, "Humor shows us as *we* are"; 307, on the educational purpose of drama; 308; 309, a words for a Masque, with music by Mr. John Eccles, Mr. Finger, Mr. Purcel, and Mr. Weldon; as playwright: *The Old Batchelour,* 310; *The Mourning Bride,* 313; *Love for Love,* 314; 314, fn., 29; 347; *The Double-Dealer,* 314; *The Way of the World,* 314, fn., 29; 319; *Squire Trelooby,* 319; as poet, 347; 356, set to music by John Eccles in 1701; 360; 370; 399, on the serenade

Conine, Pieter de, sixteenth century goldsmith and instrument maker, **V:** 3

Conrad II, eleventh century Franconian king, **II:** 238

Conrad von Zabern, 1410–1481, theorist at Heidelberg University, **III:** 272ff

Constable, Henry, 1562–1613, English poet, **V:** 257ff

Constantine IX, 1000–1055, **II:** 231

Constantine V, Byzantine emperor, **VIII:** 139

Constantine, 272–337, Roman emperor, **II:** 88; 107

Conti, Abate, seventeenth century Italian critic, **VI:** 52

Conti, Francesco, Imperial composer in Vienna in 1730, **VI:** 189, fn., 21, punished for improper gestures

Convenevole da Prata, thirteenth century teacher of Petrarch, **III:** 21

Cooke, Henry, Captain, 1615–1672, composer and choral leader of the court under James II, **VIII:** 431; 439

Cooper, Anthony, Earl of Shaftesbury, 1671–1713, known as Shaftesbury, **VIII:** 279. Durant (1963) called him the most important writer on aesthetics in modern philosophy.

Coperario, sixteenth century English composer, **V:** 218

Copernicus, Nicholaus, 1473–1543, astronomer; **III:** 1; **V:** 82, Luther rejects; **VI:** 259ff (Kepler)

Cordatus, Conrad, V: 83, Luther's correspondence with

Corelli, Arcangelo, 1633–1713, Italian musician, **VI:** 8; 53, first-hand description of his playing; 165; **VII:** 146; **VIII:** 26, fn., 16, Judged by Avison as a composer of the highest regard; 386, 419

Corio, Bernardino, fifteenth century historian; **III:** 180

Cornale, Lodovico, VI: 16, cornettist with the wind band of Venice in 1602

Corneille, Pierre, French playwright, 1606–1684, **VII:** 89; 130; 187ff, *Le Cid* (1636); *Nicomedes;* 108, *The Liar;* 227; 231; 270; 273; 283; 289; 298

Cornier de Cideville, Pierre Robert de, VII: 279, Voltaire's famous satirical definition of opera

Cornish pipes, II: 356

Cornu, early Roman trumpet, **I:** 343

Correggio, Antonio da, 1489–1534, Italian painter, **VII:** 267

Cortesi, Paolo, 1465–1510, humanist philosopher, **III:** 162, fn., 6; 168 relationship of education to the emotions; 170; 186; **VI:** 32, on words vs emotions

Corvinus, Matthias, 1443–1490, King of Hungary, **III:** 283

Coryat, Thomas, visiting in 1608, **VI:** 21, hears older consort and new strings in Rome; 22

Cossezen, an old Lombard troubadour, **II:** 373

Council of Constance, 1414–1418, **III:** 282

Council of Trent, 1545–1563, **IV:** 37ff

Count Dierichstein, VI: 128, (1667)

Count of Oliveres, Cardinal, **VI:** 90, seventeenth century Spain

Count Preiner, VI: 128, (1667)

Countess of Abingdon, English, seventeenth century, **VIII:** 325

Countess of Arcos, seventeenth century, **VII:** 10

Courperin, François, 1668–1733, French composer, **VII:** 4, weekly performances for Louis XIV; 22, on Taste; 24; 26ff, on communicating emotions and on Movement vs Time; 31, improvisation; 34, on music education

Court life, V: 342ff, Shakespeare describes the courtier, including *Hamlet* (III, ii, 345ff) where a lesson on the recorder is given, as a metaphor of the courtier playing on others, and in *Timon of Athens,* where a character, as the opposite of a gentleman, is called Apemantus; **VII:** 244ff, Voltaire on Paris society; 281 Voltaire's famous comment on spectales

Courville, Joachim, d. 1581, sixteenth century French poet, composer and singer, **IV:** 204

Cousser, J. S., conductor at Wolffenbüttel, **VI:** 216, fn., 103

Cowley, Abraham, 1618–1667, English poet, **VIII:** 65, on divine and natural knowledge; 94; 96; 99; 111; 114

Crashaw, Richard, 1613–1649, English poet, **VIII:** 99; 106; 108; 114; 117; 123; 124; 126

Crébillon, fils, Claude Prosper Jolyot, seventeenth century French writer, **VII:** 215

Créqui, Mareschal de, seventeenth century noble in France, **VII:** 229

Cricket, see Cicada

Cristoforno, Giovanni, Italian musician and sculptor, **IV:** 145

Criticism, VII: 118, La Bruyère opposed to critics; 232, Saint-Évremond, disdainful of critics; 308 (Voltaire); **VIII:** 147, (Milton); 305, several playwrights criticize the critics; 349, Pope: "A little learning is a dangerous thing"; 383; 415ff, (Shenstone)

Croce, Benedetto, 1866–1952, Italian philosopher, **I:** 3ff; 10; 12; 14ff; 22ff; 27; 35; 42; 51ff;

Croce, Giovanni, 1557–1609, Italian composer, **VI:** 126

Croft, William, 1678–1727, Restoration composer, **VIII:** 363, fn., 41

Cromwell, Oliver, 1599–1658, English political leader, **VIII:** 6; 106; 328; 353

Crüger, J., Baroque writer on the Doctrine of the Affections, **VI:** 163, fn., 36

Crusades, II: 281, on the music of the crusades

Cruz, Juana Inés de la, 1651–1695, Spanish poet, **VI:** 92

Cudworth, English philosopher quoted by Voltaire, **VII:** 250

Curtes, Mr., Jacobean composer who set poetry to music, **VIII:** 95

Cuzzoni, Francesca, 1700–1770, first generation opera diva, **VI:** 12ff; **VII:** 279; **VIII:** 462, famous singer mentioned by Lord Chesterfield

Cyclops, Greek giant, **I:** 435, fn., 36, Ovid

Cymbals, I: 88ff; **VIII:** 74, Bunyan on the listeners excitement by, and urge to dance

Cynic philosophy, I: 273

Cyrus II, the Great, 585–529, of Persia, **I:** 68; 69; 147; **III:** 212; **V:** 186

Cyrus, first century AD poet, **II:** 43

Czepko, Daniel, von, 1605–1660, German noble and poet, **VI:** 226

Dalla Casa, Girolamo, d. 1601, **IV:** 83, leader of the Venetian Civic wind band; 84 on his cornetto playing

Damian, Peter, monk and poet, **II:** 229; 232, complains of monks who hurry singing; 237

Damon of Athens, music teacher of Socrates and Pericles, **I:** 145; 220; 229

Damonidas, choral member mentioned by Plutarch, **I:** 126

Danaus, brother to Amunoph III, founder of Argos, **I:** 103

Dance, I: 73; 78; 108, military; 108, fn., 19, Athenaeus says Socrates was a dancer; 125; 148ff; 171, Sophocles; Phrynichus; Thepis, dance teacher mentioned by Athenaeus; 183ff; 209; 222, fn., 69, for exercise; 224, with singing; 233, Plato's ethics; **II:** 6, chorus lascivious dancing in sun worship; 9, dancing slaves; 195, military, sixth to eighth centuries; 255, Al-Farabi, c. 900 AD, dance is visible music; 295, Roger Bacon on two kinds of music: that which you can hear and that which you can see (dance); **III:** 39, Petrarch on decline of choral-dance; 42, Petrarch's attack on morals of; 233, fifteenth century Burgundy *basse danse;* **IV:** 174, Cardano; 194, Arbeau, French author of sixteenth century dance manual; 206, Arbeau found there was still some dancing in the church; knowledge of ancient Greek dances has been lost; dance is a kind of mute rhetoric; when mime is added to dance it has the power to stir the emotions; musicians accompanying dance are free to improvise; *basse danse* has been out of date for 40–50 years; 290 some dance still found in Spanish churches in sixteenth century; 326, Lope de Vega criticizes modern dance; 344, Cervantes gives the titles of a number of folk dances popular at the time; **V:** 74, 1519 Swiss edict against; 158, Praetorius on court dance organization; 191, Puritans consider dance evil; 286, a Morris dance with the tempo too fast making the dancers perspire; 310, dancers playing a pipe while dancing in Elizabeth England; 313, on the dangers for young ladies on dance; 315; **VII:** 16, Ménestrier on the value of trumpets in teaching horse dancing; **VIII:** 74, Bunyan on the listeners excitement by cymbals, and urge to dance; 200, music for dance in the Jacobean plays; 233 and 233, fn., 42, negative Puritan views; 244, Penn's Puritan views of dance; 405, with the fiddler; 427, only value is for posture, writes Chesterfield

Daniel, Arnaut, troubadour, **II:** 375; 377; 387

Daniel, Samuel, c. 1563–1619, English poet, **V:** 268

Daniello, Bernardino, d. 1565, Italian drama critic, **IV:** 128

Dante, 1265–1321, Latin poet, **II:** 369; 396ff; **III:** 12; **VI:** 96

Daphnis and Chloe, **II:** 40

Daphnis, aged panpipe player, sixth to eighth century, **II:** 198

Darius III, 336–330 BC, King of Persia, **I:** 69

Dark Ages, dates from the sixth century, **II:** 175ff, reflects the disappearance of secular scholarship; 178, invasion by Eastern tribes; 179, Justinian on the decay of Rome; 257, Guido's anagram on the disappearance of music during the Dark Ages;

Darwin, Charles, 1809–1882, English naturalist, **I:** 12

Dato, Carolo, Florentine noble, mentioned by Milton, **VIII:** 133

Daube, Johann, German Baroque writer, **VI:** 171

Davenant, William, 1606–1668, composer of the first opera, *The Siege of Rhodes,* sung in England, **VIII:** 10, opened a theater for music in London in 1656; 328; 367; 440

David, Hebrew king of the Old Testament, **I:** 89ff; 96; **II:** 100; **V:** 38; 40ff (Erasmus); 48; 112; 195; 264; 269; 333; **VII:** 238; **VIII:** 34; 114

Davies, Sir John, 1569–1626, English poet, **V:** 256; 275

Davison, Archibald T., 1919–1933, Boston choral conductor, **I:** 26

De Brosses, Charles, 1707–1777, French intellectual, **VII:** 140; 143; 146; 156, on opera; on church music; 160, on hearing church music

De la Rue, Pierre, 1452–1518, Franch–Flemish composer, **V:** 119

Debussy, Claude, 1862–1918, French composer, **I:** 17

Decorus, Volupius, Baroque writer on the Doctrine of the Affections, **VI:** 163, fn., 36

Deering, V: 247, sixteenth century popular music in England

Defoe, Daniel, 1660–1731, Restoration writer, **VIII:** 385ff ; 395; 401; 404

Dekker, Thomas, 1572–1632, English poet, **VIII:** 100; 210; 212ff; 215, on "canting"; 215, metaphors on music and society; 217; 218ff; 220; as playwright: 155, *The Roaring Girle,* 155; 167; 197; *The Whore of Babylon,* 157; 159; 186, fn., 47; *The Sun's-Darling,* 161; *If This be not a Good Play,* 163; 186, fn., 47; 188; 208; *The Wonder of a Kingdom,* 163; 171; 178; 179; 181, fn., 37; 185; *Old Fortunatus,* 165; 175; 176; 178; 184; 189, fn., 52; 200; *The Virgin Martyr,* 165, fn., 19; 188; 198, fn., 58; 438; *The Noble Spanish Soldier,* 165, fn., 19; 181, fn., 37; 189, fn., 52; *The Honest Whore,* 167; 176; *The Witch of Edmonon,* 167; 208; *Westward Ho,* 175; 184; 205, fn., 69; ("Enter a noyse of Fidles"); 208; *Sir Thomas Wyatt,* 179; *Satiromastix,* 181; 182; 195; 200; 204, fn., 66; *The Welsh Embassador,* 181; *Patient Grissil,* 184; 189, fn., 52; *The Shoemaker's Holiday,* 194, fn., 44; 186, fn., 47; 189, fn., 52; *Lust's Dominion,* 186, fn., 47

Delany, Patrick, Restoration poet, **VIII:** 352

Della Valle, Pietro, seventeenth century Italian critic, **VI:** 60

Demetrius, 337–283 BC, painter; **I:** 106; **III:** 170; **IV:** 326

Democritus, 460–370 BC, Greek philosopher, **I:** 153; 390; **II:** 24; 38, music does not exist; **III:** 7

Demodocus, ancient Greek blind musician, **I:** 115; 121

Demophilius, third century Roman poet/singer, **II:** 5

Demosthenes, 385–322 BC, Alexandrian orator, **I:** 287; 391; 396ff; **II:** 19

Descartes, René, 1596–1650, French philosopher and author of a *Compendium of Music;* **VI:** 6ff, instructor, and death, serving Christina of Sweden; 233; 302; **VII:** 37; 163ff; 250

Deschamps, Eustache, 1346–1406, poet and student of Machaut, **III:** 69, 83 purposes of music; 93ff, *L'Art de Dictier;* 102 on instrumentation for in or outdoor occasions

Desiderio, Gratioso, noble mentioned in Bottrigari, **IV:** 68ff

Desiderius, Bishop of Vienne, sixth century, **II:** 176

Desjardins, Jean Baptiste, oboist in the *Les Grands Hautbois,* **VII:** 2, teaching contract

Deutsch, Diana, Professor, UC San Diego, **I:** 51

Dexitheus, lyre player mentioned by Aristophanes, **I:** 175

Diamantina, La, Restoration Period lady who "played on the violin divinely and sang angelically," **VIII:** 425

Diana, Greek god, **I:** 428; 430; 432, Horace; 437

Diderot, Denis, 1713–1784, French encyclopedist, **VII:** 28, description of the emotional singing of Rameau's nephew

Dieupart, Charles, VIII: 450, 453, involved in the development of opera in England

Diodorus Siculus, 60–30 BC Greek philosopher on Egypt, **I:** 78

Diodorus, first century lyre player, **I:** 467

Diogenes Laertius, third century AD philosopher, **I:** 286; 292ff

Diogenes, 412–323 BC Greek philosopher of the Cynic School, **I:** 292; **II:** 32ff

Dionysius, ancient Greek philosopher, **II:** 27

Dionysus, mythical Greek god, **I:** 110; 156; 175; 182; 208; 244ff; 296; 321; 359

Diophantus, VIII: 271, ancient writer mentioned by Wotton

Dioscorides, second century Roman poet, **II:** 6, Cybele festival

Diotogenes, sixth century, Pythagorean School, **I:** 161

Dioysius, I: 393 (legendary ancient musician mentioned by Cicero)

Divine frenzy, **IV:** 98, Vida; 103; 195ff, Pontus de Tyard, *fureur Poétique* and *fureur divine;* 264, Montaigne on the poet's frenzy; **VIII:** 27 (Butler, 1636); 96, mentioned in a poem by Cowley

Divine, I: 88; 90, Heman, Old Testament choral leader; 317, Strabo: music puts us in touch with the Divine; 336, Plutarch: still associated with sacrifices in Roman Period of Greece; 347, fourth century BC aulos players go on strike; 352, Horace on aulos and lyres in temple of Venus; 357ff, for Roman cult gods; 358, re Hannibal; 359ff, Livy; 362, instrumental festival days: June 13, aulos; March 23 and May 23: trumpet [Varro]; 425, Tibullus; 452; 463, emperor Elagabalus played aulos and panpipes in Baal services; **II:** 6, Gibbon on music with sun worship; 6, chorus lascivious dancing in sun worship; 9, dancing slaves; 34, Philodemus: music has no effect; 43, music like religion cannot be seen; 46, a Christian should not sing love songs; 46 fn., 6, Commodianus agrees; 53ff, Egyptian religious rites; 55, transition of Greek to new Christian music; 74, on Art's divine connection: St. Justin Martyr, Origen, Clement of Alexandria; 76ff, Church music; 93, Julian reestablishes cults; 100, divine connection; 118, St. John Chrysostom Jews for still using the trumpet; 121, fourth century, pagan music vs Church music; 194, pagan rites; 279, the Great Hallelujah! of 1233, religious trumpeter; **IV:** 32, poet as prophet, divinely inspired; **V:** 37, poem in Ockeghem's honor by Erasmus—Music is something divine; 88, Luther finds the divine in music; 216, fn., 103, William Byrd writes that if you just diligently and earnestly ponder

the divine, a profound and hidden power will supply the music; **VIII:** 214, Browne on music's connection with divinity; 215, did music survive the Flood?; 343, Dryden's reference to a pagan ritual; 369, Swift on the pagan moon ritual

Dolcibene, distinguished fourteenth century performer, knighted by Charles IV; **III:** 14

Domenico da Prato, 1389–1433, Florentine writer; **III:** 10

Domesday Book, 1086, **II:** 237

Domitian, 81–96 AD, Roman emperor, **I:** 459; 506ff; **III:** 25; 33

Donatello, 1386–1466, Italian artist, **IV:** 178

Donatus, Aelius, fourth century professor of rhetoric, author of an early incomplete treatise on the theater, **II:** 92

Doni, Antonfrancesco, sixteenth century writer, **IV:** 77

Doni, Giovanni, 1594–1647, **VI:** 34, on words vs emotions; 61, on improvisation

Donne, John, 1573–1631, **VIII:** 58, syllogism on the superiority of intelligence in women; 60; 66; 69; 72; 74; 75; 93, on kinds of poets beneath respect; 95; 100; 102; 105; 112

Donnington, Robert, VI: 39, early opera melody (monody) is "one actor's cry from the heart"

Dorat, Jean, 1508–1588, **IV:** 199, sixteenth century French lecturer on classical literature.

Dorati, Nicolao, sixteenth century leader of the Lucca civic band, **IV:** 83

Dorian, a Greek style mode, **I:** 104ff; 180, fn., 41; 180

Dorilaus, early philosopher, **V:** 107

Dorion, I: 276ff, Alexandrian Period aulos player

Douglas, Lord James of Scotland; **III:** 131

Dowland, Robert, 1591–1641, son of John Dowland and author of a lute method book of 1610; **VIII:** 4

Draconites, Johannes, V: 30, 1518 letter from Erasmus recommends the young poet, Eobanus

Draghi, Giovanni, Restoration composer, created the music for Dryden's famous "Song for St. Cecilia" of 1687, **VIII:** 334

Drake, Sir Francis, 1540–1596, **V:** 241 sails with a Wait band

Drayton, Michael, 1563–1631, English poet, **V:** 257; 283ff

Drum, I: 63; 65; 67; 73ff; 81

Dryden, John, 1631–1700, English poet and one of the great English writers, **II:** 11; **VII:** 112, fn., 107; **VIII:** 321ff; major works: *The Conquest of Granada,* 322; 344; *The State of Innocence,* 323; 336; *The Indian Emperour,* 323; 329; 333; *The Rival Ladies,* 324; *Troilus and Cressida,* 324; *The Empress of Morocco,* 324; *Tyrannick Love,* 326; 331; *The Spanish Fryar,* 327; 344; *An Evening's Love,* 329; 341; *The Vindication,* 329; *The Wild Gallant,* 330; *Aureng-Zebe,* 330; 343; *The Tempest or the Enchanted Island,* 330; 334; *All for Love* [an adaption of Shakespeare's *Antony and Cleopatra*] 330; 331; *Secret Love,* 331; 335; 341, fn., 57; *The Duke of Guise,* 333; *The Indian Queen,* 335; 341; *King Arthur* [Dryden's play, music by Purcell), 336; 344; 345; *Albion and Albanius* [play by Dryden, music by Louis Grabu] 337; *Marriage A-La-Mode,* 341; *Cleomenes,* 341; *Oedipus,* 341; 342; 344; *Kind Keeper,* 341; *Amphitryon,* 342; *Love in a Nunnery,* 343; 363; 383

Du Bos, Jean-Baptiste, 1670–1742, French philosopher, **VII:** 84, renewed interest in catharsis. 110, on art and nature; 116, his *Réflexions Critiques sur la Poésie et sur la Peinture* (1719); 119; 129; 141

Duc de Joyeuse, sixteenth century French noble, **IV:** 209

Duché, Joseph, 1668–1704, French librettist and *valet de chambre* of Louis XIV, **VII:** 277

Duchess of Maine, VII: 286

Ductia, **II:** 439, a light song sung in chorus in Grocheo, 1300

Dudley, Robert, Elizabethan English nobleman, **V:** 300, dedicatee of Greene's *Planetomachia* (1585)

Duellius, Gaius, first century BC, Roman admiral, **I:** 353

Dufay, Guillaume, 1397–1474, Burgundian composer; **III:** 121; 211, already old-fashioned in the fifteenth century; 235, music for Philip the Good's banquet of the Order of the Golden Fleece in 1454; 221; 228; 231; 236; 238ff; 244

Duke Johann Friedrich, 1608–1628, instrumental church music, **VI:** 145

Duke August of Brunswick, VI: 173

Duke Henry, V: 31, Erasmus letter of 1514 reminds the duke of the importance of posterity

Duke of Brunswick, sixteenth century Germany, **V:** 154, fn., 2

Duke of Buckingham, seventeenth century, **VII:** 89

Duke of Burgundy, seventeenth century, **VII:** 235

Duke of Lorraine, VI: 128, (1667)

Duke of Noaille, seventeenth century France, **VII:** 5

Duke of Saxony, (1621), **VI:** 127

Dulcimer, VIII: 149

Dumesnil, seventeenth century leading singer of the Paris Opera, **VII:** 10; 287

Dumuzi, ancient god of Addad, **I:** 64

Duns Scotus, Joannes, thirteenth century Irish Philosopher, **II:** 230ff (on liberal arts); 299ff, on Reason and the senses; 301ff; 303

Dunstable, John, 1390–1453, English composer; **III:** 211, already old-fashioned in the fifteenth century; 221; 239

Durán, Domingo, author of the Spanish music treatise, *Lux bella* (1492), **III:** 299

Durant, Will, 1885–1981, American historian, **I:** 3ff; 249; **II:** 312; **VI:** 71; 283; **VIII:** 77; 279

Dürer, Albrecht, 1471–1528, German artist, **IV:** 178, f. 7; **V:** 4; 69ff

Duchess of Marlborough, VIII: 360

Duval, Jean-Baptiste, seventeenth century French ambassador to Venice, **VI:** 22

Dynamic symbols, II: 354, Thomas Acquinas: the intensity of a given passion varies with the active power of the agent.

Ea, ancient god of music in Babylonia, **I:** 65

Ealhhild, English queen, eighth century, **II:** 202

Earl of Arundel, English noble, **VIII:** 5

Earl of Chesterfield, Philip Stanhope, 1694–1773, English writer famous for his letters to his son, **VIII:** 407ff; 416ff; 424; 427

Earl of Cumberland, seventeenth century English noble, **VIII:** 3

Earl of Hertford (1591), **V:** 235, visit of Elizabeth I

Earl of Leicester (1575), **V:** 5; 231, visit of Elizabeth I

Earl of Roscomon, English, seventeenth century, **VIII:** 324

Earl of St. Albans, seventeenth century English noble, **VII:** 233

Earle, John, 1600–1665, chaplain to Charles II in exile; **VIII:** 216, pun on virginals and organ; 218ff

Early music, V: 45, views by Erasmus

Ebles de Sagna, troubadour, **II:** 372

Eccles, John, Restoration composer, "Master of Her Majesties Musick," **VIII:** 309, named on the cover of a Masque text by Congreve; 314, fn., 29

Echo, VI: 84, Kircher gives the famous anecdote about crossing a river; mentions a building in Pavia which could return an echo 30 times; **VIII:** 230, Hobbes, first philosopher to understand the true nature of the echo

Edemberger, Lukas, V: 89, German song writer and friend of Luther

Education, I: 271, Protagoras on basis for pay of teachers; 288ff, Eratosthenes, Strabo, Polybius; 292, Crates of Thebes, Diogenes, Diogenes Laertius; 415, Horace; **II:** 34ff; 58ff, attacks by early Church writers Turtullian, Lactantius, Clement of Alexandria, Origen; 58ff, Turtullian, Lactantius, Clement of Alexandria, Origen; 121ff, church concerns in the fourth century; 179, on the closing of the schools in the sixth century; 180, restoration by Charlemagne; 255, Al-Farabi, c. 900 AD; **III:** 166, Valla: learning music is necessary to learning the other liberal arts; 168, Cortesi: relationship of education to the emotions; 195ff, Leonardo da Vinci; 214ff, some dark views by Christine de Pizan; 216, François Villon, author of the *Great Testament* regrets his failure to take advantage of early education; 255, Nicholas of Cusa, 1401–1464, "education is learned ignorance"; 260, Brant on; 310, William Caxton, fifteenth century writer, on the importance of learning; **IV:** 36, Giulio del Bene proposes an academy following Aristotle's *Poetics;* 63, Galilei, you learn from the music; 217, du Bellay, important but music is only a recreation; 248, Montaigne on its utility, are there limits?; 250, on class size, on why we do not teach philosophy to the young; what to do with children who can't learn (strangle them); 251 too much education is bad; description of the classroom; how children are treated at

home; 269, music education should be by performance, not conceptual; 274ff, Vives was an early believer in childhood education; 275 in *Tradendis Disciplinis* (1531), nothing is more beautiful than learning; environment of the school itself; duties of the teacher; 276, encourages competition; teacher's job is to sort out levels of ability; 277, duties of the student; encourages memory; 'empty slate' theory; desires an universal language; student discipline; 278, on poetry, "the characteristic of their art is music," on the subjects of poetry, dangers in love poetry; 279, dramatic literature must be heavily edited; worries that teaching science may lead to ideas contrary to the Scriptures, thus hesitant about heathen writers such as Aristotle; importance of play; education must be used for the common good; 296, Cervantes description of Jesuit education in Spain; 328, Lope de Vega, the most educated man knows the least; **V:** 17, Erasmus on; 20, of all persons, the aristocracy are the least educated; 64ff, Johann Bugenhagen's 1528 school plan for Brunswick; 65 Frederick Sternfeld's 1529 school plan; 84ff, Luther's views, including the importance of music; 103, in 1505 the University of Leipzig appointed Sebastianus Müchelon as *lector musicae et aritmetice,* and in 1558 the lecturer in mathematics at the University of Heidelberg was expected to also teach music; 201ff, sixteenth century England; Knox presents a comprehensive plan for education of 1560; 202ff, Ascham greatly opposed to sending children to Italy for further education where they learn bad manners and bad habits; 290ff, Lyly: principal subject must be philosophy; 345ff, Shakespeare never praised formal education and in *The Taming of the Shrew* (I, iii, 25ff) a character warns not to let philosophy and the liberal arts get in the way of happiness. His most famous advice is the passage in *As You Like It* (II, i, 15ff), where he advises the importance of learning from Nature, "books in the running brooks, sermons in stone"; **VI:** 14ff, seventeenth century description of a singing school in Rome under Maestro Mazzocchi; 76ff, Marino: music education is reserved for women and children; 242ff, Leibniz; **VII:** 96–100, views of La Bruyère, Fénelon (very opposed to educating girls), Montesquieu; 258, Voltaire: if art has beauty, then the rules must be taught; **VIII:** 63, Hall on the dangers to children; 79, Bacon: society does not pay enough attention to the selection of teachers; 211, examples of extreme Puritan prejudice toward education; 242, Penn discounts too much education, for example, "The first thing obvious to children is what is sensible; and that we make no part of their rudiments"; 280, the views of Shaftesbury are those of the higher class and he complains that the literary category of "letters" has been banished from universities to distant cloisters; 322, Dryden dismisses traditional universities; 329, Dryden: both the best and worst of the modern poets will equally instruct you to admire the ancients; 378, views of Restoration philosophers

Educational Music, I: 88, Jeremiah ordered to teach music; 318, Athenaeus on philosophic reflection and educational purpose; 318, Plutarch; 355ff, Roman Republic; **II:** 110ff, Julian: the noble avoids study and performance; 256, Odo of Cluny, c. 935 AD; 257, Guido, c. 1026–1028; **III:** 13, fourteenth century summary; 128ff, "dear Walter," criticism of a music student in fourteenth century England; 156ff, Chaucer; 279, in pre-Renaissance German

universities; 299, fifteenth century Spanish writings; **V:** 48, Erasmus states *quality* music must be used for children; **VI:** 23ff, the *ospedali,* charitable instutions for orphans which featured the study of music, one of which in Venice employed Vivaldi; 66ff, Tosi; **VII:** 78ff, on new system of the Baïf Academy in Paris; **VIII:** 36ff discussion by English Baroque composers; 146, Milton's comments on music in school; 197ff, in Jacobean plays; 386, a lecture by Daniel Defoe; 463, on the coffee house tradition in London

Edward II of England, 1284–1327; **III:** 134

Edward III of England, 1327–1377; **III:** 128; 132

Edward IV of England, 1461–1470 and 1471–1483, **III:** 320

Edward VI of England, 1547–1553, **V:** 227ff, court musicians; **VIII:** 17

Effendi, Achmet, VI: 148, Turkish ambassador to Berlin in the eighteenth century

Elagabalus, 205–222 AD, Roman emperor, **I:** 463, played aulos and panpipes; **II:** 3, played organ;

Elector of Bavaria, seventeenth century, **VII:** 10

Electress Sophie, of France, VII: 234

Elisabeth Charlotte, Duchesse d'Orléans, 1652–1722, sister-in-law to Louis XIV, **VII:** 227; 232; 234; 237, on a concert postponed by weather; 238; 239; 240

Elizabeth I, Queen of England, 1558–1603, **V:** 183; 221ff; 229ff, major discussion; personal description by Roger Ascham, her tutor; performer on virginals; 229ff shortage of musicians and teachers; 230ff, court musical entertainments; 231, Elizabeth's Progresses: Kenilworth Castle (1572), 233, Norwich (1578), 236, Earl of Hertford (1591); 283; **VIII:** 1; 17

Elizabeth, Princess of Bohemia, VII: 165; 168; 177

Eltester, C., d. 1732, German poet, **VI:** 223ff

Emhab, seventeenth dynasty Egypt percussionist, **I:** 81

Emotions, I: 375, Cicero; 482ff, Pliny the Younger, Quintilian; **II:** 11ff, in communication; 12ff, on false emotions; 28, Galen, Sextus Empiricus; 71ff; 72, Tertullian; 126, fourth and fifth centuries; 148ff, St. Augustine; 253, Aurelian: Music moves the emotions; 301, thirteenth century philosophers; 302, Bacon: emotion is a form of madness; 302, Bartholomew Anglicus on emotions and speech; 302, Duns Scotus: emotions are the same as the "Will" of the intellect; 341, Thomas Aquinas; **III:** 22, Petrarch; 76ff, Machaut, 80ff, 85ff; 114ff, Gower on value; 141, Chaucer; 167ff; 197ff, Leonardo da Vinci; 216, rarely mentioned, except for Love, by fifteenth century French writers; 288, Ruiz on the universality of emotions; Love is most discussed; 291, Encina: poetry can move the emotions; pleasure and pain; 290; **IV:** 10, church distrust of emotions; 11, Machiavelli and Aretino on Love, and on the torment of Love; 32, Ficino: Love is the teacher and ruler of the Arts; 32, Pontus de Tyard describes affect of performance on emotions; 101ff, Vida, in poetry emotions are what reach the reader; Giraldi: the life force of poetry is emotions; 112, vivid example of emotions; 116, pleaing to Muses to help with emotions in poetry; 124, Guarini on the power of Love; 125, Love unaffected by Reason; 219, sixteenth century French poets; 233, Rabelais on color and emotions; Bodin on everything is subject to emotions;

253ff, Montaigne on emotions; 282, Vives and St. John of the Cross on the emotions; 329ff, Lope de Vega, love is known only by experience and further definitions of Love; **V:** 21ff, Erasmus thoughts on; 22, on Love; criticism of wives; on anger; 24, emotions block his speech; 67, Agrippa's views; 93, Luther on the ability of music to express feelings; 205, Philip Sidney: Reason and love are not connected; 346ff, Shakespeare's emphasis on melancholy; **VI:** 31ff, on words vs emotions; 37, Galilei recommends a singer attend opera to observe the physical aspects of emotion; 40, Christoph Bernard's (1649) remarkable list of emotions used in singing, on Peri's emotional singing; Berardi: music is the ruler of the passions of the soul; 51ff, on the duty of the player to express the emotions of the music; 53, to move the emotions of the audience the player must first feel the emotions himself; 53, Frescobaldi: the player must find the emotions in the music; 53ff, Giovanni Bonachelli (1642): even tempi is adjusted according to the emotions of the words; 54, Tossi on singing from the heart; 86, Kircher on the basic emotions, illustrated by the lament of Jephta's daughter in an oratorio by Carissimi; 96, Gracián follows the Church teaching that the emotions are the first step toward sin and must be overcome. "The emotions are the breaches in the defenses of the mind."; 105, Calderón on the conflict between Reason and emotion; 106, words cannot express everything; 167, and gesture; 164, on the relationship between emotion and tonality; 167, Marpurg: all music has emotion at its foundation; 206ff, Mattheson on the range of emotions in music; **VII:** 24ff, seventeenth century French on communicating feeling; 51ff, Mersenne on the association of colors and emotions; 53, the notational system is inadequate regarding the expression of emotions; 55ff, on the relationship of emotions and humors; 56, on the origin of emotional speech in man and animals; 57–68, major discussion of music and emotions; 59, Aldorise, Prosper, cited by Mersenne on the subject of emotions and laughter; 129, Raguenet on praise for the emotions in Italian music; 169ff, (Descartes); 174 Descartes on the physical manifestations of emotions; 179, Descartes: purpose of music is to communicate emotions to the soul of the listener; 186ff, on the emotions of the viewer of drama; 188ff, Corneille on the nature of Tragedy and its emotions; 192, Corneille on Love in the theater; 193, Fénelon on tragedy vs comedy; 231, Saint-Évremond, on Corneille vs Racine in how they treat the emotions in their works; 234, Saint-Évremond is not moved by the emotions of opera; 254, Voltaire discusses; **VIII:** 27, Avison on the affect of hearing the emotions in music, pointing out it never produces bad emotions; 32ff, major discussion by English writers; 65ff, Hall, very dark view of natural emotions with an extraordinary portrait of "anger"; 66, Harvey and Burton on melancholy; 66, Donne on associations between color and the emotions; 80, Bacon on the physical associations with various emotions and influence on the body; 100ff, a seventeenth century English poem calling on music to dispel Melancholy; 101, on love and music; 102, on suffering pain; 111, a poem by Herrick expressing the strong emotions in music; 209, Brown: As reason is a rebel to faith, so passion is to reason; 234ff, Locke, from his totally left-hemisphere view, sees all emotions only as variations of thought in the mind; 248, Hume assigns emotions

a much higher level of importance than earlier philosophers; 281, Shaftesbury believed emotions are genetic, which in general is true; 290ff, Hutcheson, 1694–1746, author of "An Essay on the Nature and Conduct of the Passions and Affections" (1742) helped bring England up to modern thinking on the emotions; 300, the power of music is to raise the emotions; 334, Dryden: What Passion cannot Musick raise and quell!; 380, Young, Swift and Pope; 381, Akenside; ancient philosopher, **V:** 40; 448, Addison on emotion in music

Emprepes, member of the Ephors, **I:** 129, cut the strings of a lyre;

Emser, Jerome, 1477–1527, lecturer in the humanities at the universities of Erfurt (where Luther was his student) and Leipzig, **V:** 82ff, Luther answers his criticism

En Raimbaut, troubadour, **II:** 372

Enlil, ancient god of humanity, **I:** 62

Enlulim, shepherd flutist in Sumeria, 2600 BC, **I:** 62

Ennius, 236–169 BC, Roman poet, **I:** 358

Enrique IV, the Impotent, fifteenth century king of Castile, **III:** 301

Entertainment music, I: 150, Pericles; 237ff, Plato; 265, Aristotle; 321, art vs entertainment; 337; **II:** 8ff, first three centuries; 69ff, Tertullian; 95ff; 102, grave material should have lighter moments; 119ff, fourth century, St. John Chrysostom: no more music and dance in the home, only singing of hymns; races & sports are entertainment for the Devil; 120ff, evils of the coliseum still exist and public still enjoying them; beginning to lessen due to economy; 239, court of Louis I; 279, twelfth century banquet; 280, arrival music in 1241; 282, arrival music for Richard I at Acre; 322, John of Salisbury against; 367, in twelfth and thirteenth century French Romances; 424ff, in German literature in the twelfth and thirteenth centuries; **III:** 14ff; 42ff; 102, Deschamps on instrumentation of in and outdoor occasions; 134ff, mumming in fourteenth century English; 159, Chaucer; 189, banned in 1405 at the University of Bologna; 225, on players in taverns; 234ff, the banquet of the Order of the Golden Fleece [*Toison d'Or*] of Philip the Good in 1454; 284, Brant's satire on local folk music; 301, need for; **IV:** 40, loses respect in sixteenth century Italy, Guicciardini, Machiavelli, Aretino (including music and pornography); 89, sixteenth century Italy; 120, value in Ariosto; 156, Castiglione, on laughter; but the gentleman should not *cause* laughter; 176, Cardano on simple quality of pop music; 214, sixteenth century France; 270ff, Montaigne worries about the effect on man and the great cost of large productions; 308, Cervantes, aboard ship; 310, this age so deficient in cheerful amusement; **V:** 54ff, Erasmus on entertainment music; 73, Agrippa on evils of popular music; 285, the lowest music; 382ff, examples in Shakespeare, including a portrait of the wandering minstrel in *The Winter's Tale* (IV, iv, 207ff and 276ff); **VI:** 87ff, in Marino's *Adonis* we find a description of a typical allegorical play within a play, an example of high court entertainment; 103ff, Quevedo on the ancient practice of barbers playing guitar; 120, rare example in seventeenth century Spanish theater; 231ff, Grimmelshausen describes the itinerant fiddler; **VII:** 13ff, seventeenth century street fairs in France; 161, La Bruyère and La Rochefoucauld find no interest; 241, for Louis XIV the 24 violins for banquet;

oboes and drums at his window to wake him; 242, peasant music; **VIII:** 75, Donne praises use for winter mornings; 90ff, Bacon finds the masque to be entertainment, not serious art; 97, example of a poem with the purpose of entertainment; 127, on geniune popular music; 202ff, descriptions from Jacobean plays; 220, Dekker on drums and the beer fiddler; 427, description of the dance fiddler; 428, the humble bagpipe player described; 428, on the broadside ballads and their singers; 465ff, comments on fiddle music and barbers

Eobanus, V: 30, young poet recommended by Erasmus in 1518

Epic poetry (celebrating great men and events), **II:** 91 (Julian); 438, Grocheo calls these kinds of songs, *cantus gestual;* **III:** 155, Chaucer; 214, recommended for children by Christine de Pizan; 221, in fifteenth century France; 250, Tinctoris points to the excellence of two Flemish brothers, Charles and Jean Orbus; **IV:** 104, Tasso on purpose of; components of; 106 Tasso on requirements of; 107, Giraldi on the connection between poetry and music; do not write for money; should have an educational purpose; 108, on the rules for; 316, promised by Luis de Góngora; , **V:** 349, Shakespeare's play, *Pericles, Prince of Tyre,* is a work of epic poetry

Epictetus, 55–135 AD, Roman poet, **I:** 305; **V:** 289

Epicurian philosophy, I: 273

Epicurus (342–270 BC), **I:** 283ff; 316

Epidaurians, I: 146

Epidicus, Roman playwright, **I:** 366

Erasmus, Desiderius, 1466–1536, Dutch humanist philosopher, **IV:** 167; 273; **V:** 1; 3; 7ff, major discussion; self-description; 18, self-pity description; 57; 84; 114; 201; 223

Erato, one of the Greek Muses, **I:** 210

Eratosthenes, 276–194 BC, Alexandrian philosopher, **I:** 288

Ercole d'Este, of Ferrara, 1431–1505; **III:** 179 **IV:** 77

Ereditario of Florence, wedding of 1661, **VI:** 5

Eryximachus, fifth century BC Greek physician, quoted by Plato as one who could create poets by touch even if they had no music in them, **I:** 207, fn, 36

Espinosa, Juan, sixteenth century Spanish music theorist, **IV:** 273

Este, Beatrice, d', 1475–1497, **III:** 180

Este, Isabella, d', 1474–1539; **III:** 181ff

Etherege, Sir George, 1633–1691, Restoration composer, **VIII:** 309ff, as playwright on Manners, *The Man of Mode,* 309; 311; 319, fn., 34; *She Would if she could,* 310, fn., 34

Ethos, **I:** 483ff; **II:** 133, in the context of Church music;

Etruscan Music, I: 343ff

Euclid, fourth century mathematician, **II:** 213; **VI:** 262

Eudes, English bishop, eleventh century, **II:** 239

Eumpolpus, aged lyre player, sixth to eighth century, **II:** 198

Eunomus the Locrian, famous first century lyre player, **II:** 4; 4 fn., 4;

Eunomus, II: 55 (singer under Clement of Alexandria)

Eupolis, I: 318, Eupolis: music is deep and intricate;

Euripides, 480–408 BC, Greek playwright, **I:** 169ff; 175ff; 181; 183ff; 186; 188ff; 207; 343; **II:** 17ff; 52; **VII:** 275; 284

Euryphamus, Pythagorean School, **I:** 161

Eutychides, first century Greek lyric poet, **II:** 3, owned 25 cases of music

Evelyn, John, 1620–1706, diary of an English tourist, **VI:** 4; 11; **VII:** 13, describes slave musicians in 1644; **VIII:** 18, documents first appearance of strings in English churches in 1662; 421; 422ff

Evradus Venator, II: 281, twelfth century trumpet player;

Experience, III: 140, valued above books in Chaucer; 192, Leonardo da Vinci; 288, Fernando de Rojas, fifteenth century: only comes with age; **IV:** 246, Montaigne on doctors and syphilis; **V:** 202, Ascham: year of learning is worth 20 of experience; experience makes us more miserable than wise

Eyselin, Jörg, civic musician in Memmingen, **V:** 40

Faidit, Gaucelm, troubadour, **II:** 370

Falkland, Lord, Treasurer of the Navy, **VIII:** 422, mentioned by Evelyn in 1684

Fantini, Girolamo, 1600–1675, famous trumpeter and author, **VI:** 5; 56

Farinelli, famous tenor, **VI:** 91; **VII:** 279; **VIII:** 462, famous singer mentioned by Lord Chesterfield

Farmer, Henry G., English writer, **I:** 63; 75ff

Farnese, Duke Odoardo of Parma, VI: 2

Farquhar, George, 1677–1707, Restoration actor, soldier and playwright, **VIII:** 305; 306, on drama's universality and being too close to human experience; as playwright: *The Twin-Rivals,* 305; *The Beaux Stratagem,* 314; *Love and a Bottle,* 314, fn., 29; 319; 320; *The Inconstant,* 314, fn., 29; *The Recruiting Officer,* 318; 393

Faustina, Mme, Italian singer, **VII:** 279; **VIII:** 422; 462

Federigo da Montefeltro of Urbino, 1444–1482, **III:** 182, music at court of; **IV:** 152

Feijoo, Benito, seventeenth century Spanish critic of Italian music, **VI:** 91

Feind, Barthold, 1678–1721, important German philosopher on opera, **VI:** 254ff

Feltre, Vittorino da, 1396–1415, humanist in the court of Mantua, **III:** 185

Fénelon, François, 1651–1715, French Church leader and writer, **VII:** 96ff, on education; 103ff, emotions are the central feature of communication; 106; 108; 109; 116; 118; 135ff, on the role of music in ancient and modern societies; 193; 213; 216; 218; 220ff; 224; 225

Ferdinand de' Medici, 1663–1713, patron of Alessandro Scarlatti, **VI:** 51

Ferdinand I of Naples, 1423–1494, **III:** 237

Ferdinand I, emperor, **V:** 139, in 1521 travels with a trombone consort; 144; 147

Ferdinand II of Innsbruck, 1529–1595, **V:** 137ff, instrument collection; 142

Ferdinand II, 1578–1637, become emperor in 1619, **VI:** 121; 124; 133

Ferdinand III, 1608–1657, emperor, **VI:** 83; 126, an active composer; 128; 134

Ferdinand, archduke, V: 9, 1524 letter from Erasmus, "it is too late to burn Luther"

Feriol, Charles-Augustin, VII: 291

Fernando V, of Aragon, patron of Columbus, 1474–1516, **III:** 295ff

Ferrabosco, Alphonso, 1575–1628, Jacobean composer, **V:** 218, "the father of many other composers"; **VIII:** 108

Ferrari, Ludovico, sixteenth century Italian theorist, **IV:** 43

Festa, Constanzo, sixteenth century composer, **IV:** 190

Festival at Delia, I: 143

Festival at Delos, I: 145

Festival at Delphi, I: 135; 145

Festival at Oea, I: 146

Festival of Cybele, II: 6, 138, St. Augustine;

Festival of Dionysus, I: 80

Festival of the moon, I: 85

Festivals, II: 47, Justin Martyr and Minucius Felix opposed; 48, Novatian opposed; 117, St. John Chrysostom states that God hated the theater and its music;

Ficino, Marsilio, 1433–1499, humanist and founder of the Florentine Academy and lyre performer, **III:** 164, on Plato's *Timaeus;* 173, on music therapy; 173; **IV:** 31ff; 326; **VI:** 31

Field, John, sixteenth century English Puritan writer, **V:** 220

Fielding, Henry, 1707–1754, Restoration novelist, **VIII:** 391ff; 393; 394; 396; 402

Filippo di Monte, 1521–1603, **IV:** 65, Giustiniani considered among the best composers of the 16th century; **V:** 156, mentioned by Praetorius relative to the Motet form

Finé, Oronce, sixteenth century French professor, **IV:** 193

Finger, Mr., Restoration composer, **VIII:** 309, named on the cover of a Masque text by Congreve; 314

Firmicus Maternus, Roman astronomer, **I:** 467

Flaccus, freedman of Claudius, composer named in works of Terence, **I:** 353

Fletcher, Giles, 1546–1611, English poet, **V:** 265

Fletcher, Phineas, 1582–1650, English poet whose poems "may be sung," **VIII:** 95; 97

Florence Civic Wind Band, IV: 82, sixteenth century

Flud, Robert, 1574–1637, English philosopher, physician and Rosicrucian, **VIII:** 24

Flute, I: 62; 63; 64; 65; 66; 68; 70; **II:** 49, Minerva;

Fogliano, Lodovico, sixteenth century Italian theorist, **IV:** 60

Fontanelli, sixteenth century Cardinal, **IV:** 76

Fontenelle, Bernard Le Bovier de, 1657–1757; French poet, **VII:** 117, on the development of poetry from music; 117, fn., 129, his famous dressing room comment; 308

Ford, John, 1586 to after 1639, lawyer and Jacobean playwright, **VIII:** 158, *The Broken Heart,* 158; 199, fn., 59; 200, fn., 61

Form, IV: 101, Vida on planning in poetry; **V:** 155ff, Praetorius definitions; **VI:** 123, Italian church forms which become court forms in Germany; Mattheson, 208, 210, on instrumental dance forms; **VII:** 32, Meret, on tempi in dances; 45ff, Mersenne on the various Baroque dance forms; **VIII:** 45, North calls the concerto form, which followed Corelli's lead, the bread of life for musicians

Fortunatus, d. seventh century, Greek poet, **II:** 200

Fra Angelico, 1395–1455, Italian painter, **IV:** 184, praised by Michelangelo for his piety

Fra Sebastiano del Piombo, receipient of poetry by Michaelangelo, **IV:** 190

Francisco, Signor, one of the most excellent harpsichordist in Europe, heard in 1674 by Evelyn, **VIII:** 421

Francesco da Miliano, 1497–1543, lutanist, classic illustration of the contemplative listener; **III:** 323; **IV:** 85

Francesco d'Ambra, sixteenth century playwright, **IV:** 81

Francesco de Medici, IV: 81

Francis, Duke of Brabant, sixteenth century, **V:** 5

Francisco de Hollanda, IV: 180, fn., 17, his *Four Dialogues of Painting* is a basic source on Michelangelo; 184; 191

Francisco de Quevedo, 1580–1645, Spanish poet, **VI:** 93; 100; 102

Francisco Gómez de Sandoval y Rojas, Duke of Lerma, **VI:** 89

François I of France, 1515–1547, **IV:** 76; 193ff; organization of court music under François I; 193 fn., 4, personal description by Henry VIII of England; 199ff; 211, music for the coronation of his queen; 214; **VII:** 269

François II of France, 1559–1560, **IV:** 194; 201

François Villon, c. 1431–1463, author of the *Great Testament,* **III:** 216, regrets his failure to take advantage of early education

Franz Josef, 1830–1916, Emperor of Austria, **I:** 55

Frederick I, 1122–1190, Emperor of the Holy Roman Empire, **II:** 278

Frederick II, 1194–1250, Emperor of the Holy Roman Empire, **II:** 274; 276ff; 280; 285ff;

Frederick III, 1440–1493, emperor, Holy Roman Empire, **III:** 229; 249; 277

Frederick IV of Denmark and Norway, VI: 24, records his hearing the young women of the *Ospitale della Pieta* sing in Venice, where Vivaldi was employed between 1704–1740. An English visitor reported that Vivaldi was an eunuch.

Frederick the Great, 1712–1786, **VI:** 131, complains of French influence; 171; **VII:** 2; 244; 301; 303; 314ff

Frederick the Wise, d. 1525, of Wittenberg, **V:** 76; 100, Luther on the death of church music at Wittenberg

Frederick William I, 1713–1740, **VI:** 148ff

Freschi, Giovanni, 1640–1690, Italian opera composer, **VI:** 9, *Berenice* (1680)

Frescobaldi, Girolamo, 1583–1643, seventeenth century Italy's greatest organist, **VI:** 20; 53, first-hand description of his playing; 55; 63; 71

Friedrich August I of Dresden, 1694–1733, **VI:** 124, interest in Italian opera; 127

Friedrich I, 1688–1713, **VI:** 147, the beginning of the military Hautboisten

Friedrich Wilhelm, the "Great Elector," 1640–1688, **VI:** 147

Friedrich, Count Palatine, 1486–1525, **V:** 140

Froidmont, Libert, d. 1653, **VI:** 280, anti-instruments in Church

Froissart, Jean, 1337–1405, chronicler and poet; **III:** 78ff, pleasure and pain; 80; 86; 97; 99; example of a poem in troubadour style; 131ff; 227

Fronsperger, Lienhart, V: 148, 1555 publication on army music

Fugger, Hans Jakob, V: 138; **VI:** 142

Fugger, Raimund, V: 141, German businessman at Augsburg, supporter of music

Fuhrmann, Martin, seventeenth century witness to Bach's playing, **VI:** 159

Fulcher of Chartres, d. 1130, **II:** 281

Fuller, Thomas, 1608–1661, Puritan philosopher in England, **VIII:** 210ff; 213ff; 216

Gabrieli, Andrea, 1532–1585, Italian composer, **VI:** 126

Gabrieli, Giovanni, 1554–1612, **IV:** 87, Venice church composer **V:** 157; 159; 162, Praetorius on tempo signs; 170, on the concerto style; 175; **VI:** 21ff; 126; 142; 156

Gaetani, Italian archlute player, **VII:** 146

Gaffarielli, VIII: 462, famous singer mentioned by Lord Chesterfield

Gaffurio, Franchino, 1451–1518, music theorist and head of music in the Milan cathedral, **III:** 161, fn., 1; *Practica Musicae;* 174ff, on the virtues of music; only noble music, amazed that musicians can learn harmony without study in theory; 165; 171ff; 176, Gaffurio: theory of harmony in vain unless expressed in practice; 171, cites both Cicero and Aristoxenus as believing in internal tuning; 187; **IV:** 44; 54; 60; **V:** 116; 122; **VI:** 32, on words vs emotions

Gagliano, Marco da, 1575–1642, composer of the opera, *Dafne* (1608), **VI:** 50; 53; 62

Galatea, lady in Greek poetry, **I:** 298

Galeazzo Maria Sforza, 1466–1476, **III:** 180, music at court of

Galen, b. 130 AD, famous physician, **II:** 9; 22; 26ff; 28; 185ff, on too much music; **V:** 120; 185ff; 212

Galilei, Vincenzo, 1533–1591, **IV:** 43, wrote of the disappearance of the Greek ideals during the Dark Ages; 44 found Zarlino, Glarean and Gafurius as trying to restore the old ideals; 46, misunderstands how emotions are communicated in music; 50ff; 54ff; 62; 73ff, on instrumental performance, including avoiding repeated notes; **VI:** 32, on words vs emotions; against polyphony; 37; 40; **VII:** 37

Galileo, 1564–1642, Italian astronomer, **III:** 1; **VII:** 168, his trial; **VIII:** 230

Galliard, Johann Ernst, Restoration composer, **VIII:** 363, fn., 41

Gallus, Jakob, author of *Opus Musicum* (1587), **V:** 145

Garcilaso de la Vega, 1503–1536, Spanish poet, **IV:** 317ff

Gaspare, Pallavicino, 1488–1511, **IV:** 139ff

Gasparini, Francesco, 1687–1762, Italian violinist living in London, **VI:** 24; 47ff, the noble class no longer has time to become musicians; 49, on working in London

Gausmar, Grimoart, troubadour, **II:** 372

Gautier de Coinci, c. 1218–1236, **II:** 365, use of strings in church in the thirteenth century

Gavaudan, 1195–1230, troubadour, **II:** 387

Gay, John, 1685–1732, poet and composer of *The Beggar's Opera* of 1728, **VI:** 13; **VIII:** 351; 353; 360; 365ff; 374; 423, on the decline of opera in London; 445

Geier, Martin, seventeenth century German preacher, **VI:** 178

Gelimer, King of the Vandals, 530–534, **II:** 193

Gellius, A., philosopher cited by Roger Bacon, **II:** 292;

Geminiani, Francesco, 1587–1727, violinist living in London, **VI:** 51; 53; 64ff; **VIII:** 386

Geminus, lyre-singing teacher to Marcus Aurelius, 121–180 AD, **I:** 463

Genesius, sixteenth century Spanish playwright, **IV:** 336

Genetic emotions, I: 9

Genetic information, I: 192, Plato on Soul; **II:** 296, early twelfth century treatise on Reason, part of which is genetic; **III:** 141, Chaucer: we are programmed; **IV:** 97, Vida on poetry; 109, Giraldi; 274: Vives, some knowledge handed down from God; **VI:** 237ff, Leibniz refutes Locke on "blank blackboard" metaphor; **VIII:** 231, Locke dismisses any possibility of such; 281, Shaftesbury believed emotions are genetic, which in general is true; 322 (Dryden)

Genetic music, I: 208, Plato; 267, Aristotle; 322, Lucian; **II:** 220, Cassiodorus: music is innate to man; 249; **III:** 172, Gaffurio; 265 Nicholas of Cusa: Art is in the soul, where it has been received by the artist; **IV:** 20ff, Aretino, the gift of art is genetics, not instruction, Michelangelo is the example; 22, Vasari; **V:** 37, Erasmus suggests the evidence of children proves; **VI:** 252, Leibniz on; **VII:** 20ff, Rameau's questions on genetic information; 90, (Saint-Lambert); 122, (André); , **VIII:** 43, North on Time; 101, a Herbert poem; 113, "God made man for music"; 267, (Temple)

Genthius, king of the Illyrians, **I:** 354

Geoffrey of Monmouth, twelfth century writer, **II:** 355, fn 2

Geography, V: 74, Agrippa, sixteenth century, on influences on singing; 110, on national styles of singing; 287ff, Robert Greene, 1560–1592, on the "excess of vanity" among the English; 288, comparing the English with Spain, Italy and the Danes, with similar criticism of the English by John Lyly and Philip Stubbs in 288, fn., 5; 291, Lyly, in writing about education; 291, condemns the environment for education in England; 291, Nashe condemns the subjects of poetry and history, while the study of the Arts should be the pathway to honor; Greene on the characteristics of a good teacher; 341, Shakespeare on England's exaggerated sense of pride; **VI:** 49, warnings about working in Rome and London; 83, in book 7 of his *Musurgia Universalis,* Kircher classifies music by national styles; **VI:** 156ff, on the differences between seventeenth century German and French music; 157ff, Muffant on French and German style; 158, Heinichen on the same topic; 158, Niedt, just because it is French it doesn't mean it is good; 188, Mattheson on national differences in singing; **VII:** 70, Mersenne on French vs Italian singers; 123–126, debate on French vs Italian music by Le Cerf de La Viélle and Raguenet; 127ff, Batteux; Montesquieu on the affects of climate; 138–147, On French vs Italian music, vocal and instrumental, major discussion: Maugars; Raguenet; Bonnet-Bourdelot; Le Cerf de La Viélle; Brosses [on singers], 141, Raguenet; Le Cerf de La Viélle; De Brosses [Instrumental music], Maugar; Raguenet; Le Cerf de La Viélle; De Brosses; **VIII:** 8, national styles heard at the court of Charles II; 220, on Italian music in the court in Vienna, also views of Köln and Rome; 258, Hume's curious description of the population of Knittelfeld in lower Austria; 266, Temple finds a negative influence of climate on the English character; 269, Wotton argues that Nature has nothing to do with prominence: Why are there no eminent poets

in Peru?; 330, Dryden: [The French] do out of gaiey that which would be an imposition upon us; 425, on French and Italian opera; 449, Addison on French and Italian opera

George I, King of England, 1660–1727, **VIII:** 9

George II, of England, 1683–1760, **VIII:** 353

Gerber, Christian, late Baroque critic of church music in Germany, **VI:** 178ff

Gesner, Johann, German Baroque writer, **VI:** 173, on Bach conducting

Gesualdo, Carlo, 1566–1613, Prince di Venosa, composer, **IV:** 67; 76ff, his involvement with music; **VI:** 86; 173

Ghent town band, sixteenth century, **V:** 3

Ghiberti, Lorenzo, 1378–1455, Italian artist, **IV:** 178

Gian Galeazzo, Visconti of Milan, fourteenth century; **III:** 15

Gibbon, Edward, 1737–1794, historian of Roman Empire, **II:** 6, fn., 14; 8; 87ff; 92, theater; 94; 179, on the closing of the schools; 195ff; 201; 229; 237ff

Gibbons, Orlando, 1583–1625, **V:** 247, sixteenth century popular music in England, **VIII:** 34

Gideon, Old Testament figure, **I:** 93

Gifford, Humphrey, sixteenth century English poet, **V:** 271ff; 274; 284

Gildon, Charles, 1665–1724, a writer on many topics, especially the theater, **VIII:** 274ff; 304

Gillotot, François, oboe student and servant of M. the Abbey Bouchart, in seventeenth century Paris, **VII:** 2

Giovanni da Udine, sixteenth century painter, **IV:** 23

Giovio, Paolo, contemporary biographer of Leonardo da Vinci; **III:** 191

Giraldi Cinthio, author of *Discorso intorno al Comporre dei Romanzi* (1549); **IV:** 106ff

Giraut de Borneil, 1165–1211, troubadour, **II:** 371; 375; 377ff; 379ff; 382ff; 388ff; 392ff

Gissagho, Italian composer of *Sonatas* (1608) for the "Excellent Virtuosi," the civic band of Venice, and the cornettist, Lodovico Cornale, **VI:** 16

Giuliano de Medici, 1479–1516, brother to Leo X, **IV:** 148

Giulio Cesare of Oriveto, flutist, **IV:** 85

Giulio del Bene, sixteenth century philosopher, **IV:** 36

Giustiniani, Leonardo, 1388–1446, solo singer, **III:** 163, 188

Giustiniani, Vincenzo, 1516–1582, Italian nobleman, **IV:** 49ff; 53; 55ff; 61; 65, author of *Discorso sopra la Musica* (1628); 84ff; 89; **VI:**18, his account of papal music under Urban VIII and mentions improvisation over chant; 18; 20, eyewitness to a performance by Frescobaldi

Glarean, Heinrich, 1488–1563, Swiss theorist, author of *Dodecachordon* (1547), an extensive treatise on church modes, **IV:** 44; **V:** 35, letter of recommendation by Erasmus; 104; 114ff

Glaucon, a brother to Plato, **I:** 221

Gluck, Christoph, 1714–1787, German composer, **VI:** 148, influence of Turkish Music

Gnesippus, Greek lyric poet, **I:** 175

God, I: 317 fn., 30, God played the aulos; **II:** 117, in fifth century the Church reports God hated the theater and its music; **III:** 268, Nicholas of Cusa, 1401–1464, God used the liberal

arts to create the world; **VII:** 251 (Voltaire); **VIII:** 38, Mace, God takes no pleasure from lame performance; 113

Godefridus, famous fifteenth century shawm player, **III:** 249

Goethe, Johann von, 1749–1832, German poet, **I:** 43

Goliath, killed by David in the Old Testament, **I:** 96

Góngora, Luis de, 1561–1627, Spanish poet, **IV:** 316; **VI:** 99; 102; 103, on the shrill trumpet

Gonzaga, Prince Francesco, VI: 4ff, letter of 1611 from Monteverdi giving the duties of the court wind band

Gonzalgo Roïtz, troubadour, **II:** 372

Gonzalo de Ovedo, fifteenth century Spanish writer; **III:** 296

Gorgias, Greek philsopher, fl. 450 BC, **I:** 155ff

Görner, Johann, Baroque music director at Leipzig University, **VI:** 136

Gossec, François, 1734–1829, French composer, **VII:** 11

Gosson, Stephen, 1555–1624, English Puritan, 1579 author of *The Schoole of Abuse,* **V:** 192ff; quoting Maximus Tyrius, the addition of instruments ruined theater; 194, *An Apologie of the Schoole of Abuse* (1579); 199; 206ff; 210ff; 239

Gottfried von Strassburg, fl. 1200–1210, German poet, **II:** 412ff; 418ff; 424,

Gower, John, 1330–1408, fourteenth century English counter humanist philosopher, **III:** 111ff; 115

Grabu, Louis, d. 1694, French composer of Spanish origin, **VIII:** 337; 339; 434, fn., 7; 435

Gracchus, Calius, 154–121 BC, Roman orator, **I:** 365

Gracián, Baltasar, 1601–1658, Spanish priest and philosopher, **VI:** 93ff, on Reason and the senses; 98; 102

Grammar in music (see also Harmony, Tonality, Melody, Form, Tempo), **I:** 212, Plato; 239ff; 319, Plutarch: men trained only in details of music may not be capable of judging music; 255, Aristotle; 282, ancient Greek understanding in music; 282, example of failure of grammar in music; 284, Theophrastus on failure of grammar; 285; 314ff, major discussion of Roman period of Greece; 315, confusion of scale and mode; 31, fn., 29, Epictetus placed music in same category as geometry as late as first century, AD; 319, Plutarch: men trained only in details of music may not be capable of judging music; 388; 395, Isocrates, 436–338 BC, on the differences between hearing orators vs poets, and of the contributions of music to speech; **II:** 6, third century reference to the invention of the 'Italian scale.'; 27, Empiricus: Music and Mathematics have nothing to do with grammar; 111, Martianus Capella on rhythm and time; 160ff, St. Augustine: listener of music need not know anything about the conceptual aspects of music; St. Augustine; 175ff, language grammar, sixth to eighth centuries; 177, Venerable Bede; 198, association of grammar and music, sixth to eighth century; 257, Guido, c. 1026–1028, will omit those "things which cannot be understood" ie they cannot be notated; 258, Guido found color in cadences; associates cadences with grammar; 289, thirteenth century poem on the battle between grammar and logic, music stands apart; 305, Bacon: on meters in the Old Testament,

grammarian can teach the rules, but music gives the reasons and theories for these meters. Also the "accents, longs, shorts, colons, commas and period" all belong to music; 310, the important contributions of Bacon on the nature of music and grammar, ie "accent" comes from "accino," "I sing"; 313, John of Salisbury: *Trivium* discloses the significance of all words, while the *Quadrivium* unveils the secrets of all nature; 313, fn., 11, five basic vowel sounds are common to all men; 314, Salisbury: speech teaches Reason (like music created grammar); 330 Bernard of Clairvaux finds emotions in cadences; 434ff, minor reflections in *De Musica Mensurata*, c. 1279; **III:** 176, Gaffurio: theory of harmony in vain unless expressed in practice and notation is not music; 177, Gaffurio: basic unit of pulse should correspond with human pulse; 242, Tinctoris confuses melody and harmony; 243, Time is based on mathematical proportions resulting in unperformable music; 245, on consonance and dissonance; **IV:** 11, Aretino advice to writers: express feelings not words; Segni, 1573, language, music and dance are all imitations of each other; 43ff, sixteenth century Italian music theory; theorists Ferrari and Tartaglia; 44ff, Bardi on the decline of polyphony; 47ff, views of the sixteenth century Italian theorists; Zarlino: music must not be judged by the senses alone, still thinking of mathematics; 48ff on whether theory is necessary to performance; 49, Giustiniani says both are needed; 52, Zarlino hopes for the day when aesthetics is the point and not mechanical rules; 67, Zarlino, all theory must be directed toward performance or else is vain and useless; 67, Mei: purpose of theory is to find Truth, but it is found in performance; 68, Benedetti, you cannot understand theory without performance; 110, Giraldi on the definition of Art, not the parts of speech, etc.; 112, detail can go too far; 113 warning on too much correcting and editing; 164, Cardano, the value of music must be in the present, not past; 231, Bodin on the bad influence of grammarians; **V:** 108, Ornithoparchus admits theory is understood not by the ears but "wit and reason"; 125ff, Coclico, *Compendium musices* (1552), the first treatise to emphasize performance over theory repeatedly criticizing rules-based learning; **VI:** 244, Leibniz: understanding of arts is experiential, not the product of Reason; 245 because of this, Wolff says this is why there is no philosophy of the arts or law or medicine; **VII:** 25, Rameau: in composing the "rules" take second place; Nature precedes the rules; 29, Rameau: don't listen to the rules, be swept away; 53, Mersenne: the notational system is inadequate regarding the expression of emotions; 54, the rules of harmony are not like those of geometry, which force the mind of all those who have common sense to adopt them; 70, Mersenne: the heart of improvisation is nature, not rules of division; 106, Fénelon: art discredits and betrays itself when it makes its methods known; 178, Descartes discredits "speculative music"; 179, Descartes: purpose of music is to communicate emotions to the soul of the listener; 185, Chapelain (1637), art must not only please but follow the rules of experts; 266, Voltaire: music communicates passion, not ideas; **VIII:** 68, James I, "Art is better learned by practice than speculation"; 72, Donne: listeners and players prefer improvised music rather than written music; 211, Puritan prejudice toward: "Rhetoric," the mother of lies"; "A mere scholar is an intelligible Ass"; "Fencing

is to be taught not by words but by practice"; 242, Penn discounts too much education, for example, "The first thing obvious to children is what is sensible; and that we make no part of their rudiments"; 276, music has nothing to do with Reason; 287, Shaftesbury finds the laws of music are found in Nature; 296, the pleasure of a fine composition is incomparably greater than any single part

Grandi, Alessandro, 1586–1630, church music official in Ferrara and Venice, **VI:** 21, attacks polyphony

Grassis, Paris de, IV: 75, papal Master of Ceremonies

Graun, Carl, 1704–1759, important German composer of Italian opera, **VI:** 157; 159

Gray, Thomas, 1716–1771, **VIII:** 422, a poet who also composed and performed; 424ff; 429

Great minds, IV: 109, Giraldi on the student reading epic poetry; 261, Montaigne on the damage of exposure to weak minds of inferior music; **VIII:** 27, Avison on the affect of good music on the mind

Greban, Arnoul, fifteenth century playwright; **III:** 221

Greek gods, VIII: 360, Restoration poets; 362

Greene, Robert, 1560–1592, important English writer, **V:** 188, too much music turns listeners off; 287ff, on the decay of letters and lack of honor for art; 290, on four things which dull the senses; 291, the good teacher; 292ff; 296; 300ff; 303; 306ff; as playwright: 319, *Alphonsus, King of Arragon;* 320; 322; *The History of Orlando Furioso,* 319; 320; 339ff, includes a scene where a violin is broken over the player's head; *James the Fourth,* 320; 323; 338; *Frier Bacon and Frier Bongay,* 338; 391

Gregori, Alberto, VI: 15ff, leading trombonist in seventeenth century Italy and leader of the civic band in Siena

Gregory IX, thirteenth century pope, **II:** 325

Gregory of Tours, 538–594, Church writer, **II:** 178; 209ff, on singing hymns

Gregory the Great, 540–604, pope, **II:** 176; 189ff; 194; 198, as poet; 210; 286; 324; **III:** 6

Gregory, David, Dr., seventeenth century Professor of Astronomy and English at Oxford, mentioned by Pepys, **VIII:** 432

Gresset, Jean-Baptiste, 1709–1777, French poet, **VII;** 118, found music superior to poetry for intimate communication

Greville, Fulke, 1554–1628, English poet, **V:** 254ff; 265ff; 278

Grieffenberg, Catharina Regina von, 1633–1694, German poet, **VI:** 223

Grignan, Count de, VII: 232

Grignan, Mme de, VII: 233

Grillo, Giovanni, 1570–1662, Italian composer, **VI:** 124, Italian composer who dedicated music to Ferdinand II

Grimaldi, Nicolino, Italian singer in London, **VIII:** 364

Grimmelshausen, Hans Jacob Christoffel von, 1625–1676, German writer, **VI:** 221ff; 225; 227ff

Griselius, a sixteenth century scholar of Wittenberg, **V:** 130, a poem on how music affects the listener

Grosseteste, Robert, d. 1253, **II:** 290, thirteenth century Scholastic philosopher; 296ff, on genetic Reason, 303ff; 306

Grossmann, Burckhart, seventeenth century German music critic, on the economic ramifications of the Thirty Years War, **VI:** 121f

Guarini, Giambattista, 1538–1612, Italian poet, **IV:** 122ff; 124ff; 126ff; 132; 134

Gudea, King of Sumeria, 2600 BC, **I:** 62

Guicciardini, Francesco, 1483–1540, Spanish politician and musician **IV:** 1; 5; 10, cautious attitude on traditional education; 13; 40, on entertainment

Guido Cavalcanti, 1259–1300, Italian poet, **II:** 399

Guido Guinizelli, fl. 1250–1300, Italian poet, **II:** 397

Guido of Arezzo, 990–1050, music theorist, *Micrologus,* c. 1026–1028, **II:** 236, *Prologus antiphonarii sui* on new method of teaching; 257ff, introduces staff lines; 262; **III:** 241; 299; **VI:** 182

Guilds, I: 463, first music guilds in Rome; 274, modern music guilds begin in Vienna in 1288; **III:** 101, *Confrérie de St. Julien* of 1321; 321, England fifteenth century; **V:** 4, guilds, in sixteenth century low countries, in Mons, Antwerp, Bruges; **VI:** 133ff, trumpet guilds in Baroque Germany; 146; **VII:** 11ff, bylaws of the musicians guild of Srasbourg (1606); **VIII:** 75, in England

Guillaume de Lorris, Romance of the Rose, **II:** 355ff

Guillaume IX, Count of Poitiers, troubadour, **II:** 370; 387; 393

Guillem de Montanhagol, 1233–1270, a knight of Provence, good troubadour and great lover, **II:** 370; 376; 384; 390

Guillem de Ribas, troubadour, **II:** 372

Guiraut Riquier, 1230–1292, troubadour, **II:** 391

Guittone d'Arezzo, 1235–1294, composer of sung poetry, **II:** 295ff

Gutenberg, Johannes, 1398–1468, German printer; **III:** 1

Guthere, King of the Burgundians, fifth century, **II:** 202

Gutiérrez de Padilla, Juan, 1590–1664, **VI:** 92, Spanish composer in Mexico and builder of instruments to be used in the church

Gwin, Matthew, Fellow at St. John's College, in 1582 required to each music, **V:** 230

Gwynn, Nell, 1650–1687, amatuer singer, mistress to Charles II, **VIII:** 6, uttered the most famous remark of seventeenth century England, "Be silent, good people, I am the *Protestant* whore."

Hades, I: 112, myth regarding death of music lovers;

Hadly, Mr., best flageolet player in England in 1673, **VIII:** 220

Hadrian, 76–138 AD, Roman emperor, **I:** 459; 463, who sang and played harp;

Hainhofer, Philipp, 1578–1647, **VI:** 126, visitor to Dresden court in 1629, describes music at the court

Hall, Joseph, Rev., 1574–1656, Puritan preacher, **VIII:** 63; 69

Hammerschmidt, German Baroque composer, **VI:** 205

Handel, Georg, 1685–1759, Baroque German composer, **I:** 15; **VI:** 6; 8, cantatas composed in Rome; 12, as opera conductor in London; 159; 183; 188; **VII:** 144; **VIII:** 9, fn., 38, details on his "Fireworks" music; 26, fn., 16, Judged by Avison as a composer of the highest regard; 32; 36, recalled as a teacher; 362; 367; 386; 388, Swift, as dean of St. Patrick's cathedral in Dublin, forbids church musicians from appearing in public performances—notwithstanding this ban, the premiere performance of Handel's *Messiah* was given in the same cathedral a few weeks later; 396; 413; 460

Hannibal, Roman general, **I:** 358; 472

Harington, Sir John, 1561–1612, English noble, writer, **VIII:** 2

Harmony, I: 427 (Ovid), **II:** 106; 330, Lull: arranging many voices so they are concondant; **IV:** 235, Bodin on harmony and sanity; 237 on the affect of harmony on life; 309, Cervantes, tuned instruments at a wedding; **V:** 354, Shakespeare's praise of two voices instead of one in his "Sonnet VIII"; **VII:** 80ff, Mersenne on the importance of the unison

Harp, I: 67; 69; 73; 75, house of King Antef, 18th dynasty Egypt; 76; 88ff; 134; 138, Lydian harp of 20 strings; 147; 228; 270, Aristotle; 276, on Stratonicus of Athens; 463, emperor Hadrian played harp; 475, Leaena, 4th c. AD harp girl prostitute; **II:** 199, harp playing actress named Ariadne, 6th to 8th century; 419, playing with sad passion; 427, singing harpist of the thirteenth century; 127 fine harpist, 124ff, fourteenth century English; **VIII:** 138, mentioned in Milton's song on the death of Jesus; 149

Harrington, James, 1611–1677, English author of the utopian *Oceana* (1656), **VIII:** 61; 75

Harris, James, 1709–1780, a wealthy member of parliament, wrote treatises on Music, Painting and Poetry, **VIII:** 300

Harsdörffer, Georg, 1607–1658, a German nobleman and poet, **VI:** 225ff

Hartmann von Aue, 1160–1210, German poet, **II:** 417ff; 422; 425

Harvey, William, 1578–1657, physician to the king and author of *Anatomy* (1616), **VIII:** 59; 62; 66

Hasse, Johann Adolf, 1699–1783, German composer, **VI:** 13, fn., 36; 51; 157; 188; **VIII:** 26, fn., 16, Judged by Avison as a composer of modest ability

Hathor, ancient Egyptian god of love and music, **I:** 73

Hautboisten **bands, VI:** 27, beginning in Italy in 1684; 90, Spanish ensemle led by Francesco de Baldes (or Valdes), formed between 1652–1655; 126, for court use; 127; 131, major discussion

Hawkins, John, 1719–1789, author of a *General History of the Science.and Practice of Music* (1776), **VIII:** 9; 303

Haydn, Josef, 1732–1809, **VI:** 148, influence of Turkish Music

Haym, Nicolino, VIII: 450, 453, involved in the development of opera in England

Healfdene, sixth century Danish king, **II:** 206

Hédelin, François, 1604–1676, theater critic, known as Abbé d'Aubignac, **VII:** 185

Hegelochus, first century Roman singer, **II:** 5

Heinichen, Johann David, 1683–1729, German composer, **VI:** 16, visits Venice in 1670 to study opera style; 152ff, on experience not rules and for the ear not the eye; 155, the composer cannot escape the influence of music he has heard; 158; 164; 166ff; 170; 174; 177; 183; 188

Heinrich von Morungen, d. 1222, Minnesinger, **II:** 417ff

Heinrich, German lutanist under Charles the Bold; **III:** 250

Heman, Old Testament choral leader, **I:** 88; 90

Henci d'Andeli, thirteenth century trouvère, **II:** 289

Henry I of England, 1086–1135, **II:** 274

Henry II of France, 1547–1559, **IV:** 194; 214

Henry III of England, 1207–1272, **II:** 273; 278; 285

Henry III of France, 1574–1589, **IV:** 194, description of court behavior; 205

Henry IV of England, 1399–1413, **III:** 319

Henry IV of France, 1553–1610, **VII:** 1, assassination in 1610

Henry V of England, 1413–1422, **III:** 319

Henry VI of England, 1422–1461 and 1470–1471, **III:** 320

Henry VII of England, 1485–1509, **III:** 320

Henry VIII of England, 1509–1547, composer and flautist, **IV:** 211; 214; 273; **V:** 17, l523 letter to from Erasmus; 183; 220; 223, major discussion; personal description; instrument collection; 224, "disguising"; music for his funeral; 238; 247; 276

Hentzner, Paul, German jurist (1598) records post-drama concerts, **V:** 316

Hentzschel, Caspar, seventeenth century court trumpeter, **VI:** 133, on the memorized reperoire of toccatas, sonatas

Heracleides of Cumae, 221–205 BC, historian of Persia, **I:** 69,

Heracleides of Pontus, 387–312 BC, author of a lost book on Greek music, **I:** 128; 315

Heraclitus, 540–475 BC, Greek philosopher, **I:** 156; 158; 210; **II:** 24

Heradorus of Megara, winner of the Olympiad in trumpet in 396 BC, **I:** 110

Herbert, Edward, Lord of Cherbery, d. 1648, English writer, **VIII:** 95; 98

Herbert, George, 1593–1633, English poet, rector in the Church of England and orator at Cambridge, **VIII:** 101; 103; 107ff, "Lord, place me in Thy concert; give one strain, to my poor reed!"; 108; 110, followed by a biography written by Izaak Walton; 125

Hereward the Wake, twelfth century, **II:** 279, 326, murders during a banquet

Hermes, Greek god and inventor of the lyre, **I:** 117; 127

Hermesianax, early third century, BC, Alexandrian poet **I:** 293ff; 298

Hermippus, Roman aulos player, **I:** 354, Polybius;

Hero and Leander, **II:** 100ff

Herodotus of Halicarnassus, c. 484–412 BC, historian, **I:** 68; 77; 80; 103; 141ff; **II:** 20

Herophilus, 335–280 BC, Greek physician, **II:** 96, music therapy

Herrick, Robert, 1591–1674, English poet, **VIII:** 95, called "the greatest song-writer ever born of English race." by Swinburne; 97; 98; 100; 103; 105; 111, a poem expressing the strong emotions of music; 114; 116; 117, "Upon a hoarse singer"; 121; 123; 126

Hervart, de, French noble, **VII:** 233

Herwald, John George, Chancellor of Bavaria, **VI:** 261

Hesiod, ancient Greek poet, fl, c. 850 BC, **I:** 113ff; 118, on competition; 121; 156, fn., 13; 160

Hesu, ancient Egyptian god of music and creator of the earth, **I:** 73

Heydenreich, Caspar, V: 96, 1542 correspondence with Luther on the seriousness of church music

Heywood, Thomas, 1575–1648, Jacobean writer, author of *An Apology for Actors* (1612). **VIII:** 156; and playwright, *The Golden Age,* 167; *A Woman Kilde with Kindness,* 170; *The Iron Age,* 174; 186, fn., 47; 206, fn., 72; *The English Traveller,* 179; *If you know not me, you know no body,* 181; 186, fn., 47; *King Edward the Fourth,* 181, fn., 37; 202; *Fortune by Land and Sea,* 182; *Loves Mistris,* 182; 187; 190; *Foure Prentises of London,* 183, fn., 43; 186, fn., 47; 187; *A Maiden-head well lost,* 184, fn., 44; *The Rape of Lucrece,* 186, fn., 47; 189, fn., 52; 196, *The Witches of Lancashire,* 188

Hiero, fourth century BC, Greek political leader, **I:** 142, on competition;

Hieron, ruler of Syracuse in 478 BC, **I:** 135

Hieronymus of Udine, sixteenth century Italian cornett player in Munich, **V:** 138

Hildegard von Bingen, 1098–1179, nun and philosopher, **II:** 315ff, on the soul; 330ff

Hiller, Ferdinand, 1811–1886, German composer, **I:** 25

Hindemith, Paul, 1895–1963, German composer, **I:** 11; 42

Hingston, John, 1612–1683, court organist under James II, **VIII:** 433

Hipparchion, V: 46, a leading ancient lyre player, according to Erasmus

Hippias, fl. c. 450 BC, Greek philosopher and composer, **I:** 157

Hippocrates, 460–370 BC, physician, **II:** 198; **V:** 120

Hobbes, Thomas, 1588–1679, pe;rformer on the bass viol, Restoration philosopher, secretary to Francis Bacon **VIII:** 223; 224 all thoughts have their origin in the senses, [but] the senses are located in the heart

Hoccleve, 1368–1426, English poet, fifteenth century, **III:** 304

Hodson, Mrs., Restoration Period singer, **VIII:** 314, fn., 29

Holbein, Hans, 1497–1543, German artist, **V:** 69

Hollanda, Francisco, sixteenth century sculptor, **IV:** 179; 191

Homer, ancient Greek poet, fl. c. 850 BC, **I:** 106 fn., 12; 110 fn, 26; 113ff; 146; 156 fn, 13; 160; 186; 194ff; 230; 29; 309; 399; 437; 499; **II:** 17, Longinus; 20; 40; 74; 200; **III:** 17; **IV:** 108; **V:** 119; **VII:** 136; **VIII:** 107; 141

Honestus, first century Roman poet **II:** 4, on the decay of good lyre music;

Hook, James, 1746–1827, English composer mentioned by Pepys, **VIII:** 434

Hooke, Robert, seventeenth century English physicist on music, **VIII:** 241

Hooker, Richard, 1553–1600, **V:** 212, a moderate church philosopher, countering the arguments of the Puritans; 221ff

Horace, 66–8 BC, Roman (Augustan) philosopher, **I:** 124; 352; 381, emotions; 401ff, on decay of Greek culture; 402ff, on aesthetics; 410, on the public; 412, on art music; 415 on education; 423; 426ff; 430; 451; 454ff; **II:** 321; **III:** 27; 34; 248; **VII:** 268; **VIII:** 136; 269; 373; 429

Horse ballet, VI: 4, Möller's book of 1672 recreating the design of the coat-of-arms of Lübeck on the field with men and horses; 128, for Ferdinand III, 1637–1657; for Leopold I, including description of the horse dances

Howard, Henry, 1517–1547, English poet, **V:** 262

Howell, Thomas, fl. 1568–1581, English poet, **V:** 261

Hrotswitha, tenth century nun and playwright, **II:** 233ff, *Paphnutius,* on definition of music;

Hucbald, b. c. 840 AD, Benedictine monk and theorist, **II:** 253ff, *De Harmonica Institutione,* 895 AD, a treatise on the conceptual nature of music;

Hudemann, Ludwig (1732), German poet, **VI:** 154

Hueber, Wolf, sixteenth century civic musician at Freistadt, Austria, **V:** 140

Hugh de Orléans, II: 427, Golliard of the thirteenth century; 429; 431

Humanism, IV: 43ff, sixteenth century Italian contributions; 54

Hume, David, 1711–1776, Scottish Presbyterian who became a great representative of the Enlightenment, **VIII:** 245; 246, on the senses

Humfrey, Pelham, 1647–1674, court organist under James II, **VIII:** 431; 435ff

Humors, the Doctrine of Affections, or Spirits, V: 72, Agrippa; **VI:** 85ff, Kircher; **VII:** 55ff (Mersenne); 57–68, major discussion of music, humors and emotions; **VIII:** 58, (John Burton); 59, William Harvey on the "spirits"; 116, (Cowley); 281, Shaftesbury, on the listeners of music

Hut, Abraham, Stadtpfeifer in Swickau, **V:** 148

Hutcheson, Francis, 1694–1746, Irish born philosopher, **VIII:** 290

Hutten, Ulrich von, sixteenth century German poet and humanist, **V:** 58; 114, co-author of satirical *Letters of Obscure Men* (1515)

Huygens, Christian, 1629–1695, Dutch philosopher, **VI:** 300ff; **VII:** 37

Huygens, Constatin, 1596–1687, Dutch poet and composer, **VII:** 67

Hy, ancient Egyptian name for joy related to music, **I:** 75

Hyperides, early Roman orator, **II:** 19

Hypodorian, a Greek mode, **I:** 104

Iamblichus, c. 250–325 AD, Pythagorean School, **I:** 160ff

Iba, ancient Egyptian dance, **I:** 73

Ibycus of Rhegium, c. 530–500 BC, lyric poet, **I:** 124ff, 170; **II:** 34

Ignatius, third bishop of Antioch after Peter, **VIII:** 139, created antiphonal singing in church

Iibis, mythical Egyptian god, **I:** 417

Imagination, IV: 246ff, Montaigne; 328, Lope de Vega

Imitation, II: 108; 151ff, St. Augustine; **III:** 27, Petrarch; **IV:** 17ff, sixteenth century Italy; Segni, 1573, language, music and dance are all imitations of each other; Vasari; 19, Tasso on the relationship of imitation and dialogue; 127, Ariosto vs plagiarism

Improvisation, III: 163, Pirrotta on fifteenth century "unwritten music" (improvisation); 249, Tinctoris on *cantus regalis,* the improvisation on chant; **IV:** 72ff, improvisation in church, including above the chant; 71ff, sixteenth century Italians, Bach, ensemble improvisation, etc.; 74, Galilei on aesthetic goals of improvisation, purely aesthetic goals, beauty, grace and delight of the ear, not instilling moral virtues; 227, in poem set by Hubert Waelrant of Antwerp; 305, Cervantes, description of a singer; **V:** 121, Glarean refers to improvisation over chant; 130, without the ability to do this, writes Coclico, a singer is nothing; 328, More's *Utopia* (1515) reference to improvisation; 352, Shakespeare says none!; **VI:** 42ff, in early opera; 58ff, major discussion of Baroque Period; 169ff, views of German Baroque musicians; 212ff (Mattheson); **VII:** 31, including Couperin, Bénigne de Bacilly, Mermet; 70, Mersenne: the heart of improvisation is nature, not rules of division; 80, Mersenne confirms improvisation over chant; 147, Maugars, on improvisation; 148, Bonnet-Bourdelot, on improvisation; **VIII:** 28, Playford: "divisions" are contrary to passion; 36, Avison: ornamentation is impossile to be expressed in notation; 53, North discussion; 126, reference to improvisation in Christmas music; 157, in Jacobean plays; Dekker objects to this practice; 356; 447, Addison , on the violin, first thinks of improvisation

Ingersoll, Robert, 1833–1899, American writer, **I:** 45

Innocent III, 1161–1216, pope, **II:** 285 (called for Fifth Crusade in 1217)

Innocent IV, 1195–1254, pope, **II:** 272

Innocent X, 1691–1700, pope, **VI:** 6

Innocent XII, 1691–1700, pope has opera house torn down, **VI:** 14

Inspiration, I: 216; 424, Horace; 42, Ovid; **II:** 376, of the troubadour composers; 81; **III:** 84, Machaul; 144, Chaucer; **IV:** 94, Aretino and Tosso; 99, Vida on turning inspiration into verse; 127, sixteenth century Italian playwrights: divine; **VIII:** 308, Congreve on the relationship between winds and "inspire"

Ion of Ephesus, fifth – fourth century BC, Greek Rhapsodist, **I:** 193; 212ff, Plato; **II:** 17, Longinus

Ionian, a Greek mode, **I:** 105

Ionians, I: 147

Isaac, Heinrich, fifteenth century composer, **III:** 162; 183; **IV:** 75; **V:** 138

Isabella of Castile, 1474–1504, patron of Columbus, **III:** 295ff

Isabella of Portugal, 1503–1539, wife to Philip the Good; **III:** 232

Isabella of Urbino, III: 182

Isadore of Seville, 560–636 AD, Spanish theorist, **II:** 213ff; 221, *Etymologirarum*, 222, three types of music: *harmonica, organica* [instruments], and *rhythmica* [percussion]; melody comes from *mel* [honey] refers to the sweetness of music; catalogs ten kinds of voice quality; 248; 251; 434

Isaeus, 415–340 BC, orator, **I:** 487ff, (Pliny the Younger)

Ishtar, goddess of Assyria, **I:** 67

Ismenias of Themes, early music therapist, **V:** 40

Ismenias, fourth century BC Greek aulos player, **I:** 109; 288

Ismenias, c. 63 BC – 24 AD, prisoner musician of the Scythians, **I:** 135

Isocrates, 436–338 BC Greek rhetorician, **I:** 388; 395

Ivanovich, Cristoforo, a canon at St. Marks in 1681, **VI:** 9, describes entertainments in Venice; 14, on the political advantages of public performance

Jacopo da Bologna, 1340–1386, composer; **III:** 10, complains everyone is composing

Jacopone da Todi, 1230–1306, **II:** 318, on the senses

Jacques de Liège, 1260–1330, author of *Speculum Musicae* of 1313 (*ars antiqua*), **III:** 70; 87ff

Jaime II, of Aragon, 1291–1327, **III:** 295

James I of Scotland, 1424–1437, **III:** 320

James I, King of England, and poet, 1603–1625, **VIII:** 1; 1, fn., 2, physical description of James; 16; 68, "Art is better learned by practice than speculation"; 106; 107

James II, of England, 1633–1701, **VIII:** 353; 431

Jan III of Poland, seventeenth century; **VI:** 7

Janequin, Clément, 1485–1558, French composer, **IV:** 195; 198; 201; 21 9

Jaufré Rudel, Prince of Blaia, troubadour, **II:** 370

Jean de Gerson, 1363–1429, Chancellor of the University of Paris, author of *Tractatus de Canticis*, **III:** 218ff; 226

Jean de Joinville, thirteenth century chronicler, **II:** 285ff

Jean de la Motte, fourteenth century poet, **III:** 96, list of instruments in *Remede de Fortune*

Jean de la Taille, b. 1540, soldier, poet, **IV:** 224, first introduction of the three unities in France in the preface of his play, *Saül le furieux* (1572); 224ff, the purpose of Tragedy; 225, on the audience

Jean de Muris, c. 1290–1350, *Ars nove musice,* **III:** 92ff

Jean d'Estrée, sixteenth century oboist of the king, **IV:** 195

Jeduthun, Old Testament singer, **I:** 90

Jehan de Lescurel, d. 1304, poet; **III:** 79

Jehoshaphat, Old Testament king of Israel, **I:** 91

Jephthah, Hebrew leader of the Old Testament, **I:** 97

Jeremiah, seventh century BC, Hebrew leader of the Old Testament, **I:** 97; 88, ordered to teach music

Jerome of Moravia, thirteenth century theorist, **II:** 435

Jesus, I: 112, myth regarding death of music lovers; 83, myth on two kinds of Hell; **II:** 130; 353. Thomas points out Jesus sang [he gives Matthew 26:30]; **V:** 53 (Erasmus, on trumpet signals); **VIII:** 138; 150ff, in Milton's Paradise Lost; 244 (Penn); 269, because of the then taste for Burlesque in the seventeenth century Rymer reports that in 1649 a serious treatise was published with the title, *La Passion de Nostre Seigneur, En vers Burlesques*

Joachim II of Brandenburg, 1505–1571, German noble, **V:** 134; 146

Joan of Arc, III: 212

Jochum, Eugen, twentieth century German conductor, **I:** 40

Johann Friedrich, 1608–1628, Duke of Württemberg, **VI:** 145

Johann Georg II of Dresden, VI: 125, a noble who was also a composer and student of Schütz

Johann Georg, 1571–1598, North German elector, **V:** 112; 133

Johann von Saxony, sixteenth century German noble, **V:** 139; 143

Johann von Vlatten, V: 19, letter on education from Erasmus

Johanna of Austria, IV: 81

Johannes de Garlandia, *De Mensurabili Musica,* c. 1279, **II:** 433; 435ff

Johannes de Grocheo, *De Musica,* c. 1300, **II:** 433; 436ff

John II, French king, 1350–1364, **III:** 97, list of household minstrels; 227

John of Salisbury, twelfth century Church philosopher, **II:** 313ff; 316; 318; 320ff; 322; 326

John the Fearless of Burgundy, 1404–1419, **III:** 227ff

John V of Portugal, 1689–1750, **VI:** 92

John XXII, 1324–1325 pope, **III:** 90ff, *ars antiqua*

John XXIII, fifteenth century pope; **III:** 282

John, *On Music,* c. 1100 AD, **II:** 261ff

Johnson, Samuel, 1709–1784, English writer, **VIII:** 258

Joinville, thirteenth century historian, **II:** 285ff

Jomelli, Niccolo, 1714–1774, Italian composer, **VII:** 144

Jonathan, Hebrew figure of the Old Testament, **I:** 91

Jongleur, Latin, *Ioculator,* medieval entertainer, **II:** 181; 197; 201ff, description of skills; 202, Widsith, fifth century Jongleur in Britain; 237, eleventh century England; 261, "uneducated," c. 1100 AD; 355ff, contemporary descriptions; 357 described in the *Song of William,* oldest Chanson de geste; 371; 374ff; 390ff; **III:** 159, in Chaucer a poor wanderer; **IV:** 65, "Pitio, excellent musician and jongleur" (Giustiniani, 1628)

Jonson, Ben, 1572–1637, English writer, **VIII:** 2; 94; 96; 98; 99; 103; 105; 106; 108, an Epigram for Alphonoso Ferrabosco; 112, lyrics for a song by Henry Youll; as playwright, *Volpone,* 156, 158; *Every Man in his Humour,* 158; 169; *Timber, or Discoveries made upon Men and Matter* (published 1641), 158; *Sejanus,* 159; 165; 198; *Every Man Out of his Humour,* 159; *A Tale of a Tub,* 160; *Bartholomew Fair,* 161, fn., 17; *The Alchemist,* 163; 199; *The Silent Woman,* 166; 171, fn., 26; 183; 207; *The Staple of News,* 169; 206; *Cynthia's Revels,* 171; 182, fn., 41; 192; 196; *Case is Altered,* 183; *Poetaster,* 190; 193; 207; *The Devil is an Ass,* 193, fn., 55; [Masque] *Pleasure Reconciled to Virtue,* 202

Jordan, Raimon, troubadour, **II:** 370

Josephus, first century AD, Jewish historian, **I:** 472

Joshua, Hebrew leader of the Old Testament, **I:** 86

Josquin des Près, 1450–1521, Franco–Flemish composer, **IV:** 155; **V:** 98; 119; 127ff, comments on his teaching by his student, Adrian Coclico; 138

Juan del Encina, 1468–1529, Spanish poet, **III:** 291ff, *Arte de poesia castellana;* 293, fn., 25

Juan I of Aragon, 1350–1396, **III:** 287, invited troubadours to Barcelona, first step toward humanism in Spain; 295

Juana la loca, IV: 291

Julian, 361–363 Roman emperor, **II:** 88; 90; 91, on the water organ; 93ff; 107ff, self-portrait; 110ff; 112ff

Julianus, City Prefect of Rome and fifth century poet, **II:** 101 fn., 8, public does not always want the Truth

Julius Caesar, 100–44 BC, Roman general and statesman, **I:** 352; 359; 473; 313, anecdote on speech

Julius II, 1443–1513, pope, **IV:** 177; 182; **V:** 52

Jupiter, I: 430; 455; 457

Justinian, sixth century emperor, **II:** 179

Juvenal, second century AD Roman poet, **I:** 464, satire on vocal choirs; 488; 502ff

Karl II (Charles II), 1540–1590, Archduke of Graz, **V:** 147, funeral, 1590

Karna, musical instrument mentioned in the Book of Daniel, **I:** 66

Kastner, Georges, 1810–1867, French historian, **VII:** 15

Kathros, musical instrument mentioned in the Book of Daniel, **I:** 66

Keen, Edward, VIII: 453, father of twenty children benefited from a concert in London in 1712

Keil, John, correspondent of Matthew Prior, **VIII:** 386

Keiser, Reinhard, 1674–1739, **VI:** 124, first great German opera composer; 141

Kepler, Johannes, 1571–1630, astronomer, **VI:** 233; 259, major discussion; **VII:** 40

Kessler, Johannes of St. Gall, **V:** 67, on the destruction of church art

Keyboard music, VI: 159, Germany felt pre-eminent in the seventeenth century

Khesuwer, singing instructor, Middle Kingdom, ancient Egypt, **I:** 77

Killigrew, Thomas, manager of the King's Company and Theater Royal in 1664, **VIII:** 436

Kimura, Doreen, twentieth century writer on the bicameral brain, **I:** 48

King Arthur, II: 361; 365; 367ff

King of Cyprus, III: 97

Kircher, Athanasius, 1601–1680, German born, brilliant scholar who sppent his life in Rome and author of a virtual encyclopedia, *Musurgia Universalis* (1650), **VI:** 79ff major discussion; 84; **VIII:** 116

Kirchmaier, Thomas, sixteenth century Lutheran lawyer, **V:** 144

Kirchner, Walther, twentieth century writer, **I:** 158

Klaj, Johann, 1616–1656, German poet, **VI:** 226; 230

Knabe, Martin, student of Schütz, **VI:** 122, on the economic ramifications of the Thirty Years' War

Kneller, Sir Godfrey, 1646–1723, English painter, **VIII:** 332, 340

Knight, Mrs., soprano praised by Evelyn in 1674, **VIII:** 421

Know thyself, **II:** 46, Clement of Alexandria; 107, emperor Julian

Knox, John, 1505–1572, radical English puritan leader, **V:** 201ff, a comprehensive plan for education of 1560

Köchel, Ludwig Ritter von, 1800 1877, **V:** 133, strings do not appear until after 1566 at court

Koussevizky, Serge, Russian conductor, **I:** 36; 39

Kraton of Chalkedon, fourth century BC, famous Greek aulos player, **I:** 172

Kreiger, Philipp, 1649–1725, **VI:** 149, composer of concert music for military band

Kugelmann, Johann, sixteenth century German composer, **V:** 136

Kugelmann, Paul, sixteenth century German composer, **V:** 136

La Barre, Pierre, 1592–1656, organist to Louis XIV, **VII:** 11

La Bataille des VII Ars, **II:** 289, thirteenth century poem by Henri d'Andeli;

La Beaupré, c. 1637–1657, French actress, **VII:** 273

La Borde, Jean Benjamin de, 1734–1794, French opera composer, guillotined during the French revolution, **VII:** 272; 273

La Bruyère, Jean de, French philosopher, 1645–1696, **VII:** 85; 89, bicameral mind; 96; 103; 105, on artists and society; 107; 118; 134ff; 161; 186ff, on the emotions of the viewer of drama

La Comtessa de Dia, fl. c. 1160, rare female troubadour, **II:** 377

La Font de Saint Yenne, period of Louis XV, **VII:** 84, everyone has the right to form his own opinion

La Fontane, eighteenth century French poet, **VII:** 308

La Maupin, seventeenth century soprano at the Paris opera, **VII:** 9

La Mothe-Fénelon, François, 1651–1715, French philosopher, **VII:** 85

La Motte (Antoine Houdar), 1672–1731, French poet and musician, **VII:** 117; 308

La Rochefoucauld, François de, 1613–1680, French philosopher, **VII:** 88ff, on the bicameral mind; 90; 102, finds all emotions to be variations on self-love; 107, on Truth; 109; 161

La Valiere, Madame, mistress to Louis XIV, **VIII:** 444

Lactantius, 250–325 Church philosopher of rhetoric, **II:** 43; 51, against theater; 57; 59ff; 67ff, on the senses, mind and soul; 70ff; 72ff; 75

Lalande, French Baroque composer, **VII:** 160

Lambert, Michel, vocal teacher, court of Louis XIV, **VII:** 4; 122; 270

Lamia, third century BC, single-pipe girl, **I:** 278

Lampetides, lyric poet, murdered in performance, **I:** 425, Ovid; **II:** 89

Lamprus, teacher of music and dance of Sophocles, **I:** 171

Lampugniani, VIII: 26, fn., 16, Judged by Avison as a composer of modest ability

Landini, Francesco, 1335–1397, blind composer, **III:** 10

Laneham, Robert, 1572, reports on ceremonies for the arrival of Elizabeth I at Kenilworth Castle. **V:** 231

Langer, Susanne K., twentieth century philosopher, **I:** 44ff

Langland, William, fourteenth century English writer, **III:** 105; 112, on the soul

Language, I: 30, on ancient languages; **III:** 269, Nicholas of Cusa, 1401–1464, understood that Music expresses feelings and was the origin of language; it is language which expresses the senses; Adam was created with a complete language (German), the root of all other languages; **V:** 45, range in speaking by Erasmus; **VII:** 247ff, Voltaire on the development and use of language

Lanier, Nicholas, in charge of court music of Charles II of England, **VIII:** 7ff

Laniere, John, Jacobean composer who set poetry to music, **VIII:** 95

Lassus, Orlando, 1532–1594, Franco-Flemish composer, **IV:** 65, 226; **V:** 62; 74; 77, forecasting the Baroque in 1593; 138; 144; 147; 218; **VI:** 126

Latomus, V: 36, treatise's value questioned by Erasmus

Lauterbach, Anthony, V: 88, 91; reports on his conversations with Luther

Lawes, Henry, 1595–1662, Jacobean composer who set poetry to music, **VIII:** 95; 123; 137, a composer Milton praised

Lawes, William, 1602–1645, Jacobean composer who set poetry to music, **VIII:** 95; 123

Layamon, author of thirteenth century Romance, *Brut,* **II:** 366

Le Cerf de La Viélle, Jean Laurent, 1647–1707, French aristocrat, **VII:** 14; 123, on French vs Italian music; 140; 142; 146

Le Châtelain de Couci, d. 1203, trouvére, **II:** 383

Le Couvreur, Adrienne, 1692–1730, French actress, **VII:** 270; 279; 287

Le Jeune, Claude, 1525–1600, French composer, **IV:** 205; **VII:** 48

Leaena, fourth century AD harp girl (prostitute), **I:** 475

Lechler, Benedict, b. 1594, German Baroque theorist **VI:** 168

Leclair, Jean-Marie, 1697–1764, French composer, **VII:** 147

Lee, Edward, sixteenth century English scholar, **V:** 13, 1520 Erasmus letter on being attacked by

Lee, Nathaniel, 1648–1692, Restoration playwright, **VIII:** 303, comments on the low quality of both theater and poetry; as playwright: *Nero,* 303; *Rival Queens,* 303; 309; 313; 319; *Lucius Junius Brutus,* 305; 318; *Oedipus,* 306; 311, fn., 22; 313, fn., 28; 314; 317; *Gloriana,* 309; *Sophonisba,* 311, fn., 19 and 20; 318; *Theodosius,* 311, fn., 21; 313; 314, fn., 30; *Constantine the Great,* 313, fn., 28; (with Dryden), *The Duke of Guise,* 314, fn., 30

Leibniz, Gottfried Wilhelm, 1646–1716, mathematician, philosopher, **IV:** 161; **VI:** 233ff, on brain function; 237, genetic knowledge; 239ff, on the senses; 242 on education and memory; 248ff, Leibniz: music is still a branch of mathematics, but comes to understand this is too limited; 250, Leibniz: Music is a form of Truth; 251, Leibniz on the perception of music; 252, Leibniz on the genetic aspects of music; 256, recommendations for a World Fair; **VII:** 83; 247; 308

Leipzig Stadtpfeifers, **VI:** 136, Bach serves on jury to examine Carl Friedrich Pfaffe

Leo v, ninth century Byzantine emperor, **II:** 238

Leo x, 1475–1521, pope, **IV:** 75, sang, composed and studied with Isaac; 89, hunting routine, 96; 135; **V:** 13, Erasmus letter to on being criticized for his translation of the New Testament; 80, letter from Luther

León, Fray Luis de, b. 1527, Spanish poet and professor, **IV:** 311, on the political climate for poetry in late sixteenth century Spain; 316

Leonardo da Vinci, 1452–1519, **III:** 180, at Milan; 192ff, as a musician; **IV:** 91, 112

Leone, Ambrogio of Nola, V: 36 "famous philosopher" discusses music with Erasmus

Leopold I, 1658–1705, emperor, **VI:** 126, an active composer; 128; 239, fn., 57, Leopold calls for music on his death,

Les Grands Hautbois of Louis XIV, **VI:** 90; 131; **VII:** 2

Lesage, Alain-René, 1668–1747, French playwright, **VII:** 210, Turcaret; 217; 222; 225

Lessius, Leonard, 1554–1623, Dutch philosopher, **VIII:** 114

Libanius, b. 314 AD, last philosopher of the old Greek tradition, **II:** 107

Liberal Arts, I: 317, fn., 29, Epictetus placed music in same category as geometry as late as first century, AD; **II:** 140ff, St. Augustine; 175ff, Cassiodorus; 230, begin to reappear, 10th century; Scotus; 236, music first to reemerge; 272, universities students moving away from in favor of skills for employment; 288ff, in Paris university curriculum in thirteenth century; 295, Roger Bacon: purpose is to know God; **III:** 20, Petrarch still includes Music; 166, Valla: learning music is necessary to learning the other liberal arts; 268, Nicholas of Cusa, 1401–1464, God used the liberal arts to create the world; **IV:** 217, Marguerite de Navarre on the study of; **V:** 292, Greene condemns the liberal arts in Elizabethan England; **VI:** 242, Leibniz on the "dark side" of the liberal arts; **VII:** 117, Segrais on music's special status in the liberal arts; **VIII:** 80, for Bacon the foundation for the professions; softens manners; 139, according to Milton, the Saxons were the first among which they first flourished; 205

Ligatures, **II:** 439, in Grocheo, 1300, phrasing, not short-hand for copyists

List, G., d. 1720, German poet, **VI:** 232

Listener, (also see Public and Audience), **I:** 213; 217ff; 193, Plato; 238ff, audiences; 264, Aristotle; 270, Aristotle on feelings of; 388; 395, Isocrates on the difference of hearing orators vs poets (musicians); **II:** 37, lullaby: infant needs no knowledge; 103; 160ff, St. Augustine: listener of music need not know anything about the conceptual aspects of music; 169, St. Augustine; 260, Guido, 1026–1028; 331, music reaches the heart of the listener; 396, in a poem by Dante; 419ff, thirteenth century German contemplative listeners in Strassburg's *Tristan;* Grocheo on the effect on the listener of the music of the different parts of the Mass; **III:** 33, Petrarch; 94ff, new emphasis on importance of the listener in fourteenth century; **IV:** 101, Vida, emotions are what reach the heart; 108, Giraldi, on the power the poet has over the emotions of the listener; 115ff, examples of contemplative listener in sixteenth century Italian poetry; 168ff, Cardano on the affect of the elements of music on emotions; 307, Cervantes, contemplative listener; 341, contemplative listener in Lope de Vega; **V:** 130, a sixteenth century poem on how music affects the listener by Griselius of Wittenberg; 188, Robert Greene writing in 1587 creates a story about Pan in order to make his point that too much music turns off the listener; 214, Lodowick Bryskett, *A Discourse of Civil Life,* many examples of corruption are caused by the music we listen to; young men must be more selective as listeners; 218, John Case, in *The Praise of Musicke* (1586), on how specifically music soothes the listener; 219, examples where music fails to soothe the listener; 310, contemplative listeners in Elizabethan England; **VI:** 33, Zarlino on the effect of emotions on the listener; 200, Mattheson on identifying the contemplative listener; **VII:** 179, Descartes: purpose of music is to communicate emotions to the soul of the listener; **VIII:** 30, Avison, Handel

and Talbot on the contemplative listener; 48, North: music requires some responsibility from the listener; 73, Bunyan suggests that to be a contemplative listener one must have some education in music first; 121ff, Wither: by your face we can know what your heart perceives; 125, heart must be in the right place when listening to church music; 215, Walton: what man hears is conditioned by his perspective as a listener; 273ff, Wotton on the "skilled" listener of music vs the "common" listener; 289, Shaftesbury on the importance of the contemplative listener; 401, contemplative listener in Restoration fiction; 438, Pepys reaction as a contemplative listener of Dekker's *Virgin Martyr*

Listenius, Nicolaus, 1500–1550, German theorist, author of *Musica* (1537), **V:** 112ff, taught at Wittenberg as a colleague of Luther and Melancthon

Liszt, Franz, 1811–1886, Hungarian pianist, **I:** 26; 39; 45ff; 49ff; 56

Literature, II: 355ff, French Romances and Chansons; de Geste of the twelfth and thirteenth centuries; 395ff, Italian literature of the twelfth and thirteenth centuries; 410ff, German literature in the twelfth and thirteenth centuries; **III:** 1ff humanism begins with Petrarch and Boccaccio

Lituus, early Roman trumpet, **I:** 343

Livius Andronicus, fl. c. 240 BC, **I:** 353, Roman actor and singer

Livy, Titus, 59 BC – 17 AD, Roman historian **I:** 344ff, on Etruscan music; 359ff; 364; 366

Locatelli, VIII: 26, fn, 16, judged by Avison as being a composer defective of in harmony and invention, music "fit for children"

Locke, John, 1632–1704, English philosopher whose education was in ancient languages, rhetoric, logic and medicine, resulting in an almost total left-hemisphere view of the world, **VI:** 237ff; **VII:** 247; **VIII:** 231;

Locke, Matthew, 1621–1677, Jacobean composer for the King's wind band, **VIII:** 7

Lodge, Thomas, 1558–1625, English poet and playwright, **V:** 196ff, writing in support of the arts, *A Defence of Poetry, Music and Stage-plays* (1580); 260; 293; 303ff; 308ff; as playwright (with Greene): 319, fn., 16; *A Looking Glass for London;* 321; 330; 332; 335; 337

Lomazzo, Giovanni, sixteenth century philosopher, **IV:** 13

Longinus, first century author of *On the Sublime,* **II:** 11ff; **VII:** 107

Longus, early Christian poet of *Daphnis and Chloe,* **II:** 7, 40

Lope de Vega, Félix, 1562–1635, Spanish playwright, **IV:** 313ff; 317; 325ff, in theater emotions are supplied by the music; **VI:** 93; 105

Lord Herbert of Cherbery, Edward, d. 1648, Jacobean poet whose poetry was set to music, **VIII:** 95; 98

Lorenzo the Magnificent of Florence, **III:** 182ff, music at court of and funeral music, 185, singing while traveling

Lottich, Jacob, seventeenth century German poet, **VI:** 138, poem in praise of tower music

Louis I, King of France, 814–840, **II:** 239

Louis IX ("St. Louis") of France, 1214–1270, **II:** 285, organized Seventh Crusade in 1248;

Louis VII of France, 1120–1180, **II:** 281, first crusade

Louis XI of France, 1423–1483, **III:** 213, a strange man who dressed as a pilgrim.

Louis XII of France, 1498–1515, **IV:** 194

Louis XIII of France, 1601–1643, king and composer, **VI:** 893; **VII:** 1ff; 11; 128; 269

Louis XIV of France, 1638–1715, **IV:** 194; **VI:** 5; 27; 131; 157; **VII:** 1ff; 5, functional music for the king; 14; 16; 75; 85, fn., 7; 139; 210, fn., 38, the king's famous remark to the door servant; 227, fn., 2; 229; 235, as a singer; 236; 238; 240 on an evening entertainment; 241 more funcional music; 243; 246; 269; 270; 273; 277; 279; **VIII:** 340; 444

Louis XV of France, 1710–1774, **VII:** 9; 84; 243

Lovelace, Richard, 1618–1657, English poet who named the composers who set his poetry to music; **VIII:** 104; 111, "Dialogue for Lute and voice"; 120

Löwenstern, Matthäus Apelles von, 1594–1648, German writer and musician, **VI:** 223

Lübeck, Henrich, V: 148, extant sixteenth century trumpet choir music

Lubuissière (La Bassire), VI: 132, leader of the court Hautboisten in Berlin

Lucanus, Roman poet, **I:** 469

Lucian of Samosata, 125–180 AD, satirist, **I:** 310; 322; 337; 464; 500, a banquet of the gods

Lucilius, first century Roman poet, **II:** 7; 9

Lucius Anicius, Roman general, **I:** 347

Lucius Flaccus, fl. c. 19 AD, Roman consul, **I:** 352, played trumpet

Lucretius, 99–55 BC, Roman writer, **I:** 347; 357; 369ff; 392

Lucrezia, Borgia, 1480–1519, daughter to Alexander VI, pope, **IV:** 88, wedding, arrival ceremonies in Rome

Ludovico Sforza, 1481–1499, **III:** 180, music at court of

Ludwig III, Duke of Württemburg, 1568–1593, **V:** 137, instrument collection; 143; 149

Luigi del Cornetto of Ancona, cornett virtuoso, **IV:** 84

Luis de Góngora, 1561–1627, Spanish poet, **IV:** 316

Lull, Ramón, 1232–1315, **II:** 312, frowns on the new translations of Greek philosophy; 317, on senses; 325ff; 330

Lully, Jean-Baptiste, 1632–1687, French composer, *surintendant, Musique de la Chambre* under Louis XIV, **VI:** 157; 161; 170; 188; 281; **VII:** 4; 5 conducting the music of the *les plaisirs de l'île enchantée* (1664); 8, his official positions under King Louis XIV; 11; **VIII:** 23; 122; 141; 145; 237; 267; 269; 270; 272; 273; 274; 313; 449

Lute, I: 76, in ancient Egypt; **III:** 250, Tinctoris found the most gifted players Pietro Bono of Ferrara and Heinrich, a German in the service of Charles the Bold; **IV:** Galilei on arranging for 60 parts; **V:** 315; **VIII:** 111; 117; 121; 137, Milton's preference; 139; 143; 144; 193, fn., 55; 262; 421

Luther, Martin, 1483–1546, **IV:** 4; **V:** 1; 8ff, his movement followed by Erasmus; 63ff, on education; 75; 79, major study; 79, self-description as a young priest; 112; 203; 253; 325; **VII:** 253

Lyceum, I: 249, Aristotle's school

Lycurgus, ninth century BC general, **I:** 111, battle music; 141, as creator of choral competitions; **IV:** 148

Lydgate, John, 1370–1450, English poet, fifteenth century, **III:** 303ff; 311

Lydian, a Greek mode, **I:** 104ff

Lyly, John, 1554–1606, sixteenth century English poet, **V:** 189, music education may not be 'unfit,' but has nothing to do with virtue; 272, on the darker emotions of music; 288, fn., 5; 290; as playwright: **V:** 315, *Sapho and Phao;* 334; 335; *The Maydes Metamorphosis;* 316; 325; 330; 337; *Campaspe,* 319; 327; 328; 331; 332; *The Woman in the Moone,* 319; 321; *Endimion,* 320; 324; 326; 336; *Loves Metamorphosis,* 325; *Midas,* 328; 334; *Mother Bombie,* 336

Lynche, Richard, fl. 1596–1601, English poet, **V:** 263

Lyre, I: 63; 68; 69; 78; 86ff; 105; 117ff, lyre players called "Theioi," the divine; 118, singing for character purposes in banquets; 127, Terpander; 129, Timotheus of Miletus; 160; 161, as a metaphor for bodily health; 169; 171ff; 175, Dexitheus, lyre player mentioned by Aristophanes; 182ff, 214ff, in concert; 224ff, use in education; 467, players Terpnus and Diodorus given large cash gifts by the emperor Vespasian, 69–79 AD; **II:** 4, Honestus on the first century decay of good lyre music; 5, third century player, Simylus; 90, "with a frequent quill"; 100, Christian metaphor of the lyre; 198; 200; **IV:** 34, Bruno, sixteenth century Italy: lyre has become the instrument of charlatans; **V:** 45, Erasmus on the fable of Aspendus

Lyric poetry, II: 200, 6th to 8th century

Lysimachus, second century BC, famous Roman aulos player, **I:** 354, Polybius

Lysippus, ancient Greek sculptor, **I:** 373, Cicero

Maarten van Dorp, V: 12, 1525 Erasmus letter on the death of

Maban, eighth century singer of older Church songs, **II:** 212

Mace, Thomas, 1613–1709, English theorist at Cambridge, **VIII:** 23, cannot understand how popular music could be a subject of discussion; 26, on the loss of seriousness in English music; 32; 35; 36 on music education; 37ff on singing church music

Macedonius, poet, sixth century, **II:** 198ff

Machaut, Guillaume, 1300–1377, French composer and poet, **III:** 69ff; 94ff, on the listener; 37, on church ceremonies; 39, on military music; 40, entertainment; **VI:** 29

Machiavelli, Niccolò, 1469–1527, Italian writer; **IV:** 2; 5; 11ff; 13ff; 39ff; 126, on pleasure and pain; 130; 132ff

Macran, Henry, I: 282, Greek translator of Aristoxenus, says we cannot know anything important about Greek music

Madonna of Cimabue, 13th century art work in the Church of Santa Maria Novella, Florence, **I:** 52

Maffei, Raffaello, 1451–1522, Italian humanist, **IV:** 4; 70;

Maffei, Scipione, Baroque music critic, **IV:** 70; **VI:** 56

Magadis, ancient Greek string instrument, **I:** 106

Magini, Francesco, composer and professor in the conservatory in Rome, **VI:** 16, composer of a 1700 manuscript in Berlin for a civic band

Magnus, Albertus, b. 1193, philosopher, **II:** 301ff, on emotion in man and animals; 307ff, *De animalibus*

Mahler, Gustav, 1860–1911 Austrian composer, **I:** 39; 55; **II:** 263

Mairan, French Baroque poet mentioned by Voltaire, **VII:** 308

Mairet, 1604–1686, composer of *Sophonisba,* **VII:** 273

Malebranche, Nicolas, 1638–1715, French philosopher, **VII:** 91

Mallulf, Bishop of Senlis, sixth century, **II:** 210

Malvezzi, sixteenth century composer, **IV:** 82

Mandeville, Bernard, 1670–1733, Dutch philosopher, **VII:** 261

Manniche, Lisa, twentieth century authority on ancient music, **I:** 73ff

Mao, 1893–1976, Chinese leader, **I:** 98

Marcabru, 1129–1150, troubadour spoke badly of women and love, **II:** 370; 386; 393

Marcellinus, Ammianus, fourth century, last great Roman historian **II:** 90ff; 91ff, theater; 94ff, on the use of trumpets; 96ff

Marcello, Benedetto, 1686–1739 Italian composer, **VI:** 48, *Theater in the Modern Style* (1720); 51; 63, satire on improvisation; 69, in satire of church forms; **VII:** 160

Marchand, Louis, 1669–1732, leading Baroque French organist, **VI:** 170

Marchetto of Padua, 1274–1319, **III:** 5ff, on *musica speculativa* and *musica practica,* and on the etymology of "voice," which is "vota," the heart; 8, music surpasses the other arts in Beauty

Marco del Pino da Siena, a student of Michelangelo, **I:** 5

Marcus Aurelius, 121–180 AD, Roman emperor, **I:** 323; 459; 463; 480; 487ff; 494

Marduk, god of ancient Akkad, **I:** 64

Marenzio, Luca, 1553–1599, Italian composer, **V:** 218

Mareuil, troubadour, **II:** 370, made love to patron's wife

Margaret of Austria, regent for the Low Countries, visiting Mechelen, sixteenth century, **V:** 3; 139

Margareta Theresa of Spain, VI: 128, (1667)

Margherita de' Medici, 1612–1679, of Florence, **VI:** 2

Marguerite de Navarre, 1496–1549, sister to François I of France, mother to Henry IV, **IV:** 217ff, on the study of the liberal arts; 220; 222; 226ff; 234

Maria Bárbara de Braganza, 1711–1758, Spanish patron of Domenico Scarlatti, **VI:** 91

Maria Casimira, 1641–1716, widow of Jan III of Poland, Queen of Poland, **VI:** 7, activity in Rome, hiring Domenico Scarlatti

Maria d'Aquino, natural daughter of Robert, King of Naples, **III:** 45

Maria Eleanora of Brandenburg, mother to Christina of Sweden, **VI:** 6

Maria Theresa, 1717–1780, Empress of Austria and a singer, 1717–1780, **VI:** 126

Maria, Infanta of Savoy, 1620, **VI:** 2

Marie de France, twelfth century writer, **II:** 356ff, some of her Romances attributed to a jongleur; 362ff

Marie-Thérèse, visits Louis XIV in 1664, **VII:** 5

Marino, Giambattista, 1569–1625, author of *L'Adone,* **VI:** 71, on the senses; 85; 87

Marius, Marcus, d. 82 BC, Roman politician, **I:** 398

Marivaux, Pierre de, 1688–1763, French playwright, **VII:** 194, *The Game of Love and Chance;* 205, *Double Infideliy;* 208, *Money Makes he World Go Round;* 214; 215; 221

Mark Anthony, I: 467, Roman emperor

Markham, Gervase, 1568–1637, English poet, **VIII:** 70

Marlowe, Christopher, 1564–1593, English playwright, **V:** 315, *Tamburlaine The Great;* Part I and Part II; 319, fn., 16; 320; 322; 326; 331ff; *The Massacre of Paris,* 319, fn., 16; *The Troublesome Reign and Lamentable Death of Edward the Second,* 319, fn., 16; 334; 338; *Faustus,* 320; 325; *The Massacre at Paris,* 324; *The Jew of Malta,* 334; **VIII:** 155

Marolles, Michel de, abbe, 1600–1681, French churchman, **VII:** 13

Marot, Clément, sixteenth century French poet, **IV:** 215

Marpurg, Friedrich, 1718–1795, German composer and theorist, **VI:** 154; 167; 170

Marquis de Termes, seventeenth century French noble, **VII:** 241

Marsh, Robert, twentieth century American writer on education, **I:** 50

Marston, John, 1575–1634, poet and playwright until 1607 when he became a minister, **VI:** 115, as playwright: **VIII:** *Antonio and Mellida,* 157; 159; 165, fn., 19; 176; [Part Two] 177; 178; 180, fn., 33 and 34; 182 [Part Two]; 182, fn., 41; 183; 185; 186; 186, fn., 46; 190, fn., 53; 196; *The Fawn,* 157, fn., 7; 185; 187; *The Malcontent,* 162; 169; 182, fn., 41; 184; 189; 200; 204; *The Insatiate Countess,* 164; *Women Beware Women,* 169; *No Wit, no Help Like a Woman's,* 170; *A Trick to Catch the Old One,* 170; *What you Will,* 173; 182; 193; *The Tragedy of Sophonisba,* 180, fn., 33; 182; 183; 186; 200; *The Dutch Courtezan,* 190; 191; 193, fn., 55; 196; 200; [Masque] *Montebank's Masque,* 203

Martellio, Pier Jacopo, seventeenth century Italian writer, **VI:** 12, in praise of the new Italian opera form

Martial, Latin poet, **V:** 19

Martin le Franc, 1441–1442, **III:** 211, on the newer emotional style in Dufay and Binchois.

Marvell, Andrew, 1621–1678, English poet and secretary to Milton, **VIII:** 102; 104, a poem which is a virtual history of music; 119; 122; 223

Mary Tudor, Queen of England, 1553–1558, **V:** 228, minstrels playing for Philip of Spain

Mashrokita, musical instrument mentioned in the Book of Daniel, **I:** 66

Massaino, Tiburio, 1550–1608, Italian comoposer, **VI:** 71

Masson, Charles, seventeenth century theorist, **VII:** 26, Time or Measure vs Movement

Mattheson, Johann, 1681–1764, German composer and writer, **VI:** 124; 132, hears Hautboisten in Hannover in 1706; 139, his *Ehren-Pforte* (1740) which includes biographical mention of Bach and Reiche; 142, an account of peasant music; 143 on church music; 163; 177, against polyphony; 181ff, major discussion, The old debate, music as mathematics or feeling, continued and in his book *Das Neu-Eröffnete Orchestre* (1713) Mattheson argues the case for feeling, saying music communicates with the inner soul. He was attacked in publications by Johann Buttstedt and Johann Fux, but supported by Handel and Johann Kuhnau; 183ff, Mattheson continues with discussion of mathematics and measurement resulting with an attack on polyphony; 186ff, on the "Art of Gesticulation" or *Hypocritica,* the communication of emotions through movement and face (central to conducting); 188 and 191, Mattheson on national differences in singing; 189, in the decay of music in society; 192, in the classification of music in which the singer is the highest aesthetically because melody is the primary element in music which communicates feeling; 193ff a lengthy discussion of writing good melodies; 198, "Movement" is associated with emotions; 200, on the purposes of music (all tied to feelings); 215, Mattheson on the requirements and education needed for the conductor; **VIII:** 36, on music education

Matthew, book of the Old Testament, **I:** 112; **VIII:** 99

Matthias, 1557–1619, Emperor, Holy Roman Empire, **VI:** 129

Maugars, André, violist and secretary to Cardinal Richelieu in Paris, **VI:** 17ff, visits Rome in 1639; 19, on *Stile recitativo* in church music; **VII:** 128; 138; 144; 147; 150, on opera

Maurice, seventeenth century Prince of Nassau, **VII:** 178

Maurus, Rabanus, ninth century author of the *Life of Mary Magdalene,* **II:** 233

Maximian, 286–305 AD, Roman emperor, **I:** 459; 463, first music guilds in Rome

Maximilian I, emperor, **IV:** 5; 291; **V:** 103, in 1501 added poetry to the arts curriculum at the University of Vienna; 140, seeks wind players in 1502

Maximilian II, Emanuel, Elector, 1679–1726, **VI:** 125

Maximilian II, 1564–1576, emperor, **IV:** 131; **V:** 103; 114; 139; 140; 142

Maximilian III, Joseph, 1745–1777, **VI:** 125, a noble and viola da gamba virtuoso and composer in Munich

Mazarin, Cardinal, 1602–1661, chief minister under Louis XIII, **VII:** 1

Mazzocchi, Virgilio, VI: 15, famous singing teacher in Rome and head of music at St. Peter's

McLuhan, Marshall, 1911–1980, **I:** 30, on ancient languages

Mechelen town band, sixteenth century, **V:** 3

Medwall, Henry, b. 1461, English poet, **III:** 306ff

Mei, Girolamo, 1519–1594, Italian historian, **IV:** 24ff, on moving away from the old Scholastic philosophy toward an art of feeling; 25, theory vs practice; away from mathematics; 26, purpose is not entertainment; catharsis; 67, purpose of theory is to find Truth, but it is found in performance; 91, on the characteristics of poetry

Meister Eckhart, German pre-Renaissance humanist, **III:** 255

Melanchthon, Philippus, 1497–1560, **V:** 9, 1520 letter from Erasmus; 62, 65, on education; 69; 76; 90, letter from Luther; 112; 125

Meles, ancient Greek harp player, father of Cinesias, **I:** 215

Melk monastery music, VI: 145

Melody, VI: 193ff, Mattheson gives an extraordinary analysis of the characteristics of a good melody. **VIII:** 21, Avison: the foundation of harmony and expression

Melpomene, Greek god, **I:** 427, Horace

Melville, Sir James, sixteenth century English courtier, **V:** 229, hears Elizabeth I play virginals

Memory, II: 146; 148, St. Augustine; 184, Alcuin; 249, Aurelian: unless imprinted in the memory music is not retained; 434, is easier in poetry than prose; **III:** 288, Ruiz: fear of God is the beginning of wisdom, hence the importance of memory—painting, writing and sculpture were invented for the purpose of keeping things in the memory; **IV:** 18, support of Nature; **VI:** 133, on the memorized trumpet choir repertoire; 243, Leibniz; **VIII:** 72, Donne on the value of music as a tool for memory

Menander, 342–291 BC Greek playwright, **I:** 111ff; 179; 184; **II:** 83, two versions of Hell; 200

Mendelssohn, Felix, 1809–1847, German composer, **I:** 12; 14; 25; 37

Mendieta, Geronimo, sixteenth century in Mexico, **IV:** 290

Menecrates, kithara player given a palace and estate by Nero, **I:** 467

Ménestrier, Claude, 1631–1705, French scholar, **VII:** 16

Menicuccio, an Italian musician mentioned by De Brosses, **VII:** 141

Mercury, Greek god, **I:** 426, Horace; 430; 432

Meret, Louis Bollioud de, VII: 32, on tempi in dances

Merit, ancient Egyptian god, the personification of music, **I:** 74

Merlo, Alessandro, sixteenth century singer in the Sistine Chapel, **IV:** 65, sang bass with a variety of improvisation new and pleasing to the ear of all: (1575)

Mermet, Louis Bollioud de, late Baroque French critic, **VII:** 32

Mersenne, Marin, 1588–1648, French philosopher, **IV:** 203; **VI:** 79; **VII,** 15 on the psychological value of the military trumpet; **VII:** 37–82, major discussion; 38, on the old mathematics basis of music; 41, on the senses; 44, aesthetics and classification of music; 46, the perception of music, humors and emotions, emotions and color and notation; 68, performance practice, vocal and instrumental; 78, the Baïf Academy; 79, church music; 165; 172ff; 180; 181ff; **VIII:** 224

Merulo, Claudio, 1533–1604, composer, **VI:** 126

Mesomedes, kithara teacher to the emperor, Caracalla,188–217 AD, **I:** 463

Metastasio, Pietro Abate, 1698–1782, opera librettist, **VI:** 13, discusses the direction toward entertainment in Italian opera in 1750; 15; 36; 51; **VII:** 157; **VIII:** 461, mentioned by Lord Chesterfield

Metopus, fifth century BC, Greek philosopher, **I:** 153

Meyerbeer, Giacomo, 1791–1864, German composer, **I:** 26; 29

Meyerowitz, Jan, twentieth century American composer, **I:** 16

Meysonnier, Lazare, professor at Lyons, **VII:** 171

Michael de Verona, sixteenth century composer, **V:** 124

Michael VII, 1071–1078, emperor, **II:** 231ff

Michelangelo, 1475–1654, Italian artist, **I:** 5; 6; 34; **IV:** 4, The Church's view of the *Last Judgment* paintings; 18; 21, as an example that Art comes through genetics, not instruction; 91; 177ff; 339, fn., 58; **VI:** 1; 96; **VII:** 267

Michelin town band, III: 231, regular concerts in fifteenth century

Midas of Acragas, famous aulos player in 490 BC, **I:** 126

Middleton, Thomas, 1570–1627, English playwright, **VIII:** 155, *The Family of Love,* 155; *The Spanish Gipsy,* 157; 187; 189, fn., 52; *Blurt, Master-Constable,* 164; 196; 206; *Michaelmas Term,* 166; *A Fair Quarrel,* 168; *Your Five Gallants,* 168; *A Chaste Maid in Cheapside,* 174; *The Witch,* 176; 189, fn., 52; *Mayor of Queenborough,* 185; 200; *More Dissemblers Besides Women,* 189, fn., 52; 196; 197; *A Mad World, my Masters,* 195; *Women Beware Women,* 200; four published Masque texts, see 204, fn., 67

Milan, II: 276, civic band in 1268;

Milanuzzi, Carlo, sixteenth century organist of Venezia, **IV:** 86

Military music, I: 111, use of aulos in ninth century BC battle by Lycurgus; 146ff; 349, Livy on songs by soldiers; 363ff, Roman Republic; 472ff, Polybius; **II:** 7; 94, slow notes of trumpets; 97, soldier songs for entertainment; 195, dance, sixth to eighth centuries; 238, first *carroccio* in 1037, Milan; 244, battle, ninth – eleventh centuries; 245, soldiers singing; 365, in twelfth and thirteenth century French Romances, including King Arthur, *The Song of Roland;* 367 singing soldiers; 422, in German literature in the twelfth and thirteenth centuries; **III:** 132ff, fourteenth century English; 233, wind bands for battles in fifteenth

century Burgundy, including Philip's "great cat."; 300, music from the time of Fernando and Isabella; **IV:** 39, Machiavelli's discussion; 118ff, in Tasso; 228; 309, Cervantes, music of the Moors; 322, Luis de Camões; **V:** 147ff, in sixteenth century Germany; 284; 373, various trumpet signals in military references by Shakespeare; 381ff; **VI:** 27, Hautboisten band arrive in Italy from Paris in 1684 for the wedding of Vittorio Amadeo II; 115, 119, miliary drums in in seventeenth century Spanish theater; 146ff, including the role of the trumpeter; concert music; 147, first standing armies; miliary Hautboisten is only oboes and bassoons; 148, "Turkish Music,"; 149, concert music by Johann Philipp Kreiger; first military music school founded under Frederick William I; 281, pre-Hautboisten painting in the Low Countries; **VII,** 16, on the military timpani; 18, on the introduction of the Hautboisten in the French military; 18, military concert during the Battle of Mons in 1691 and Siege of Namus in 1692; 160, thoughts by Du Bos; 240, on the capture of timpani; 316 (Voltaire); **VIII:** 17ff, rules for trumpet- and drum-majors; 126ff, on getting ready for war; 152, in Milton's *Paradise Lost*; 160, "a troop Musick" used in Beaumont and Fletcher's *The Little French Lawyer*; 201ff, references in the Jacobean plays; 317ff, a number of examples involving military music in the Restoration plays; 370ff, (Congreve, Addison, Thomson, Swift, and Pope); 371ff, Young and Prior, on music giving courage to the soldier; 444, Pepys reports Louis XIV had trumpets and timpani accompany him to his mistress' house

Milton, John, 1608–1674, English poet, **VI:** 6; **VIII:** 93; 129, major discussion

Minerva, Greek goddess made the first flute, **I:** 109; 111; **II:** 49, fn 15;

Minstrel, II: 203, Britain, sixth to eighth century; **III:** 14, large groups assemble for noble ceremonies, vocal minstrels described; 97, list of household minstrels of John II, French king, 1350–1364; instruments mentioned in poems of Froissart; 120ff, state of in fourteenth century, 121ff Langland's description of the minstrel, Hawkin, or 'Active Life'; 134 indoor trumpets; 150ff, Chaucer's description of a Minstrel School; 225 punishment in fifteenth century France; **V:** 141, in sixteenth century Germany; 144; 237, sixteenth century England; 237ff; attacks on by Gossen and Stubbs; 243, concerts; 244, discipline problems; **VIII:** 15, the final period of the English minstrels

Minturno (Antonio Sebastiano), d. 1574, **IV:** 129, author of *The Art of Poetry* (1563)

Minucius Felix, second-third century Roman philosopher, **II:** 47ff, against festivals; 53, rituals with percussion; 64; 73

Miriam, sister to Moses, Old Testament figure, **I:** 92; **II:** 295

Mixolydian, a Greek mode, **I:** 104

Mizler, Lorenz, German Baroque writer, on Bach's improvisation, **VI:** 171

Modes in Greek music, I: 227, Plato; 268, Aristotle; 270, fn., 84, Aristotle's distinction between notation and style of; 315, Roman period of ancient Greece; 315, confusion of scale and mode; national characteristics; **V:** 114ff, the most extensive modern discussion on

Molière (Jean Baptiste Poquelin), 1622–1673, French playwright, **VII:** 6ff, his participation in the *les plaisirs de l'île enchantée* (1664), in which he acts and sings!; 183; *La princesse*

d'Élide, 6; *The Learned Ladies*, 193; *Don Garcia of Navarre*, 193; *The Compulsory Marriage*, 7, 193, 207, 211; *The Sicilian, or Love makes a Painter*, 194, 206; *The Blunderer*, 194; *The Affected Ladies*, 196, 201, 209; *Don Juan*, 196; *The Impromptu of Versailles*, 196; *The School for Wives Criticized*, 197, 204; *The Countess of Escarbagnas*, 198, 209; *Tartuffe*, 199, 233; *Le Bourgeois gentilhomme*, 5, 7, 11, 201, 208, 210; *Love the Best Physician*, 205; *Monsieur de Pourceaugnac*, 205, 207; *The Princess of Elis*, 205, 209; *The Hypochondriac*, 205; *The Magnificent Lovers*, 207, 209; *Les Facheux*, 210; *The Mock-Doctor*, 210; 233; 264; 270; 273; 289; 296; **VIII:** 450

Molina, Tirso de, pseudonym for Fray Gabriel Téllez, 1581–1648, Spanish playwright, **VI:** 105, as a playwright, *Tamar's Revenge; Damned for Despair; The Trickster of Seville*

Möller, German military theorist (1672), **VI:** 4

Monk of Montaudon, fl. 1180–1215, troubadour, **II:** 375; 394

Mons band guild, sixteenth century, **V:** 4

Monsieur des Yveteaux of Paris, seventeenth century noble of Paris, **VII:** 233

Monsieur, brother to Louis xv, **VII:** 10; 238

Montagu, Mary Wortley, seventeenth century English writer, **VIII:** 458

Montaigne, Michael de, 1533–1592, French writer, **IV:** 243ff

Montalto, Alessandro, Cardinal, 1571–1623, Italian musician, **IV:** 66, "played Cembalo excellently and sang in a sweet and sensitive style," Giustiniani (1623)

Monte, Filippo di, 1521–1608, Flemish composer, **IV:** 65; **V:** 156

Montemayor, Jorge de, of Portugal, d. 1561, **IV:** 293, writer of pastoral romances

Montesquieu, Charles de Secondat, Baron de, 1689–1755, French philosopher, **VII:** 86; 100, on education; 103; 127, on the affect of different climates; 137, on the role of music in ancient and modern societies; 213; 217; 224

Monteverdi, Claudio, 1567–1643, Italian composer, **IV:** 67; **V:** 180, mentioned by Praetorius; 316, *Orfeo*, fanfares to begin play; **VI:** 1ff; 4ff. 21; 31; 34ff, on the difference between the words of the text and the emotions of the text; 50; on communicating emotions, 54, Monteverdi, a sinfonia is needed to prepare the minds of the audience; 54, on rehearsals; 126

Monticelli, VIII: 462, famous singer mentioned by Lord Chesterfield

Monvoisin, Catherine, seventeenth century noble lady and provider of poison to needful nobles, **VII:** 238

More, Henry, seventeenth century, **VII:** 177

More, Sir Thomas, 1478–1535, Archbishop of Canterbury, **V:** 7, comments on Erasmus; 18; 201; 205ff, on pleasure and pain; 212, *Utopia* (1515); 254, his poem "To a Courtier"; 260; 262; 265; 277; 328, *Utopia* (1515) reference to improvisation

Moritz, Landgraf of Hesse-Cassel, sixteenth century German noble, **V:** 134ff, description of his musical establishment; 137, instrument collection; 142

Morley, Thomas, 1557–1602, English writer, **V:** 184, on the well-rounded Englishman, of one embarrassed because he cannot sight-sing; 215ff, sixteenth century English writer; 245, dedicates *First Book of Consort Lessons* of 1599 to the Waits; 260

Moschus, fl. 100 BC, Alexandrian poet, **I:** 293ff; **V:** 46, an unskilful ancient lyre player, according to Erasmus

Moses, thirteenth to twelfth century BC, Hebrew leader of the Old Testament, **I:** 86; 88; 90; 92; 97

Moussorgsky, Modeste, 1839–1881, Russian composer, **I:** 42

Mouton, sixteenth century composer, **V:** 138

Movement (see Tempo)

Mozart, Wolfgang Amadeus, 1756–1791, Austrian composer, **I:** 17; 21; 28; 54; 410; **VI:** 126; 148, influence of Türkish Music in his *Abduction from the Seraglio*

Müchelon, Sebastianus, V: 103, lector in music and arithmetic at the University of Leipzig.

Muffat, Georg, 1653–1704, German composer, **VI:** 157; 159; 161ff, 169; 170; 174

Müller, Johann, early Renaissance German humanist, **III:** 253

Murphy, Gardner, twentieth century writer, **I:** 47

Musaeus, fifth century poet, **II:** 100; *Hero and Leander*

Muses of ancient Greece (see also: Apollo, Calliope, Diana, Dionysus, Erato, Melpomene, Mercury, Minerva, Nymphs, Orpheus, Pan, Terpsichore, Urania), **II:** 99; 103, for use as leisure in school; 106; **V:** 249ff, Spenser's tribute to the Greek muses; **VIII:** 153, in concert (Milton); 205; 357

Muset, Colin, jongleur, fl., 1230, **II:** 374ff; 376, played fiddle; 378; 388

Music Academies, IV: 31ff, sixteenth century Italy, Ficino in Florence

Music and Theater, I: 353ff, Roman Republic; 355, Ovid; **V:** 242ff, use of Waits

Music at Court, II: 276ff, for meals under Richard I; Emperor Frederick II returning from the crusade; 278, marriage of Henry III of England in 1236; **III:** 179ff, music under the fifteenth century Italian courts; 186, court of a cardinal described by Cortesi; 214, arrival ceremonies; 227ff, the Burgundians of the Low Countries; 277, on the court music of Frederick III, 1440–1493, and his son, Maximilian I as seen in *The Triumph of Maximilian I;* The Congress of Vienna in 1515; royal weddings; 284, Maximilian I, dining alone; 295 fourteenth and fifteenth century Spain court wind ensembles; 319ff, fifteenth century England and Scotland; **IV:** 77ff, sixteenth century Italians, Ercole d'Este, Duke Alfonso II of Ferrara; 193ff, organization of court music under François I, including the *Joeurs d'instrumens de haulxbois et sacqueboutes,* which became the *Les Grands Hautbois* under Louis XIV and the *Hautboisten* of the late Baroque; 291, Philip I of Spain, 1504–1506, son of Maximilian I and husband of the tragic Juana, his court ensembles playing on ships; 327, Lope de Vega on skills needed at court, including singing; **V:** 133, sixteenth century German nobles, Johann Georg, 1571–1598; Albert V of Munich; Philipps von Hessen; 134, Moritz, Landgraf of Hesse-Cassel; Joachim II of Brandenburg; Christian I of Saxony; 136, Abert Duke of Prussia; 137, Ludwig III, Duke of Württemburg; Christian I

of Saxony; Ferdinand II of Innsbruck; 139, Maximilian II, 1564–1576, trumpets are named "musical" and "not musical"; 143, court church services; coronations; 180, Praetorius on the concerto principle, with changing concerti consorts, for banquets; 181 alternation of dance movements with differing tempi; 282ff on the arrival of nobles, including Elizabeth I; 288ff, on the characteristics of the courtier in the Elizabethan court; 304, outdoor water machines, water powered birds; **VI:** 1ff, extensive examples of seventeenth court entertainment music; 123ff, during the German Baroque; 126, Phililpp Hainhofer, a visitor to Dresden court in 1629, describes at the court; **VII:** 1ff. various ensembles under Louis XIII; 2ff, various divisions under Louis XIV, the *Écurie,* the *Chapelle,* the *Chambre* and the *Maison Militaire,* major discussion; **VIII:** 5, the court music of Charles I of England; 7 coronation music for Charles II; 8, retrenchment of court music in 1679 in England; 8, North on the various national styles heard at court; 8, music in the court of William and Mary (1689–1694); music in the court of Anne of England; 172, in Chapman's play, *All Fools,* there is a lengthy exchange on the cultural training of the young courtier, including ability in music

Music contests, I: 76; 111; 125ff; 141ff, contests; 232, Plato's discussion of choir contests; 466, at a banquet; 467, associated with theater plays; 468ff, Nero; **V:** 328, in Lyly's *Midas* is a contest between two musical gods, Apollo and Pan

Music education I: 323, Roman period of Greece; 324, decay in first century AD; 326, Aristides Quintilianus, late third century AD, major discussion; 447ff, Virgil, Ovid, Propertius, Tibullus; 495ff, major Quintilian discussion; **II:** 123ff, St. Gregory Nazianzus on the importance of practice; 159ff, St. Augustine: Reason is at the center of teaching, but the listener of music need not know anything about the conceptual aspects of music; 289ff, little advance in thirteenth Scholastic philosophy; **III:** 218, important for nobles; **IV:** 166ff, Cardano on value; does not weaken morals; right-hemisphere techniques; 167, exception: having private singing teachers in your home to work with children; **V:** 201ff, John Knox's comprehensive plan for education of 1560 includes music; 218, Henry Peacham, 1576–1643, wrote that Ferrabosco was "the father of many other composers"; 364, Shakespeare's depiction of a private lesson on the lute; **VIII:** 271, Wotton finds it curious that while mathematicians are conversant with earlier writers, musicians are not

Music education, early systems, I: 68; 76, 1570 BC, Egypt; 78, Plato; 78, last century BC Egypt; 84; 87; 98; 107ff; 112, aulos schools at Olypiodorus and Orthagoras; 127, choral school of Melanippides, c. 450–413 BC; 127, choral school of Philoxenus, 435–380 BC; 127, choral school of Timotheus, end of the fifth century BC; 129, boys lyre school; 131, Xenodamus, leader of a sixth century BC music school; 211ff; 219ff, Plato's discussion; 264ff, Aristotle; 325ff, teachers; **V:** 201ff, John Knox's comprehensive plan for education of 1560 includes music; **VI:** 174, German Baroque views on improvement; 175ff, on Niedt as a piano teacher; 177, on Bach as a piano teacher; **VII:** 33ff, theories of Saint-Lamert; 34 views of Couperin; 35, Rameau on the development stages of composing; 159, Batteux

praises the Italian music education; **VIII:** 54, North in support, including the teaching of some performance practice subjects

Music Festivals, I: 244ff, Plato's ideal plan; 452ff, religious festivals: Tilbullus, Virgil, Horace, Propertius, Ovid;

Music for Oratorical support, I: 365, Caius Gracchus of Roman Republic, Quintilian calls the instrument a *tonarion*

Music for Processions, II: 423, including string players, in German literature in the twelfth and thirteenth centuries; **III:** 321, London fifteenth century; **IV:** 88, Lucrezia, Borgia, 1480–1519, wedding, arrival ceremonies in Rome; 291, Charles V arriving in Valladolid in 1517; **V:** 4, low countries, sixteenth century *Ommegangs;* 226, for the arrival of Charles V in 1522; Anne Boleyn arrives; Edward VI's coronation; 380 (Shakespeare); **VI:** 16, the 1602 Bologna band described in procession

Music for Prophesy, I: 364ff, Catullus poem 64; **II:** 305, Roger Bacon; **VI:** 114 (Calderón) in seventeenth century Spanish theater

Music for the Hunt, II: 421, in thirteenth century German *Nibelungenlied;* **III:** 159, Chaucer; **III:** 214, already complex signals; **IV:** 89, Leo X; 143, Guarini; **V:** 235, musicians and singer perform while Elizabeth I shoots deer in 1591; 376; 377; **VI:** 115, (Calderón); **VIII:** 372, Restoration poets describe

Music for the Tournament, II: 422, *Erec,* German literature in the twelfth and thirteenth centuries; **III:** 68, Boccaccio; 158, Chaucer; 225ff, described by Christine de Pizan; 301, wedding of Enrique IV; **IV:** 119, Tasso; 211, one in which Henry II was killed; 227, Marguerite de Navarre; **V:** 284, poem by Peele; 313 (Sidney)

Music Guilds, (also see *Confrérie de St. Julien*): **I:** 463, legalized by the emperor Serverus Alexander, 208–235 AD

Music literature, III: 174, Gaffurio: only noble music; 177, liberal arts, 175, Quintilian, and Timagenes, music is the most ancient of the liberal arts; **VI:** 52, Tosi: sing only the best music

Music of the Spheres, I: 73; 83; 163ff; 250, Aristotle; 477; **II:** 105; 128, St. Ambrose; 215, one of the three categories of music by Boethius; 222, Isidore of Seville; 233, Hrotswitha; 249, Aurelian; 437, Grocheo, 1300, says this is nonsense; **III:** 164, Ficino commenting on Plato's *Timaeus;* 165, Gaffurio; 238ff, Tinctoris rejects this idea; 288, Ruiz: Astrology cannot be called 'mere accident'; 315, John Lydgate, fifteenth century; **IV:** 32, reference by Ficino; 50, Zarlino tends to believe in; 196, Tyard; 267, Montaigne; 287, Salinas opposes; 320, Spanish poets; **V:** 72, Agrippa; 104 (Cochlaeus, 1511); 107 (Ornithoparchus, 1517); 117, Glaren (1547) has doubts; 278, poem by Greville; 304 (Nashe); 353 (Shakespeare); **VI:** 79, Basile in his *Muse napolitane* (1635); 85, Kircher discusses this in book 10 of his *Musurgia Universalis* (1650); 109 (Molina); 192 (Mattheson); 260ff, Kepler on; 300, Spinoza rejects the idea, but some important thinkers, such as Newton and Christian Huygens, 1629–1695, were not so sure; **VII:** 38ff (Mersenne); **VIII:** 23 (Peerson); 24ff, Flud and Simpson; 105; 140ff, (Milton); 164ff, references in Marston and Dekker and in 165, fn., 19, additional references

to Webster, Dekker, Chapman, Marston and Beaumont and Fletcher; 312 (Villiers); 320 and 320, fn., 35 (Farquhar); 333, 335 (Dryden); 353ff, (Thomsom and Pope); 400

Music Performance, I: 215, Plato; 351, purpose in early Rome; 352, not appropriate for nobles; 352ff, exceptions Chrysogonos and Gaius Duellius; 353, Sallust reports a rare noble lady singer; 353ff; 393, Dioysius, legendary ancient musician mentioned by Cicero; 500ff, Pliny the Younger on recitals in the home; 501, Tacitus on the financial difficulties of the young artist; **II:** 5, private performances in noble homes; 112ff, Julian on aesthetics of performance; 162, St. Augustine provides wrong answer regarding brain function; 163, St. Augustine on money or art?; **III:** 37, Petrarch observations; 119ff, fourteenth century English philosopher values, state of minstrels; 128 *musica ficta;* 247, Tinctoris: Music is performance; **IV:** 28, Cellini on the life of the musician; 32, Pontus de Tyard describes affect of performance on emotions; 59, on style and performance, views among sixteenth century Italian theorists; on the meaning of the word *Concerto;* on large groups, tuning, "grace" is the most important quality of performance; 68ff sixteenth century Italians, increased tuning problems; 71ff improvisation; 73 Galilei, on instrumental performance, including avoiding repeated notes; 79, women's orchestra of Ferrara, the Nuns of S. Vito; 81, *intermedi* in Florence; **V:** 133, in German speaking countries, winds were predominant until after 1550; 243, concerts by Waits in late sixteenth century England; performance, **VI:** 51ff, on the duty of the player to express the emotions of the music; 52, Geminiani: good taste must be learned, is a gift of nature and cannot be learned by rules; 53, first-hand description of Corelli's playing; 53, to move the emotions of the audience the player must first feel the emotions himself; 53, Frescobaldi: the player must find the emotions in the music; 53ff, Giovanni Bonachelli (1642): even tempi is adjusted according to the emotions of the words; 54, Tossi, on singing from the heart; 173, Heinichen: one must play for the honor and perfection of the performance; **VII:** 129, Raguenet on praise for the emotions in Italian music

Music purpose, I: 427, Horace, to soothe; 438, Propertius, attracting girls; **II:** 221, Cassiodorus: to educate and soothe; **III:** 80ff, Machaut; 117ff, fourteenth century English philosophers; 147ff, Chaucer: to communicate feeling; 172ff, fifteenth century writers; 174, Gaffurio; 218ff; 239ff, Tinctoris; 194ff; 296ff; 315ff, John Lydgate, fifteenth century; **IV:** 30ff, in sixteenth century Italy; 52ff; 113, Tasso; 148ff, in Castiglione; 164ff, Cardano; 226, sixteenth century French poets; 288, Vives and Victoria; 304, Cervantes; 316, Luis de León on restoring the soul; 317 Lope de Vega; 318, Luis de Góngora; 319, Garcilaso de la Vega and Lope de Vega, to express grief; 339ff, in the Spanish sixteenth century theater; **V:** 2, Susato on the purpose of music (1551); 38ff, Erasmus views affect of music on emotions; 75 (Agrippa); 90, views of Luther; 91 famous 1530 letter to Ludwig Senfl; 92 Luther's poem on the ability of music to soothe and comfort; 93 Luther on the ability of music to express feelings; 94 to affect the character of the listener; 131, in a sixteenth century poem by Noel Bucholczer; 218, John Case, in *The Praise of Musicke* (1586), on how specifically music soothes the listener; 218, Bryskett, offers a curious explanation of how a lullaby calms

children; 219 examples where music fails to soothe the listener; 269ff; 302, Greene, woo the ladies; 331ff, views of the Elizabethan playwrights; 355, Shakespeare's discussion; **VI:** 50ff, in Baroque Italy; 85, in seventeenth century Italian lierature; 109ff, in seventeenth century Spanish theater; 161ff, views of German Baroque musicians; 168, Kuhnau to unify feelings after a period of discord; 200ff (Mattheson); 211, the King of Spain anecdote; 223, German views reflecting the war years; 253ff, Leibniz on; **VII:** 128–134, French Baroque philosophers views by Maugars, Rivault (on the affect of wisdom on the face); 129, Raguenet on praise for the emotions in Italian music; 129, Du Bos on views of the emotions which seem correct today; 131, Batteux, brilliant discussion of man's forms of communication; 205, as expressed in seventeenth century French drama; 309ff (Voltaire); **VIII:** 27, views of English Baroque writers, Butler, Avison; 69ff, views of seventeenth English writers: Donne and Hall to soothe (Hall: for those who howl in the night of their afflictions); 70ff, music therapy; 72, Donne, for courtship and aiding memory; 173–179, views among the Jacobean playwrights; 217, Puritan views; 309ff, views of Restoration composers; 333ff, (Dryden); 359–362, Restoration poets; 419, (Shenstone, Chesterfield and Samuel Butler)

Music Therapy, I: 83; 105; 481, Xenophilus, fourth century BC, lived 105 years without aging, attributed to music; 306ff, Anglicus, including madness; **III:** 173; **IV:** 239, Rabelais satire on; 267ff, Montaigne; **V:** 39, discussed in a 1522 letter of Erasmus to Pope Adrian VI; 40, long discussion of; 217 (Peacham, 1576–1643); 275ff; **VI:** 83, in book 9 of his *Musurgia Univrsalis,* Kircher discusses music therapy including here the Tarantula spider story; 211, including an example from eighteenth century America; 211, fn., 90, source for a specific Rondo which can be used as a cure for the tarantula bite; **VIII:** 70ff, including Burton's description of the St. Vitus Dance and Burton on melancholy; 108, (Herbert); 113, a plea for; 114ff, David cures the rage of Saul; 218; 267, (Temple); 288, (Shaftesbury)

Musical form, I: 216, Overture; **II:** 435, Jerome of Moravia, thirteenth century, "repetition is pleasing"

Musical humor, IV: 31, sixteenth century Italy

Musical instruments, III: 276, on the fourteenth century improvement of the shawm; **VI:** 81, the cornett is missing in mid-seventeenth century Rome (Kircher); 82, Kircher's famous cat keyboard; **VIII:** 69, Bunyan equates the cry of the beggar with a 'shrill trumpet'; 123, in praise of instruments used in the church; 198 Tubicines and Tibicines; 335, Dyden's subjective description of instruments; 400, Swift, in Gulliver's Travels, describes a giant spinet; 447ff, Addison equates instruments with personality

Mylius, W. M., German writer in 1686, **VI:** 168

Myron, ancient Greek sculptor, **I:** 373, Cicero

Nagel, Hans, sixteenth century member of the Antwerp civic band, **V:** 3

Nagy, Gregory, writer on Pindar, **I:** 123

Nanino, Giovanni Maria, 1543–1607, **IV:** 65, Giustiniani considered him among the best composers of the sixteenth century; 67

Naples, Italy, I: 5

Napoleon, I: 55

Narcissus, 206 BC, music slave **I:** 356, educational contract

Nardo, Matteo, sixteenth century Italian philosopher, **IV:** 31

Nashe, Thomas, 1567–1601, English writer, **V:** 184, from *The Unfortunate Traveller,* considered by some to be the first English novel; 287, fn., 2, on tying the murder of pope Sixtus V, 1585–1590, to the origin of solfege; 297ff; 301; 321 *Summers Last Will and Testament,* 331, 336; 391

Nature, II: 21, Longinus; 105, musical sounds in Nature; 110; 128, music of Nature; 187, Csssiodorus: "Art conquers Nature"; 320, John of Salisbury, Arts tied to Nature; 359, Art vs Nature; **III:** 30, Petrarch on various arts relative to Nature; 53, Boccaccio; 84, Machaut; 145 vs Art in Chaucer; 170, Alberti: Art is not an imitation of Nature, but of beauty; 266 Nicholas of Cusa: Art and Nature are the same thing; **IV:** 15, Bruno, the credit for Art goes to Nature; 18, Vasari on Nature and Art; 18, Aretino on imperfections in Nature; 50ff, vs Art among sixteenth century Italian theorists; 100, Vida on value for rest; 101 imitation of Nature; 110, Giraldi: Nature produces the poets, but art makes the orators; 127ff, does Art copy Nature or vice versa? In the works of Pordonone one cannot tell which; 185ff, Michelangelo on Nature vs Art; 263, Montaigne, art cannot imitate Nature; **V:** 199, Philip Sidney (1595), all art is related to Nature; 327ff, Art vs Nature in Elizabethan playwrights; 345ff, Shakespeare's famous advice on the importance of learning from Nature, "books in the running brooks, sermons in stone" **VI:** 98, Gracián: Art can improve Nature; 107, Calderón presents both sides of the question whether Art can copy Nature in his *The Devotion of the Cross* (III, i) and in *The Painter of his Dishonor* (II, lines 1137ff); 154ff, on the role of Nature in Art; 246, Leibniz on Art and Nature; **VII:** 25, Rameau: Nature precedes the rules of composition; 106, Pascal on Nature and beauty; 109ff, Art vs Nature, views of seventeenth century French philosophers; 177, Descartes: Art should imitate Nature; 193, Fénelon on Nature vs Tragedy; 194ff, Molière on Nature vs Art; **VIII:** 82ff, (Bacon); 103, on Nature vs Art, Jonson in reference to Shakespeare; 104, Lovelace: Art should not surpass Nature; 134, Milton on Art and Nature; 135; 164, on the relationship of Art and Nature, here Beaumont and Fletcher and Jonson; 212, Browne: Nature is not at variance with Art … Nature is the art of God; 269, Wotton argues that Nature has nothing

to do with prominence: Why are there no eminent poets in Peru?; 287, Shaftesbury finds the laws of music are found in Nature; 323ff, (Dryden); 415. (Shenstone)

Navarro, Spanish playwright, **IV:** 325

Nebuchadnezzar, 1,000 BC, **I:** 65, his ensemble in Old Testament; **VII:** 324

Negligence (*sprezzatura*) or *Nonchalance* or *rubato,* **IV:** 111, Giraldi on writing poetry; 149, 151, Castiglione; 178, Michelangelo; **VI:** 38, Caccini, "noble negligence" and Playford (1647) "graceful neglect"; 43ff

Neidhart von Reuental, fl. 1210–1237, German poet, **II:** 413

Nepos, Cornelius, 100–22 BC, Roman historian, **I:** 352

Neptune, Greek god, **I:** 430, Horace

Nero, 37–68 AD, Roman emperor, singer, **I:** 459ff; 468ff; 474; **V:** 106

Nestor of Nicaca, ancient Greek poet, **II:** 5

Neumes, II: 330, Bernard of Clairvaux explains their purpose

Neuschel, Hans, sixteenth century instrument maker in Nürnberg, **IV:** 75; **V:** 136

Newton, Isaac, 1642–1727, the greatest mind in English history, 1642–1727, **VI:** 233; **VII:** 247; 271; 320; **VIII:** 237

Neyschl, leader of the indoor band of Maximilian I, **III:** 277

Nicholao, Signor, VIII: 421, "stupendous violinist," heard by Evelyn

Nicholas of Cusa, 1401–1464, German cardinal, **III:** 254, does not recognize the senses, everything is Reason; 255, education is learned ignorance; 268, God used the Liberal Arts to create the world

Nicholas V, 1447–1455, pope, **III:** 161, supported humanities

Nichols, John, chronicler of court of Elizabeth I, **V:** 229, fn., 28; 230

Nicocles, King of Cyprus, **I:** 276

Nicolini, VIII: 454, famous opera singer in London in 1710; 462

Niedt, Friedrich, d. 1717, German theorist and piano teacher, **VI:** 158, Just because it is French it doesn't mean it is good; 175ff, as a piano teacher

Nikaure, singing instructor, 2494–2487 BC, ancient Egypt, **I:** 77

North, Francis, brother to Roger North and correspondent with Newton, **VIII:** 240

North, Lord, grandfather to Roger North, **VIII:** 4, description of his household music

North, Roger, 1651–1734, English lawyer and writer on music, **VI:** 36, fn., 23, says the original opera of the Camerata was all melody; **VIII:** 4; 5; 7; 18; 41ff, Major section; 42, on Time and ritornello principle, on universality; 43ff. North classification of music: solitary (made for ones self), social (natural emotions), ecclesiastical, and theatrical; 44 the primary purposes of music are to please and to communicate emotions; 45 on the universality of emotions; 45, found great value in the further study in Italy; 45, North calls the concerto form, which followed Corelli's lead, the bread of life for musicians; 46, Music is the representation of Humanity in all its states; 48, on the Italian tempo terms; 49, North discusses communication of emotions at length; 51, North on singing; 52, on programming; 53, on improvisation; 54, on music education; 56, demeans chant

Northbrooke, John, fl. 1567–1589, English Puritan minister, **V:** 189ff; 209ff; **VI:** 37, on church singing

Norton, Thomas, sixteenth century playwright, **V:** 318

Novatian, 200–258 AD, Church writer, **II:** 48ff, against festivals; 50, against theater; 56ff, coliseum description; 79, on aesthetics of Church music

Nucius, J., Baroque German writer on the Doctrine of the Affections, **VI:** 163, fn., 26

Numa Pompilius, seventh to eighth century BC, Roman king, **I:** 347

Numerian, third century Roman emperor, **II:** 8

Numerology, II: 79, fn 102, on the number seven; 258, Guido, 1026–1028, chooses Seven after days of week for the organization of pitches in notation; 315, Hildegard von Bingen on seven parts of the head; **VIII:** 25, Simpson on the number seven

Nuns of S. Vito in Ferrara, IV: 79ff, women's orchestra

Nürnberg Stadtpfeifers, VI: 135 (in 1643)

Nymphs, mythical musical maidens, **II:** 42

Obrecht, Jacob, 1457–1505, Dutch composer, **V:** 35, the music teacher of Erasmus

Occupational Music, I: 473 (Seneca); **II:** 7ff; 95; **III:** 42, Petrarch on; **III:** 131, fourteenth century English; **IV:** 63, Zarlino says it is music from the angels which relieves labor; 64, woodcut shows three peasants singing three-part polyphony to relieve their labor; 117, shepherds; 148, Castiglione; 191, Michelangelo on the goatherd; 226, Joachim du Bellay; 323, love song by the makers of instruments of war; 344, in Cervantes, a housewife as she sweeps and scrubs; **V:** 47, title of ancient gladiator's song mentioned by Erasmus; 158, comments by Praetorius; 339, three servants sing with lyrics included

Ockeghem, Johannes, 1410–1497, Flemish composer, **III:** 211, already old-fashioned in the fifteenth century; 238, criticized by Tinctoris for breaking the old rules and musicians who are up to date with their reading; 241 recalls Guido's observation that the singer who does not know the rules is an animal; **IV:** 164; 164, fn., 17; **V:** 37, poem in his honor by Erasmus—Music is something divine; 119

Odeum, ancient Athens concert hall, **I:** 145; 278

Odington, Walter, fourteenth century music theorist, **III:** 110ff

Odo of Cluny, 878–942 AD, **II:** 236 (*Enchiridion musices*); 256, introduces letters to represent pitches, purpose is to better train boy singer

Ogier, François, seventeenth century drama critic, **VII:** 183ff

Oglonus, Leo, sixteenth century music teacher to Cardano, **IV:** 159

Oldenburg, Henry, correspondent with Newton in 1675, **VIII:** 239; 241

Oldham, John, 1653–1683, Restoration poet, **VIII:** 356, a poem set to music by "Dr. Blow"

Olympus, a Phrygian aulos player in ancient Greece, **I:** 130

Omeis, Daniel, 1646–1708, a German professor of poetry, **VI:** 224

Opera, VI: 9ff, discussion of early seventeenth century opera in Italy; 15, early comic opera begins in seventeenth century Naples; Metasstasio began his career; the role of the public; 41, on the remarkable emotional singing in the first operas, testimony by Peri, Caccini and Cavalieri; 254ff (Feind); **VII:** 149–159, major discussion; 233, Saint-Évremond is critical; 234ff seventeenth century views of nobles; 271ff, discussion by Voltaire; **VIII:** 22, Christopher Simpson notes that opera is still (1667) something of a stranger in England; 28, Playford on the affect opera has on its listeners; 269; Rymer a harsh critic; 277ff, Gildon discusses opera; : 308, Restoration views against opera; 336, Dryden's discussion of opera; 363–367, Restoration poets views; 401ff, described in Restoration fiction; 422ff, Restoration writers on manners view opera; 425, on French and Italian opera; 453–462 in Restoration England

Organ, II: Water organ, 4ff, description by Tertullian; 90, Julian describes; **V:** 105, Cochlaeus, 1511, says that in ancient times the air supply came from elephant skins; 220, on the

destruction of organs by the Puritans under Henry VIII; **VI:** 20, first-hand account of the playing by Frescobaldi, Girolamo, 1583–1643, seventeenth century Italy's greatest organist; **VII:** 76, Mersenne on tonality and the colors of organ pipes; **VIII:** 138; 149

Organum, **II:** 306, the general name of all instruments of music, according to Bartholomew Anglicus; **VI:** 80, the generic name for instruments (Kircher)

Origen, 184–254 Alexandrian philosopher, **II:** 52ff, opposed to theater; 61ff; 66; 74ff; 77

Ornaments, VI: 64ff, ornaments in the Baroque style; 214ff (Mattheson); **VII:** 31; 105, Fénlon compares ornaments in speech with those in music; **VIII:** 35ff, Butler "too much ornamentation is offensive to the ear," Purcell "let the singer alone," and when one plays written music is is automatically past tense, Burney

Ornithoparchus, Andreas, b. c. 1490, German theorist, author of *Musice Active Mirologus* (1517), **V:** 106ff

Ornstein, Robert, twentieth century writer on the bicameral brain, **I:** 47

Orologgio, Alessandro, d. 1633, Italian composer, **VI:** 126

Orpheus, Greek god, **I:** 420; 431, Ovid; 437; 447; 500; 507; **II:** 40; 106; 186; 200; 243; 307; 361ff; **IV:** 7; **VIII:** 79, for Bacon, a metaphor for education; 122; 144; **VIII:** 217; 267; 272

Ottheinrich, elector at Heidelberg, sixteenth century, **V:** 142

Ottoboni, Pietro, Cardinal, 1667–1740, **VI:** 8, host of an academy; **VII:** 141

Ottonelli, Giovanni, a Jesuit priest in Rome in 1652 opposed to women singers, **VI:** 14

Otway, Thomas, 1652–1685, Restoration playwright, **VIII:** 309, as playwright: *Alcibiades,* 309; *Fall of Caius Marius,* 313, fn., 28; *The Orphan,* 315; *The Soldiers Fortune,* 318; *The Cheats of Scapin,* 319; *Friendship in Fashion,* 319; 408

Overbury, Thomas, 1581–1613, English poet and Puritan philosopher, **VIII:** 211; 213; 214; 216; 217; 219

Overtone series, I: 210, Plato

Ovid, 43 BC – 17 AD, Roman Lyric Poet, **I:** 103; 344, on aulos music; 347; 355, wants *Heroides* performed with music; 423ff; 426ff; 435, fn., 36; 402; 405; **II:** 200; 308; **IV:** 265; **V:** 30; 84; 86; **VIII:** 322

Paculla Annia, Roman priestess, **I:** 360, Livy

Padilla, Pedro de, sixteenth century Spanish poet, **IV:** 314

Padovano, Annibale, 1527–1575, Venetian School composer, **V:** 138

Paget, secretary to court of Henry VIII, **V:** 226, on the king's search for foreign players

Painting, II: 32, Diogenes: an artist should listen to music while he paints, to capture correct character; 33, Philodemus: painting must be filled with divine inspiration; **VIII:** 256, Hume on painting

Palermo civic band, VI: 16, mentioned in a civic document of 1619

Palestrina, Giovanni, 1525–1594, Italian composer, **IV:** 65, Giustiniani considered him among the best composers of the sixteenth century; **V:** 168, mentioned by Agazzari; **VI:** 178

Palladas, fifth century poet, **II:** 102

Pamphili, Benedetto, 1653–1730, grand nephew to Pope Innocent x, **VI:** 6

Pan, Greek god, **I:** 103; 121; 295; 357, origin; 420; 432ff, Virgil, Ovid, Tibullus; 440; **II:** 42, myth of the invention of the echo; 200, sixth to eighth century; **V:** 188, Robert Greene writing in 1587 creates a story about Pan in order to make his point that too much music turns off the listener; 328; **VIII:** 190

Panpipe flute, I: 186; 317, fn., 30; **II:** 8, early Roman construction; 90, played more like an harmonica; 198ff;

Papius, Andreas, 1550–1581, Italian music theorist [on behind the notes], **VI:** 184

Paris (city of), II: 287, thirteenth century university;

Paris, Matthew, 1200–1259, artist and chroniclers; **II:** 272; 276; 280; 290; 296

Parmenides, sixth–fifth century BC, founder of the Eleatic School, **I:** 155

Parrhasius, ancient painter, **I:** 403, Horace

Pascal, Blaise, 1623–1662, French philosopher, **VI:** 6; **VII:** 84, all reason is reduced to sentiment; 86ff, on the bicameral mind; 101ff, negative view on the value of emotions and pleasure; 106ff, on Nature and beauty; 109; 260 (Voltaire); 263ff

Pasquini, Italian Baroque harpsichordist, **VII:** 146

Pasquino Bastini, Vincenzo, second cornet in the Lucca civic band, **IV:** 83

Pathos, I: 483ff

Patrizi, Francesco, 1529–1597, Venetian philosopher, **IV:** 95, on nature of sung poetry

Paul III, 1468–1549, pope, **IV:** 76, his wind bands; traveled with four; 194, travels with four bands

Paulinus, Bishop of Nola, 354–431; **II:** 90ff; 95; 104

Paulus Maximus, I: 435, friend of Ovid

Paulus Silentiarius, d. 150, poet, **II:** 197ff

Peace of Westphalia, 1644, end of the Thirty Years War, **VI:** 121

Peacham, Henry, 1576–1643, English writer on etiquette of Gentlemen, **V:** 134; 188, a gentleman should not be involved in popular music (an ordinary fiddler); it takes time away from important things; 204, 208; 217ff; 223

Peckham, John, 1230–1292, Archbishop of Canterbury, professor at Paris, **II:** 333

Pedoamis, Ascpmois, first century writer, **V:** 45

Pedro III, of Aragon, 1276–1285, **II:** 274

Peele, George, b. 1558, Elizabethan playwright, **V:** 319, *David and Bethsabe,* 331; 333; 338; *The Arraignment of Paris,* 319; 329ff, includes music for a double choir; 335; 336; *Edward I,* 319, fn., 16; 323; 335, fn., 90; as playwright: **V:** 319, *David and Bethsabe,* 331; 333; 338

Peerson, Martin, 1572–1650, English composer, **VIII:** 23

Peire d'Alvernhe, fl. 1150–1180, troubadour, **II:** 371ff; 373; 384; 387; 393

Peire de Monzó, troubadour, **II:** 372

Peire Rogier, troubadour, **II:** 371

Peire Vidal, troubadour, spoke badly of others, tongue cut out by a noble, **II:** 370

Penn, William, 1633–1718, Puritan preacher and after moving to America gave his name to one of the states, **VIII:** 241

Pepin, king, 714–768 AD, **VIII:** 139

Pepusch, Gottfried, VI: 132, leader of the court Hautboisten in Brandenburg; 149 director of the first military band school in Potsdam in 1724–1750

Pepusch, Johann Christoph, VI: 132 brother to Gottfried and composer for Hautboisten

Pepys, Samuel, 1633–1703, English politician, amateur musician and author of a famous diary of the years 1660–1669, **VIII:** 11; 431ff

Perception of Music, VII: 46ff, (Mersenne); 49, Mersenne: music has to do with the expression of emotions, therefore a single line of music must be the most striking; 50, assuming that the center of the emotions is in the words, not the music, great emphasis must be placed on how a song is performed, etc.; 51, but the composer must be inspired also and Nature is also involved, the artist is born, not made by art; 54, the rules of harmony are not like those of geometry, which force the mind of all those who have common sense to adopt them; 54ff, you can only judge music by hearing; 55ff, on the relationship of emotions and humors; 56, on the origin of emotional speech in man and animals; 57–68, major discussion of music, humors and emotions; 126ff, (Batteux); : 180ff, Descartes major discussion; 263, Voltaire discussion on the perception of art; 268; **VIII:** 85ff, Bacon views, including recommending an experimental acoustic studio; 230, Hobbes is the first to fully understand that music is in the mind, not the instrument. His proof: the echo; 239, Newton believed the vibrations of light and sound must be corresponding, but could not prove it; 446, Addison on silence

Percussion, I: 178, "bones", timbrel; 182ff, timbrel; 185, bells; 190, triangle and iambuca; 251; **II:** 6, great drum in Cybele festival; use in ritual; 199, cymbal player, sixth to eighth century; 285, signals under Saladin in third crusade; 356, associations with the jongleur; **III:** 219,

on the tuning of the naquaires (prototype timpani); **IV:** 305, Cervantes: all drummers are jokers; VII, 16, on the military timpani; 77, loud church bells can cause miscarriage; **VIII:** 75, Bunyan: "hideous" drums serve Lord Lucifer; 395, playing timpani for a birth; 427, use of timpani on boats on the Thames during times of fog

Performance Practice, II: 258, Guido on *musica ficta;* 263, John c. 1100 AD, lack of agreed pitch [recommends monochord]; finds correspondence of cadences with business; 266, John, 1100 AD recommends music other than singing; 393, comments by troubadours, **III:** 155ff, characteristics in Chaucer; 177, Gaffurio on vocal practice; **IV:** 132, Aretino, talented women performers are a problem for husbands; 155, Castiglione, older men should not perform in public; 165, Cardano on ethnic music; 167ff, negative comments on singers and instrumentalists; 227, improvisation, don't sing without drinking; 288, Tomás de Sancta Maria (1565), aesthetic rules for keyboard playing; 304ff, Cervantes; **V:** 42ff, views by Erasmus; 139, Maximilian II, 1564–1576, trumpets are distinguished "musical" and "not musical"; 160ff, Praetorius discussion; 161, *musica ficta;* on numbering rests and measures of a movement; seating plan for singers; 162, on common time and alla-breve signs; on using Italian words for tempi; on *rubato;* 163, on changing dynamic markings; on *lento gradu;* fermata on next to last harmony; 164, on shaping cadences; on the requirements of good singing; 165, on *Intonatio* and *exclamatio;* on ornaments; 166, on thorough-bass; 168 on church music; 169 on the Church Concerti for multiple choirs (on the make-up of consorts and twelve instrumentation formats); 179, on tuning and warming-up at home; 276ff, hints in sixteenth century English poetry; 281, a poem by Lyly says the music will not sound well unless the bass line can be heard; 287, fn., 2, according to Thomas Nashe, 1567–1601, pope Sixtus V was poisoned by the King of Spain, whom he had invited to dinner. The following pope sent someone a note reading, *Sol Rex me facit* (the King of Spain made me pope); in Elizabethan England, **V:** 303, Sidney, technique of an 'echo' song; Greene, alternating playing a pipe and singing; Lodge mentions an instrumental performance of a madrigal, after which a guest improvises a new text to the melody just heard; 303ff, Greene on an instrumentalist conveying or not passion; **VI:** 42, in early opera: *recitar cantando;* 54, major discussion of Baroque Period; 81, the cornett is missing in mid-seventeenth century Rome (Kircher); 82, Kircher's famous cat keyboard; 102, Gracián: Nothing should be ended by breaking it off suddenly and completely; 168ff, German Baroque views on dynamics and tempi; 205ff (Mattheson), all instrumental music must be a specific emotion; 212, on singing; **VII,** 17, on French seventeenth century coordination of drum cadences and feet; Saxe on the psychological relationships with the drum cadence; 28ff, examples of strong emotions expressed in performance; 30ff, seventeenth century French views, including Charpentier, Couperin, Saint-Lambert; 68ff, major discussion by Mersenne, including vocal matters; French and Italian singers; improvisation; on matters of instrumental music; 107, intention and performance must be all of the one pattern (La Rouchefoucauld); 107, Boileau on Truth and the sublime in performance; 129, Raguenet on praise for the emotions in Italian

music; 147, Maugars, on improvisation; 148, Bonnet-Bourdelot, on improvisation; **VIII:** 31, on expressing ones self, on vibrato, freedom in time, on the performer's relationship with the composer; 34ff, major discussion by English writers: Gibbons, Playford "Art admitteth no Mediocrity", Simpson, North, Mace on the pyramid principle, Butler "too much ornamentation is offensive to the ear"; 50, North discussion, including the curious recommendation for intentional lack of unison between two violinists; 72, Donne: listeners and players prefer improvised music rather than written music; 90, Bacon: melodic quarter tones are possible; vibrato is like light playing on water; 116ff, specific detail by Jacobean poets; 145, Milton on the importance of modulation; 310, several plays mention idioms of French singing; 451ff, on improvisation and tuning

Pergolesi, Giovanni, 1710–1736, Italian composer, shortest lived of any famous composer, **VII:** 144; 159; **VIII:** 425

Peri, Jacopo, 1561–1637, Italian composer and singer, **IV:** 85; **VI:** 9, *Euridice;* 30; 36; 40, Christoph Bernard's (1649) remarkable list of emotions used in singing, 41, apparent reference to the ancient Greek Rhapsodist

Pericles, 495–429 BC, Athens leader educated in music, **I:** 144; 150; **III:** 36

Persius, 35–62 AD, Roman poet, **I:** 466

Pesanterin, musical instrument mentioned in the Book of Daniel, **I:** 66

Pesarino, seventeenth century composer whose song "A che del Quantomio" was set to poetry, **VIII:** 95

Peter Abelard, 1079–1133, **II:** 311, tries to bring Reason into church thinking

Peter I, King of Cyprus, **III:** 10, honors Landini

Peter the Deacon of Pisa, sixth century, **II:** 180

Petrarch, Francesco, 1304–1374, early humanist poet, **III:** 1ff, begins humanism in literature; 8; 10; 12; 17ff; 45ff; 324; **IV:** 142; **VII:** 323

Petronius, 7–66 AD Roman courtier and writer, **I:** 357; 474

Pezel, Johann, 1639–1694, **VI:** 137, composer of German Baroque wind band music; 139, *Hora decima* and *Fünff-stimmigte blasende Music*

Pfaffe, Carl Friedrich, VI: 136, auditions for Leipzig Stadtpfeifers

Pfefferkorn, Johannes, V: 57, social commentator sixteenth century Germany

Phalereus, Demetrius, fourth BC century writer, **V:** 21

Phalèse, Pierre, sixteenth century publisher, **V:** 3, fn., 11

Pherecrates, fifth century BC playwright on the decay of music culture, **I:** 274

Philemon the Younger, ancient playwright, **IV:** 260

Philetaerus, 343–263 BC, Greek politician and military leader, **I:** 111, special Hell for music lovers; **II:** 83

Philidor, Jacques Danican, d. 1708, member of *Les Grands Hautbois,* including instruments owned, **VII:** 2ff; 18 (1690)

Philip I of Castile, 1478–1506, son of Maximilian I; **III:** 230; **IV:** 291

Philip II of Macedonia, c. 338 BC, father of Aristotle, **I:** 109; 273, defeat of the Greeks

Philip II of Spain, d. 1598, **VI:** 89. 90, Austrian wife sponsored private academy of music

Philip III of Spain, 1598–1621, **VI:** 89; 128

Philip IV of Spain, 1621–1665, **VI:** 90, ordered an Hautboisten ensemble imported abroad

Philip of Hessen, fifteenth century German noble, **IV:** 76

Philip the Bold of Burgundy, 1363–1404, **III:** 227

Philip the Good, 1419–1457, of Burgundy, **III:** 228ff, personal description; 280

Philip v of Spain, 1683–1746, **VI:** 90ff, with his second wife, Maria Luisa of Savoy, French musicians begin to arrive in Spain, including Domenico Scarlatti, teacher of the Princess Maria Bárbara de Braganza and the tenor Farinelli

Philip van Wilder, V: 226, in charge of Henry VIII's wind instruments; 276, anonymous poem on his death

Philip, Archduke, V: 24, 1503 letter to from Erasmus on emotions blocking speech

Philip, Duke of Anjoy, VI: 90

Philip, Duke of Stattin-Pomeria, (1602) records pre-drama concert, **V:** 317

Philippe de Commynes, 1447–1511, French writer; **III:** 214ff, one should openly express profound emotions; 223

Philippe de Vitry, 1291–1361, French composer, author of *Ars Nova,* **III:** 32; 92ff

Philippe, Duke of Orléans, regent for Louis XV; **VII:** 9

Philipps von Hessen, sixteenth century German noble, **V:** 133ff, hunting practice; 147

Philippus, second century Roman poet, **II:** 7

Philodemus of Gadara, first century Epicurean philosopher, **II:** 29ff, anti-Music; 33

Philosophy, II: 139, St. Augustine on pagan philosophy; 220, Cassiodorus on the division of philosophy; 230ff, secular philosophy nearly disappeared in Dark Ages; 311, first modern translations of Greek philosophers begin in c. 1150; 312 effect on monks; 318, John of Salisbury: philosophy is impossible during sex; **VII:** 252ff, Voltaire discusses

Philoxenus, early Greek aulos player, **I:** 292, early Greek composer mentioned by Arcesilaus; 298

Photius, fifth century BC Greek philosopher, before Plato, **I:** 155

Phrynis, ancient Greek lyre player, **I:** 129

Phyrgian, a Greek mode, **I:** 104ff

Pico della Mirandola, Gianfraancesco, 1470–1533, philosopher, **III:** 161, fn., 2; **IV:** 5ff, on mind, senses and soul; 6, role of imagination; 15; 17

Pierre d'Auvergne, 1130–1170, French poet; **III:** 31

Pierre de Prost of Bruges, fifteenth century instrument maker; **III:** 228

Pietro di Bartolomeo, fourteenth century trumpeter in Treviso, **III:** 11

Pictro, Signor, VIII: 421, a singer in the court of Christina of Sweeden heard by Evelyn, who also mentions, in 421, fn., 62, a murder committed by Queen Christina which we have not read elsewhere

Piles, Roger de, 1635–1709, French philosopher, **VII:** 83

Pindar, c. 518 BC, lyric poet, **I:** 123ff; 146ff; 289; 499; **II:** 17, Longinus

Pino, Marco, 1521–1583, artist from Siena, **I:** 5

Pirrotta, Nino, modern scholar, **III:** 163, on fifteenth century "unwritten" music (improvisation)

Pitio, IV: 65, "excellent musician and jongleur" (Giustiniani, 1628)

Plaser, Ulrich, civic musician in Memmingen, **V:** 140

Plato, 429–347 BC, (see also Glaucon), **I:** 78, on Egyptian educational system; 83; 103ff; 108; 130; 141; 153ff; 157; 173; 181; 191–247, major discussion; 495; 512; **II:** 20; 107; 139, St. Augustine; 213; 218ff; **III:** 36; 37; 164, Ficino comments on *Timaeus*; 257; 261; **IV:** 50; 114; 142; 230; 236; 271; **V:** 186; **VI:** 30ff; 34; 37; 280; **VII:** 136ff; **VIII:** 166

Plato, first century AD lyre player, **II:** 40;

Plautus, 254–184 BC, Roman playwright, **I:** 354; 362; 366ff, on single-pipe girls; **IV:** 279; 334

Playford, John, 1623–1687, English writer, **VI:** 38; **VIII:** 5, author of *An Introduction to the Skill of Music* (1674); 25, laments the low state of the arts; 32; 34; 37

Pleasure and Pain, I: 198ff, Plato; 256, Aristotle; 309, Athenaeus; 384, Cicero; **II:** 27, Sextus Empiricus; 146, St. Augustine; 185ff, Boethius; 412, on pleasure and pain, 300ff, Duns Scotus on "many intellections"; 339, Thomas Acquinas; 359; **III:** 23, Petrarch; 50ff, Boccaccio; 77ff, Machaut; 78ff, Froissart; 115, Gower; 142, Chaucer; 167ff, fifteenth century philosophers: Poliziano finds more pain than joy in Love; 168, Boiardo: Love improves a man; 198, Leonardo da Vinci; 216, poem by François Villon; 217, Christine de Pizan: pleasures lead to evil; **IV:** 12, Bruno, Machiavelli, Guicciardini; 126, Machiavelli; 163, Cardano; 180, Michelangelo; 197, sixteenth century France; 220, sixteenth century French poets; 221 du Bellay on the physical nature of pain; 233, sixteenth century prose; 257ff, Montaigne; 283, Vives on; 298, Cervantes; 314, de Padilla, Lope de Vega; **V:** 25, Erasmus on; 205ff, views of Sir Thomas More; 294ff, Greene, Sidney; 326ff, Elizabethan playwrights; 348, Shakespeare, they are connected; **VI:** 243, Leibniz; 237, Böhme finds Nature much at the heart of pleasure and pain; 297, Spinoza; **VII:** 185, (Chapelain, 1637); 255 (Voltaire); 306 (Voltaire); **VIII:** 67, (Hall); 101 (Herbert); 102 (Marvell); 133, (Milton); 227, (Hobbes); 250, (Hume); 260, (Berkeley); 282, (Shaftesbury); 380; 411

Pleasure, I: 188; 215ff, pleasing the audience; 292, anti pleasure in music; **II:** 69ff, Tertullian; 126, fourth and fifth centuries; 146ff, St. Augustine;

Pléiade, sixteenth century group of French poets, **IV:** 195; 199ff

Pliny the Elder, 23–79 AD, Roman writer, **I:** 464; 477ff; 479, details on the aulos and its reeds; 480, on the origin of instruments and their inventors; 488; 493; 498ff

Pliny the Younger, 62–113 AD, Roman lawyer, **I:** 355; 465; 475; 482; 487ff; 499ff; 508ff

Plotinus, 204–270 AD, Greek philosopher, **I:** 303ff

Plutarch, 46–120 AD, historian, **I:** 68, fn 25; 69ff; 104ff; 111ff; 118; 124; 126ff; 129; 135; 144ff; 156; 158ff; 172; 188; 260; 275ff, on the decay of music culture in the fourth century BC; 289; 306ff; 316, acoustic; 318ff, on judging music; 321, effeminate symbol of decay; 324ff; decay in music education; 336; 348; 365; 473; 512; **IV:** 230; 260; 265; 266; 268; 269; **V:** 46; 194

Poellnitz, K. L. von, VI: 25, visitor to Venice in 1729

Poetry, I: 423, Horace complains "everyone is a poet"; 313; **III:** 204ff, Leonardo da Vinci vs painting; 291; 292, Encina, on the difference between a poet and a troubadour; 314, Lydgate, fifteenth century English, on poets; **IV:** 56, on the relationship of words and music 52, Zarlino hopes for the day when aesthetics is the point and not mechanical rules; 92, Bruno: versifiers are not poets; Aretino: too many people are writing poetry; 100, Vida on the rules of; 101ff on language of; 105 definition of by Tasso; 108, Giraldi, on the power the poet has over the emotions of the listener; 110, Giraldi on the definition of Art, not the parts of speech, etc.; 121ff, Ariosto on poets; 129ff, Minturno (1563): imitation is the basis of all poetry; 264, Montaigne on Plato's analogy of the magnet; on the poet's frenzy; on the poetry needed by women; 299, Cervantes on; **V:** 29, Erasmus on; 207ff, sixteenth century English views; 253, on the changing religious scene in sixteenth century England; **VI:** 100ff, on the poor reputation (due to the Church) of seventeenth century Spanish poetry; **VII:** 112–118, views of Baroque French philosophers, including Boileau's *L'Art Poétique* (1674); 115 on poetry's contribution to civilization; 117, on the development of poetry from music; 118, Chaulieu, 1631–1720, believed that poetry in aiming at eloquence lost the art of singing; 118, Gresset found music superior to poetry for intimate communication; 297, Voltaire on Drama as Poetry; 301, Voltaire on a short history of rhyme; **VIII:** 83, (Bacon); 93–127, Jacobean poetry major section; 94ff, some poetry was still being sung; 97, poetry for prophesy and to stir the emotions; 97ff, examples of poetry describing various aspects of our twin brain hemispheres; 106, Odes in honor of aristocrats; 116, on performance practice; 119ff art music; 211, Browne: poetry is music in words; music is poetry in sound; 212ff several Puritan examples of their dim view of poets … they will not even be welcome in Hell; 228, discussion by Hobbes; 265, fine discussion by Temple, including its purposes; 271 Wotton finds epic poetry too complete, "Men should rise from the table with some appetite remaining …"; 286, Shaftesbury on an interesting discussion on the development of poetry in England; 301, Harris on the problems of combining music and poetry; 303, Lee, Nathaniel, 1648–1692, Restoration playwright, comments on the low quality of both theater and poetry; 324ff, 329; Dryden on poetry; 382, Restoration philosophers discuss

Poetry, Sung, I: 423, Horace; 499; **II:** 90, fourth and fifth centuries in low regard; 136, St. Augustine; 313, John of Salisbury on poetry being language or music; 295ff, Italian examples from the twelfth and thirteenth centuries; 409, German literature in the twelfth and thirteenth centuries; **III:** 12, proof Petrarch sang his poetry; 39ff, Petrarch on troubadours as art song; 126 fourteenth century English philosophers; 172, Calmeta believed music had to give up some individuality due to text; 178, Gaffurio: music must emotionally support the words; 187; 219, in fifteenth century France; **IV:** 32, Ficiino: emphasis must be on the words; 95, Patrizi: is the communication one of music or language?; 96, Vida; 173, Cardano on music with words; 200, on the *Pléide* in sixteenth century Paris; 213, Calvin found the music more dangerous than the words; 286, Vives classifies all poetry under heading of music; 312, Luis de León on singing to an audience

which pays no attention; **V:** 215, Thomas Morley, *A Plain and Easy Introduction to Practical Music* (1597), music must please the ears as well as being capable of being defended by reason; music must match the emotions of the words; 261, the poetry of Thomas Wyatt, 1503–1542 was intended to be sung; 348, a passage in Shakespeare's *Two Gentlemen of Verona* (I, ii, 83ff) suggests some poetry was still sung during the Elizabethan Period; 348ff, Shakespeare's discussion; 108, Calderón gives the purpose of poetry to please everyone; **VII:** 118, Chaulieu, 1631–1720, believed that poetry in aiming at eloquence lost the art of singing; 279, Voltaire says this tradition developed into the larger choral forms; **VIII:** 29, Simpson: advice to composers on making music reflect words; 94ff; 415, (Shensteone)

Polidori, Ortensio, seventeenth century Italian composer, **VI:** 17

Poliziano, Angelo, 1454–1494, epic poet, **III:** 162ff, good humanist perspective of Italian society; 167ff, pleasure and pain; 172; 183ff; 185; 187; 189

Pollux, second century Greek writer, **I:** 472

Polo, Gil, d. 1591, Spanish writer of pastoral romances; **IV:** 293ff

Polybius, c. 200 to c. 118 BC historian, **I:** 289; 354; 473, military signals; **VII:** 137

Polyclitus, ancient Greek sculptor, **I:** 373, Cicero

Polyhymnia, one of the ancient Greek Muses, **I:** 210

Pomponius Secundus, first century AD poet, **I:** 491

Pons de Capdueill, 1196–1236, troubadour, **II:** 385

Ponte, Petrus Caecus de, sixteenth century Dutch humanist who settled in Paris, **V:** 1

Pope, Alexander, 1688–1744, Restoration poet, self-educated, as being a Catholic, he was not allowed to attend the English universities, **II:** 11; **VIII:** 348; 352; 353; 357ff; 360; 362; 367; 368, proposes Raphael as the conductor of the heavenly choir; 369 (O Death! where is thy Sting?); 370; 371; 372; 373; 392; 404; 412 ; 415; 422; 423

Popular music, I: 270, Aristotle, instruments; **V:** 247, titles of popular songs in sixteenth century London; **VI:** 142, an account of peasant music by Mattheson; **VIII:** 161, fn., 17, actual titles given; 374, includes some titles of actual popular songs of the Restoration; 379; 380; 382; 384

Pordage, VIII: 422, a Roman singer heard by Evelyn in 1685

Pordonone, IV: 128, sixteenth century playwright mentioned by Aretino

Porphyry, c. 233–305 AD, Pythagorean School, **I:** 158ff; 303

Porpora, VIII: 26, fn., 16, Judged by Avison as a composer of modest ability

Porrus, king who fought Alexander the Great; **III:** 9

Potot, Pierre, seventeenth century French oboist in Germany, **VI:** 131

Pouplinière, Alexandre-Jean-Joseph Le Riche de la, 1693–1762, wealthy financier and supporter of private concerts n Paris, **VII:** 11

Praetorius (born Schultheiss), Michael, 1571–1621, author of *Syntagma Musicum* (1619), **II:** 438; **III:** 273 *Syntagma Musicum* (1619); **IV:** 71; 208; **V:** 77; 104; 139, trumpet choir

sonadas; 153, major discussion; 154, Kapellmeister for the Duke of Brunswick and later in Wolfenbüttel; **VI:** 17; 121; 145, conducts at Naumburg; 163, fn., 36

Pratinas of Phlius, Greek aulos player in 500 BC, **I:** 130; 321, on music becoming entertainment

Précieuses, a salon in Paris which Molière attended, **VII:** 196

Prelude, I: 216; **VI:** 54, Monteverdi, a sinfonia is needed to prepare the minds of the audience

Prévost, Abbé Pierre, 1697–1763, French writer, **VII:** 214

Price, Gervase, leader of the royal trumpets under James II, **VIII:** 444

Printz, J. C., Baroque German writer on the Doctrine of the Affections, **VI:** 163, fn., 36

Prior, Matthew, 1664–1721, Restoration poet and philosopher, **VIII:** 360; 372; 378; 379

Procopus, 500–565, Byzantine historian, **II:** 193ff

Pronomus of Thebes, c. 440 BC professional aulos player, **I:** 274, teacher of Alcibiades

Propertius, 50–16 BC, Roman Lyric Poet, **I:** 419; 423; 437ff; 439, Cynthia; 448ff; 455

Prosdocimus de Beldemandis, fifteenth century Italian theorist; **III:** 172

Prose, IV: 265, Montaigne, the purpose of prose is delight; on the historian; 299, Cervantes on; **V:** 31, Erasmus on; 32, the importance of an elevated style

Prosodia, a professional song form in ancient Greece, **I:** 130

Protagoras, 490–420 BC Greek Philosopher before Plato, **I:** 196; 271; **II:** 22

Protogenes, ancient painter, **IV:** 150

Psammetichus I, leader of Egypt, I; 103

Psellus, Michael, 1017–1078, Byzantine monk and philosopher, **II:** 231; 237, on contemporary choral composition

Pseudo-Dionysius Areopagite, fifth-sixth century, Church philosopher, **II:** 183ff; 186; 209ff

Ptolemaeus Philadelphus, 283–246 BC, **I:** 352

Ptolemy Auletes, 81–52 BC Egyptian ruler, **I:** 76

Ptolemy, 285–246 BC Egyptian ruler, **I:** 81; 273; **II:** 213; 336; **III:** 90; **VI:** 261

Ptolemy, 85–165 AD, astronomer, **VII:** 56; **VIII:** 271 (here "Ptolemee")

Public and Music (see also Listener and Audience), **I:** 238ff, audiences; 263, Aristotle; 389ff, Cicero on the audience; 410ff, Horace; 424, Horace; **IV:** 23ff, sixteenth century Italy opposed to public, who know nothing; : 62ff, views among sixteenth century Italian theorists; 190, Michelangelo distrusts; 266, Montaigne—leave them aside; 274, Vives believed education and recreation should be above the common crowd; 337, Lope de Vega against the public; **V:** 33, condemns the public; 88, Luther on the relationship of size of public and quality of the event; 301, Nashe finds the public undiscerning with respect to music; **VI:** 98, Gracián: men should have nothing to do with the taste of the broad public; **VIII:** 209, Brown: the multitude; that numerous piece of monstrosity

Pucci, Antonio, fourteenth century singer; **III:** 12

Puligo, Domenico, 1492–1527, Italian painter, **IV:** 18

Purcell, Daniel, Restoration composer, **VIII:** 309, named on the cover of a Masque text by Congreve; 314, fn., 29; 355

Purcell, Henry, 1659–1695, English composer, **I:** 15; **VIII:** 8; 11; 35; 314, rn. 30, composed original songs for Lee's, *Theodosius;* 336, 337, 340; 386

Puritan Movement in seventeenth century England, **VIII:** 4; 155, attempts to close theaters

Puttenham, George, sixteenth century literary critic, **V:** 208

Pyramus and Thisbe, **II:** 137

Pyrrhiche, an ancient Greek dance, **I:** 108

Pyrrho, 360–270 BC, of Alexandria Septic School, **I:** 283ff

Pythagoras, 570–490 BC, Greek philosopher, **I:** 73; 76; 83; 153, Archytas; 158ff, Porphyry and the Pythagorean School; 160, Iamblichus; 161, Euryphamus and Diotogenes; 165, Archytas; 191; 250ff; 299; 304; 307; 317; 322; 334; 477; 495; **II:** 36, on music and character; 60; 114; 125, on the location of senses; 213; 220, Cassiodorus; 248; 336; 437; **III:** 257; 267; **IV:** 154; 236; **V:** 17, Erasmus: who gives a fig?; 40ff (Erasmus); 193; 197; 324; **VI:** 76; 261; **VII:** 39 (Mersenne); **VIII:** 96; 141; 217; 219; 459

Pythodlides, According to Aristotle, Pythodlides was a music teacher to Pericles, of the fifth century BC, **I:** 145

Quadrivium and **Trivium,** **II:** 109, fifth century; 313, John of Salisbury: *Trivium* discloses the significance of all words, while the *Quadrivium* unveils the secrets of all nature

Quagliati, Paolo, 1555–1628, Italian canzona composer, **VI:** 21

Quantomio of Pesarino, seventeenth century composer in London, **VIII:** 95

Quevedo, Francisco de, 1580–1645, Spanish poet, **VI:** 93; 100ff

Quickelberg, Samuel, sixteenth century German humanist, physician, **V:** 74

Quinault, Mdlle, French actress, **VII:** 290

Quinault, Philippe, 1635–1688, French poet, **VII:** 267; 270; 271; 272; 273; 274; 308; 313

Quintilian, 35–100 BC, Roman rhetorician, **I:** 365; 467; 477ff, music of the spheres; 483ff, on communicating the emotions; 489; 495ff, on music education; 499; **III:** 175; **VI:** 187

Quintus Fabius, 280–203 BC, Roman general and politician, **I:** 349

Quirini, Cardinal, seventeenth century bishop of Bescia, **VII:** 283

Rabanus Maurus, ninth century, **II:** 233

Rabelais, François, 1494–1553, **IV:** 229ff, on the decline of life in general; 233 on color and emotions; 239ff; 265; **VII:** 268

Racine (born La Ferté-Milon), Jean, 1639–1699, French playwright, **VII:** 183; *Andromache,* 194; *Berence,* 198; *The Theban Brothers,* 198; *Phaedra,* 198; *Athaliah,* 207; 231; 238, his murder of his mistress, Thérèse du Parc; 89; 130; 248; 270; 273; 283; 298

Raguenet, François, 1661–1722, French writer, **VII:** 123ff; 139; 141; 144; 153, on opera

Rahere, d. 1144, jongleur in employ of Henry I of England, **II:** 274

Raimbaut d'Orange, 1150–1173, jongleur, **II:** 374ff; 376; 390; 393

Ralegh, Sir Walter, 1552–1618, English poet, close to Elizabeth I, **V:** 268; 275, on the death of Prince Henry in 1612

Rameau, Jean-Philippe, 1683–1764, French composer, **VI:** 159; **VII:** 9; 11; 20ff, questions on genetic music information; 23 on Taste; 25 on communicating feeling in the notation; 28, expression of emotions by Rameau's nephew; 29, don't listen to the rules, be swept away; 29, harmony; 267; 273ff; 281; 313ff; **VIII:** 26, fn., 16, judged by Avison as a composer of the highest regard, being "graceful and spirited"

Ramos de Pareja, fifteenth century professor at Salamanca, author of Musica practica, (1482); **III:** 299

Raphael, sixteenth century artist, **IV:** 18ff, Vasari on Raphael's art vs Nature; 91; 184, critical comment by Michelangelo; 188; **VI:** 245; **VII:** 320; **VIII:** 368

Raphel (Sanzio Reffaello), 1483–1520, Spanish playwright, **IV:** 18

Ratgeb, Jörg, sixteenth century painter, **V:** 68

Rauerij, seventeenth century Venetian publisher, **VI:** 21

Reason, II: 142, St. Augustine; 149; 125, on the location of senses; 157, St. Augustine; 183ff, Boethius, the only happiness; 249, Aurelian: music unites Reason and body; 313ff, major discussion by twelfth and thirteenth century philosophers; 357, Reason vs Love, in *Romance of the Rose;* **III:** 47; 73; 106ff; 199ff, vs emotions in Chaucer; 164, fifteenth century Alberti says Reason must rule; 193, Leonardo da Vinci, is confirmed only by the senses; 304ff, John Lydgate, *Reson and Sensuallyte,* fifteenth century England; **IV:** 124, Guarini says Reason must obey the senses; 179, Michelangelo: Reason is interrupted by Love; 244ff, Montaigne; **VI**; 94ff, Gracián and the Church emphasis on Reason; **VII:** 247, Voltaire on how poorly Reason had been valued; **VIII:** 60ff, Reason vs emotions, Bunyan, Donne; 61, Burton, Harrington; 77, Bacon classified the mind as consisting of Memory, taught through history, Imagination, taught through poetry, and Reason, taught through philosophy; 78, the emotions are a threat to Reason; 162, Chapman: Fortune, not Reason, rules the state of things; 163, Jonson: Art must be based on Reason; 209, Brown: As reason

is a rebel to faith, so passion is to reason; 248, interesting thoughts by Hume; 276, music has nothing to do with Reason; 378, Wycherley on Reason and emotions

Reese, Sam, twentieth century writer on the bicameral brain, **I:** 47

Reggio, Pietro, VIII: 422, singer heard by Evelyn in 1684

Regius, Henricus, 1598–1679, professor of medicine in Utrecht, **VII:** 165; 169

Reiche, Gottfried, 1667–1734, German composer, **VI:** 139ff, member of Leipzig Stadtpfeifers and composer for them; his dedication for his *Neue Quatricinia;* and his death in 1734

Reinmar, c. 1150–1210, **II:** 411, German Minnesinger

Religious Music (see Divine and Church Music)

Rencia, Anna, seventeenth century soprano in Venice, **VI:** 11; **VIII:** 425

René of Anjou, III: 225, late fifteenth century banquet

Repertoire, I: 226ff, good and bad; 230ff, influence on character; 235, choral;

Reuchlin, Johannes, V: 57, social commentator sixteenth century Germany

Rewer, singing instructor, 2563–2423, ancient Egypt, **I:** 77

Rhapsodist, I: 113ff; 118; 193, Plato on Ion; 212ff; 323, Strabo describes performer, Anaxenor; 499, fn., 2, performance style still evident in Roman Imperial Period; **II:** 113, description of style by Julian; 313, Julius Caesar anecdote a hint of old rhapsodist technique?; **VI:** 41ff

Rhau, Georg, V: 88, published religious music with preface by Luther in 1538; 93

Richard I of England, 1157–1199, **II:** 275, noble singing society; 277; 287ff; 388, as composer

Richard II of England, 1377–1399; **III:** 128; 130ff

Richard III of England, 1483–1485, **III:** 320

Richardson, Mr., composer of a song in Farquhar's *The Inconstant;* **VIII:** 314, fn., 29

Richardson, Samuel, 1689–1761, Restoration novelist, **VIII:** 391; 392; 393, 394; 395; 397; 398; 402

Richelieu, Cardinal in France, 1585–1642, minister under Louis XIII, **VI:** 17; **VII:** 1, French minister; 138; 183; 187ff; 284

Riemenschneider, Tilmann, sixteenth century German wood carver, **V:** 68

Right-hand Prejudice, II: 124, fourth century; 142, St. Augustine on Jesus; 316, John of Salisbury; **III:** 113, Richard Rolle; **IV:** 93, Tasso; : 232, Bodin; 295ff, Cervantes in *Don Quijote;* **V:** 16, Erasmus; 344 (Shakespeare); **VI:** 222 (Grimmelshausen); **VII:** 249 (Voltaire); 295 (Voltaire); **VIII:** 62, (Donne), (Bunyan); 99ff, references by Jacobean poets; 131, (Milton); 163, Dekker, two references from his plays; 210, discussion by Sir Thomas Brown, physician

Rinuccini, librettist for Peri's *Euridice,* **VI:** 9

Rivault, David de Flurance, chief tutor to Louis XIII; **VII:** 11; 128, on the affect of music on man

Robert de la Magdelaine, singer under Philip the Good; **III:** 228

Robinson, James, III: 3, fn., 3, in praise of Petrarch

Rogier, Peire, toubadour, **II:** 371

Rohan-Chabot, Chevalier, 1683–1760, French noble, **VII:** 279

Roïtz, Gonzalgo, troubadour, **II:** 371

Rojas, Fernando de, 1479–1541, Spanish playwright; **III:** 288, **IV:** 332; 337

Roland, nephew to Charlemagne, **II:** 237; 357; 366ff, *The Song of Roland*

Rolle, Richard, fourteenth century English poet; **III:** 110; 113ff, on the soul; 117ff; 124; 126

Rollin, Charles, late Baroque writer on gesture, **VI:** 189

Romagnesi, Jean-Antoine, 1690–1742, French playwright, **VII:** 270

Roman emperors and senators as musicians, I: 459, Calius Calpurnius Piso; Caligula, 12–41 AD; Nero, 37–68 AD; 462, Titus, 79–81 AD; Domitian, 81–96 AD; Trajan, 52–117 AD; Hadrian, 76–138 AD; Marcus Aurelius, 121–180 AD; Caracalla, 188–217 AD; Elagabalus, 205–222 AD; Severus Alexander, 208–235 AD; Maximian, 286–305; Theodoric, 489–526 AD;

Roncesvalles, a Spanish village famous at the time of Charlemagne, **II:** 237

Ronsard, Pierre de, 1524–1585, leading poet and humanist of sixteenth century France, **IV:** 200ff; 201 cites leading composers: Josquin des Prez, Willaert, Jannequin, Arcadelt, Orlando Lassus; 219; 221; 223ff; 226; **VI:** 33, on words vs emotions

Rore, Cipriano de, 1516–1565, Franco-Flemish composer, **IV:** 65, Giustiniani considered among the best composers of the sixteenth century; **VI:** 126

Roscius, Sextis, 126–62 BC, famous Roman actor, **I:** 388, chief thing is good taste, which cannot be taught; **II:** 152

Rossi, Bastiano, sixteenth century court official, **IV:** 82

Rossi, Luigi, seventeenth century composer in Rome, **VI:** 18, his theater work, *Il palazzo incantato* lasted eight hours in performance; 71

Rossini, Gioacchino, 1792–1868, Italian composer, **I:** 25

Roszal, Theodore, twentieth century writer, **I:** 47

Rousseau, Jacques, [not Jean-Jacques Rousseau], seventeenth century violist, **VII:** 22, on Taste; 26, on Movement vs Time

Rousseau, Jean-Baptiste, 1671–1741, **VII:** 117, as poet he wrote libretti for operas; 308

Rousseau, Jean-Jacques, 1712–1778, French philosopher, professional music copyist and composer, **VI:** 23, in his *Confessions,* records his hearing the young women of the *Mendicanti* sing in Venice two years after the death of Vivaldi; **VII:** 3

Rowley, William, sixteenth century playwright, **V:** 317

Rubeanus, Crotus, German teacher and publisher, sixteenth century, **V:** 58; 114, co-author of satirical *Letters of Obscure Men* (1515)

Rubini, Nicolo, seventeenth century chaplain in Rome, **VI:** 17, also a famous cornett player, known as "Il Cavaliere del Cornetto," but was murdered.

Rudolf II, sixteenth century, **V:** 150

Rufinus, V: 46, a leading ancient lyre player, according to Erasmus

Rufus, Conradus, V: 30, 1518 letter from Erasmus recommends the young poet, Eobanus

Ruiz, Juan, Spanish poet, fourteenth century, **III:** 287ff, wrote *The Book of True Love*

Ruspoli, Prince of Rome, supporter of Handel, **VI:** 8, host of an academy

Sacadas, ancient Greek composer of choral odes, **I:** 129, Plutarch

Sacchetti, Franco, c. 1335–1400, **III:** 7ff, emotions and senses block the intellectual side of man; 7, pain is relative; 10; 12; 14

Sackville, Charles, 1638–1706, Earl of Dorsset, **VIII:** 363

Sackville, Thomas and **Thomas Norton,** authors of the earliest Elizabethan play, *Gorboduc* of 1570, **V:** 318

Saint-Evremond, Charles, de, 1613–1703, French noble, diarist, **VI:** 255; **VII:** 89, bicameral mind; 151, on opera; 190; 227; 228; 229; 230; 231, on Corneille vs Racine in how they treat the emotions in their works; 232; 233ff; 237; 238

Saint-Lambert, Michel de, French theorist, **VII:** 22, on Taste; 33, on music education; 90, genetic musical information

Saint-Simon (Louis de Rouvroy), Duke of, 1675–1755, **VII:** 229; 235; 236; 238; 240

Saladin, twelfth century, **II:** 282, third crusade; 285

Salazar, Anonio de, 1650–1715, Spanish composer in Mexico, **VI:** 92

Salinas, Francisco, 1513–1590, blind theorist and organist at Salamanca, **IV:** 287, on aesthetics of music, music of the spheres; 316

Sallaert, Anthonis, seventeenth century Dutch painter, **VI:** 279

Sallust, 86–34 BC Roman historian, **I:** 353, account of noble lady singer, Sempronia; 369; 382

Salpinx (Greek trumpet), **I:** 343

Salutati, Coluccio, 1331–1406, Church humanist, **III:** 6, Virgil should be read allegorically of the mysteries of Church faith

Salvian, fifth century Church writer, **II:** 116ff; 120ff

Sambyke, musical instrument mentioned in the Book of Daniel, **I:** 66

Sanctis, Francesco de, nineteenth century writer; **III:** 2ff, in defense of Boccaccio

Sandoval y Rojas, 1552–1625, Duke of Lerma, Spain, **VI:** 89

Sannazaro, Jacopo, 1456–1530, Italian poet, **IV:** 114ff; 118

Sappho, c. 640–550 BC, lyric poet, **I:** 124ff; 294; 298; 423ff; 466; **IV:** 223; **V:** 207; **VI:** 202; **VIII:** 121

Sardanapalus, heathen king, **III:** 264

Sargon I, Semitic king of Mesopotamia, **I:** 62

Saturn, Greek god, **I:** 416; 457

Saul, Hebrew leader of the Old Testament, **I:** 91; 96; **VIII:** 34

Savonarola, Girolamo, 1452–1498, Florentine friar, politician; **III:** 162; 183; **IV:** 88

Saxe, Maurice de, 1696–1750, French general, **VII,** 17

Saxo the Grammarian, Danish historian, **V:** 71

Scacchi, Marco, seventeenth century Italian music critic, **VI:** 82

Scaliger, Julius, 1484–1558, IV:129, in his *Poetics* (1561) adds to Aristotle's purpose of Tragedy, that it must also be educational; **VI:** 238

Scandello, Antonio, 1517–1580, German composer, **V:** 142

Scarlatti, Alessandro, 1660–1725, Italian composer, **VI:** 7; 49, on working in Rome; 51, as a composer has tried to express the emotions, the most important consideration; **VII:** 144; 159; **VIII:** 26, fn, 16, Judged by Avison as a composer of the highest regard, being "bold and inventive"

Scarlatti, Domenico, 1685–1757, Italian composer, **VI:** 7; 49; 91

Scheibe, Johann, b. 1708, German Baroque writer, **VI:** 157; 159; 172; 174

Scheidt, Samuel, 1587–1654, German composer, **VI:** 173; 178, still liked the old polyphonic style

Schein, Johann, 1586–1630, music director at St. Thomas in Leipzig, **VI:** 135

Schélandre, Jean de, French playwright, **VII:** 183, *Tyr et Sidon* (1628)

Scherffenstein, Wenzel Scherffer von, 1603–1674, court organist for the dukes of Brieg, **VI:** 226ff

Schmelzer, VI: 129, German composer wrote for the Austrian horse ballet of 1667

Scholasticus, Leontius, first century poet, **II:** 40

Scholes, Percy, 1877–1958, English journalist, **I:** 25

Schöner, John, 1477–1547, **V:** 57, on the environment for the arts in sixteenth century Germany; 133

Schubert, Franz, 1797–1828, Austrian composer, **I:** 43

Schumann, Christoph, 1726 Stadtpfeifer contract, **VI:** 137

Schumann, Robert, 1810–1856, German composer, **I:** 27; 50

Schütz, Heinrich, 1585–1672, German composer, **IV:** 87, on Gabrieli; **V:** 177; **VI:** 71; 122ff, on the economic ramifications of the Thirty Years' War; 124; 125; 127; 129; 145; 169; 222; 225

Schuurman, Maria, 1607–1678, Dutch linguist, philosopher, **VI:** 277; **VII:** 164

Scopas, ancient sculptor mentioned by Horace, **I:** 403

Scribes, II: 178, comments on manuscripts

Scuola di San Rocco, IV: 87, school performance in Venice, sixteenth century

Sebastiano, sixteenth century painter, **IV:** 20

Sebillet, Thomas, 1512–1589, author of *Art Poétique* (1548); **IV:** 224

Sedley, Sir Charles, 1639–1701, Restoration playwright, **VIII:** 304, finds more enthusiasm for sermons than for plays; as playwright: *Bellamira,* 304; *The Mulberry Garden,* 314; *Antony and Cleopatra,* 317; as poet, 359; as philosopher, 385

Segni, Agnolo, sixteenth century Italian, **IV:** 17, language, music and dance are all imitations of each other

Segrais, J.R. de, 1624–1701, French poet, **VII:** 117, on music's special status in the liberal arts

Sempronia, early noble Roman lady singer **I:** 353

Sendrey, Alfred, writer on Antiquity, **I:** 61; 63; 73f; 85ff

Seneca the Elder, first century AD, Roman writer, **I:** 470

Seneca the Younger, 3 BC – 65 AD, Roman writer, **I:** 471; 500, on Orpheus and Apollo; 508; **II:** 302; **III:** 25; 43; **IV:** 269; 265

Senesino (Francesco Bernardi), 1680–1750, **VI:** 15; **VIII:** 458, a famous castrato

Senfl, Ludwig, 1486–1543, German composer in Munich, **V:** 91; 138

Senses, I: 196ff; 285; 303ff; 371ff, major Cicero and Lucretius discussion; **II:** 65, Tertullian; 66, Clement of Alexandria: knowledge comes from the senses; 67ff, Lactantius, on relationship of senses, mind and soul; 71, senses lead to sin; 103, Ausonius: what the eye sees is retained longer than what the ear hears; 125ff, including St. Ambrose on the location of; 142ff, St. Augustine; 183ff, Pseudo-Dionysius Areopagite; 297, Grosseteste: there is genetic Reason which did not come from the senses; 297ff, Roger Bacon on the sense; 316ff, major discussion by twelfth and thirteenth century philosophers, Ramón Lull, Hildegard von Bingen; 318 Jacopone da Todi; 338, Thomas Aquinas; **III:** 48, Boccaccio; 106ff; 194, Leonardo da Vinci, 207ff; 254, 258ff, Nicholas of Cusa, 1401–1464, German cardinal does not recognize the senses; 258ff; **IV:** 9, Church's distrust in; 93, Tasso: it is wrong to trust the senses—even Aristotle made this mistake; 124, Guarini says Reason must obey the senses; 162, Cardano, hearing is superior to sight; 147, Montaigne; 248, do we have more senses than we are aware of?; 280ff, St. John of the Cross, sixteenth century *ars antiqua* Church philosopher; 281, man must remain empty of all sensory satisfaction which is not for the glory of God; diminishes self-appreciation; **V:** 190, Northbrooke (1577) attracts both senses and Reason; 200, Bryskett, sixteenth century, the senses are responsible for all evil things; **VI:** 71, Marino (1623) writes the ear is the only door to the soul; 95. Gracián on the senses, including why we don't have earlids; 239ff Leibniz; **VII:** 41ff, Mersenne on the correspondence between taste and color with music; 91–96, Malbranche centers everything in the soul, much nonsense; 166ff, (Descartes); 250ff, Voltaire discussion; **VIII:** 62, Harvey sees the validity of the senses; 63, Hall on sight and hearing; 79, for Bacon the greatest pleasure was that associated with the left hemisphere, surpassing any pleasures of the senses; 81 on the value of the individual senses; 163, Beaumont and Fletcher, in *The Little Thief*, consider hearing more important the seeing; 224, 226 Hobbes: all thoughts have their origin in the senses, [but] the senses are located in the heart; 246: Hume on sensation and reflection; 290ff, Hutcheson in an important discussion, classifies and connects the senses with emotions

Serenades, III: 278, satire by Sebastian Brant, 1494; **IV:** 34ff, sixteenth century Italy; **VI:** 209, unusual discussion by Mattheson; **VII:** 222ff; **VIII:** 193ff, descriptions from Jacobean plays; 316; 399, (Congreve); 452ff, Addison with humorous examples

Servius Tullius, sixth century BC, king of Rome **I:** 345

Severinus, Bishop of Cologne, fourth century, **II:** 211

Severus, Alexander, 208–235 AD, Roman emperor, **I:** 459; 463; **II:** 3, played aulos, organ and lyre

Sévigné, Françoise-Margarie, 1646–1705, seventeenth century aristocratic lady in Paris, **VII:** 232; 233; 234; 236; 238; 240; 241

Sévigné, Marie, marquise de, 1626–1696, French author, **VIII:** 6

Sextus Empiricus, second century philosopher, **II:** 21ff; 23ff,

Sforza, Bianca Maria, 1472–1510, **III:** 184

Sforza, Francesco, 1401–1466, of Milan; **III:** 184

Sforza, Ludovico, 1481–1499 of Milan; **III:** 174; 180

Sforza, Giangaleazzo, 1469–1494 of Milan; **III:** 180

Shaftesbury (see Cooper, Anthony)

Shakespeare, William, 1564–1616, **IV:** 160; 210; **V:** 341, as playwright: *Othello,* 355; 378; (**VIII:** 268); *Cymbeline,* 341; 361; *A Midsummer Night's Dream,* 341; 344; 364; 366; *Timon of Athens,* 342; 349; 352; 366, fn., 86; 370; 372; 375; 379; *Twelfth Night,* 342; 343; 349; 359; 361; *Troilus and Cressida,* 342; 344; 367, fn., 92; 370, fn., 109; 371; 372, fn., 119; 373; 381; *As You Like It,* 342; 346; 349; 357; 380; 383; *The Winter's Tale,* 343; 352; 384ff; (**VIII:** 328); *Hamlet,* 343; 347; 350; 351; 369; 382; *The Two Gentlemen of Verona,* 343; 347; 348; 360; *Richard II,* 343; 345; 357; 358; 363; 366, fn., 86; 367, fn., 92; 369; 373; 374, fn., 133; *Richard III;* 366, fn., 86; 367, fn., 92; 369; 370, fn., 105; 371, fn., 110; 374; 374, fn., 133; *King Henry IV, Part I;* 366, fn., 86, 372; 373, fn., 123; 374; 374, fn., 130; 375; 381; *King Henry IV, Part II;* 366, fn., 86; 383; *King Henry VI, Part I;* 366, fn., 86; 367, fn., 92; 368; 372; 372, fn., 119; *King Henry VI, Part II;* 366, fn., 86; 367; 367, fn., 92; 370; 371; 374; *King Henry VI: Part III,* 344; 367; 367, fn., 92; 368; 370; 371, fn., 113; 372; 373, fn., 123; 374, fn., 131; *Romeo and Juliet,* 344; 347; 354; 356; *All's Well That Ends Well,* 346; 361; 366; 367, fn., 92; 368; 375; 382; *Macbeth,* 346; 351; 357; 367, fn., 92; 370, fn., 105; 371; 372, fn., 119; 378; *The Comedy of Errors,* 347; *Much Ado About Nothing,* 347; 353; 354; *Pericles, Prince of Tyre,* 349; 362; *The Taming of the Shrew,* 350, 353; 364 (the famous lute private lesson); 366; 381; *The Merchant of Venice,* 353; 354; 358; 359; 363; 368; 370; 379; 382; *Henry the VIII,* 355; 360; 366, fn., 86; 368; 370; 380; 381; 382; *The Tempest,* 356; 363; 383; *The Merry Wives of Windsor,* 358; (**VIII:** 304); *Titus Andronicus,* 366; 366, fn., 86; 368; 369; *Measure for Measure,* 366; 378; (**VIII:** 328); *Love's Labour Lost,* 366; (**VIII:** 328); *Anthony and Cleopatra;* 366, fn., 86; 367, fn., 92; 370, fn., 105; 371; 372, fn., 119; 383; (**VIII:** 331, an adoption by Dryden); *Henry V;* 367, fn., 92; 373, fn., 123; 375; 380; 382; *King Lear;* 367, fn., 92; 370, fn., 105; 370; *King John,* 373, fn., 123; 374, fn., 130; *Coriolanus,* 369; 370, fn., 105; 372, fn., 119; 373, fn., 123; 374, fn., 131; 375; **VI:** 105; **VII:** 289; **VIII:** 103; 155; 268, Rymer, a rare critic of; 304; 328, Dryden criticizes Shakespeare; 331; 383

Shamash, god of ancient Akkad, **I:** 64

Shenstone, William, 1714–1763, Restoration poet, **VIII:** 361; 362; 363; 407ff; 409ff; 411; 412ff; 415ff; 417; 423; 428; 429

Sheridan, Thomas, 1687–1738, Restoration poet, **VIII:** 350

Shirley, James, 1596–1666, Jacobean playwright, died in the London fire of 1666, **VIII:** 181, *The Cardinal,* 181; 191

Sidney, Sir Philip, 1554–1586, important English writer, **V:** 183, fn., 3, on Italian men; 198, writing in support of the arts, *The Defence of Poesie* (1595); 200; 204, on the importance of

the liberal arts; 258ff; 264ff; 273, elegy on his death by Spenser; 289, Reason is defenseless against feminine beauty; 292, 295; 301; 303; 305ff; 391

Sidonius, fifth century French poet, **II:** 89; 91; 96ff; 102

Siena civic band, VI: 15ff. led in seventeenth century by Alberto Gregori

Sigemund, Norse mythical hero, **II:** 207; 245

Sigismund, 1368–1437, emperor, Holy Roman Empire, at the Council of Constance, 1414–1418, **III:** 283; **V:** 146

Signora Settimia, solo singer, **VI:** 2, performance described for the 1608 wedding of Duke Odoardo Farnese of Parma and Margherita de' Medici

Silanion, Roman sculptor mentioned by Pliny the Elder, **I:** 498

Silesius, Angelus, Baroque German poet, **VI:** 221ff; 229

Silhon, Jean, de, 1596–1667, French philosopher, **VII:** 172

Simone de Lionardo, seventeenth century German trumpeter in Florence, **VI:** 5

Simonides, c. 556 BC, lyric poet, **I:** 125ff; 175ff; 29, "poet of Ceos,"; 310; 355

Simpson, Christopher, d. 1669, English composer, **VIII:** 22, complains most people prefer "light and airy" music

Simylus, first century Roman lyre player, **II:** 5

Singers, IV: 66, "the ladies of Mantua and Ferrara are highly competent," Giustiniani (1628); 84, Silvio Antoniano (1570); 171ff, Cardano on the qualities and technique of the voice; 305ff, art song in Cervantes; **V:** 110ff, Ornithoparchus (1517) on precepts for singers; 130 without the ability to do this, writes Coclico, a singer is nothing; 164, see Praetorius discussion on good singing; 306ff, on singers conveying, or not, their emotions, in Elizabethan England; **VI:** 37, Galilei recommends a singer attend opera to observe the physical aspects of emotion; Northbrook on style of church singing; 40, Christoph Bernard's (1649) remarkable list of emotions used in singing, on Peri's emotional singing; 48ff, Benedetto Marcello satires the social statue of singers; 49, Tosi offers advice on employment in courts; **VII:** 44, Mersenne on the aestetics of the voice and singing; **VIII:** 51, (North); 117, a Herrick poem speaks of singing turning man into an angel

Singing Societies, II: 275, thirteenth century England

Single-pipe girl, prostitutes, **I:** 187; 239; 278, Lamia, third century BC prostitute; 336ff; 366ff, Roman Republic; 475, emperor bans use of single-pipe girls; **II:** 106, here a boy

Sirens, the ancient tale of singing and sailors, **II:** 308

Sixtus, v, pope, 1585–1590, **V:** 287, fn., 2, said by Thomas Nashe to have been poisoned by the King of Spain, whom he had invited to dinner. The following pope sent someone a note reading, *Sol Rex me facit* (the King of Spain made me pope)

Skelton, John, 1460–1529, English poet, **V:** 255; 265; 274; 277

Slave music, VII: 13, slave musicians on a gally in the port of Marseilles in 1644

Slesius, Angelus, 1624–1677, pseudonym for Johann Scheffler, German author, **VI:** 221ff

Smart, Peter, early seventeenth century Protestant preacher opposed to music, **VIII:** 17

Snefrunufer, singing instructor, sixth dynasty, ancient Egypt, **I:** 77

Socrates, 469–399 BC, Greek philosopher, teacher of Plato, all of whose writings some attribute to Socrates, **I:** 108; 141ff; 192ff; 281, fn., 86; 495; **II:** 35ff; 52; 60; 428; **III:** 36; 255; 257; 261; **IV:** 114; 142; 154; 245; **V:** 295; **VII:** 136; **VIII:** 243

Soler, Francisco, 1625–1688, **VI:** 91, composer of three extant Masses with voices and wind band

Solo singer, I: 188; 425, murdered in performance; **II:** 356, Marie de France: the best singers are the most criticized; **III:** 156, Chaucer

Solomon, 1,000 BC, Hebrew king of the Old Testament, **I:** 86, his 245 singers; 91; 94ff

Solon, 630–558 BC, Greek philosopher, **I:** 103

Somerville, William, 1682–1742, Restoration poet, **VIII:** 372

Sophocles, 495–406 BC, Greek playwright, **I:** 169ff; 174; 185ff; 298; 343; **II:** 17, Longinus; 52; **VII:** 275; 284

Sordel, c. 1200–1270, troubadour, **II:** 380; 392

Soriano, Francesco, 1548–1621, **IV:** 65, Giustiniani considered among the best composers of the sixteenth century

Soul, I: 254, Voice is the expression of the soul; 304, Plotinus; 378, Cicero; 381; **II:** 62ff, Tertullian; 125, St. Basil on purification of; 183, Boethius; 315, Bernard of Clairvaux: Reason is found in the soul; Hildegard von Bingen nonsense on how the soul runs the body; **III:** 165, Gaffurio: organized like cosmic, but Ugolino says no, human music organizes it, not cosmic; **IV:** 27, Valgulio finda a natural disharmony in the soul; **V:** 36, Zeno, Greek philosopher quoted by Erasmus, the soul is a "self-moving harmony, and for this reason can be caught up and carried away by harmonious things"; 345, the brain and soul create thought (Shakespeare); **VII:** 251ff, Voltaire discusses; **VIII:** 77, Bacon finds that soul is a divine gift, it can only be understood through divine inspiration; 259, Berkeley holds that soul, spirit, self, etc., are all of the mind

Spanberg, Johann, V: 113ff, a poem on the virtues of music, which is well-paid in Germany

Spatato, Giovanni, sixteenth century Italian theorist, **IV:** 60

Spee, Friedrich, 1591–1635, a German poet, then priest, **VI:** 224

Speer, Daniel, 1636–1707, **VI:** 139ff, composer for Stadtpfeifers

Spenser, Edmund, 1552–1599, English poet, **V:** 249; 266; 270ff; 273; 280; 282; 285ff

Speusippus of Athens, 408–338 BC, **II:** 24

Spinoza, Benedict, 1632–1677, philosopher, **VI:** 233; 283ff

Spurinna, Roman lyric poet, **I:** 499

St. Ambrose, 374–397, Bishop of Milan, **II:** 121ff; 125ff; 127ff; 129; **III:** 6; 35; 66

St. Augustine, 354–430, **II:** 135ff; 167, on conducting; 301; 311; **III:** 6; 35; 105; **V:** 190; **VII:** 156

St. Basil, 330–379 AD, **II:** 45, description of a Christian; 46, a Christian should not laugh; 107; 115ff; 119; 123ff; 125ff; 129ff; 132

St. Cecilia, VIII: 334ff, (Dryden); 354–362, Restoration poets in honor of

St. Columba, of Ireland, 521–597, **II:** 210ff

St. Cuthbert, 634–687, Anglo-Saxon monk, **II:** 211, singing to otters; 212, on style of psalm singing

St. Cyprian, third century Church father, **II:** 46, a Christian should not sing love songs

St. Francis of Assai, 1181–1226, **II:** 311

St. Gregory Nazianzus, fourth century Church writer, **II:** 116ff; 123ff; 131

St. Jerome, 347–420, Church father, **II:** 122; 132ff; 353; **III:** 6; 254

St. John Chrysostom, 347–407 AD, **II:** 95; 107; 115ff; 117ff; 121ff; 124ff; 127ff; 129ff; 131; 134

St. John of the Cross (Juan de Yeppes y Alverez), 1542–1591, *ars antiqua* Spanish poet and Church philosopher, author of *The Ascent of Mount Carmel;* **IV:** 279ff, on the senses; 282 in *The Spiritual Canticle,* he mentions 'silent music,' obtainable through meditation; 312ff, don't rely on the senses

St. Justin Martyr, 100–165, early Church writer, **II:** 47, against festivals; 74

St. Paul, c. 5–67 AD, **II:** 262; **V:** 48ff

St. Paulinus of Nola, 354–431, Church writer, **II:** 90; 95; 100; 131

St. Thomas Acquinas, 1224–1274, **II:** 333, major discussion, Reason vs senses, pleasure and pain, emotions

Stamitz, Johann Wenzel Anton, 1717–1759, **VII:** 11

Statius, 45–96 AD, court poet to the emperor Domitian, **I:** 506ff

Steele, Richard, 1672–1729, Restoration writer, **VIII:** 310, as playwright: *The Tender Husband,* 310; 314; *The Funeral,* 314, fn., 29; as poet: 363; 363, fn., 41 two poems published with music by William Crofts and Johann Ernst Galliard; 364, mentions he wrote a play, *The Tender Husband;* 445, began the *Tatler* in 1709; 446; 451

Sternfeld, Frederick, sixteenth century German educational philosopher, **V:** 65

Stesichorus of Himera, 610–550 BC, Greek Lyric poet, **I:** 123ff; 175; **II:** 20

Stettin Stadtpfeifers, VI: 137, letter of application

Stewdl, leader of the trombones in Maximilian I's church band, **III:** 278

Stockmann, Ernst, 1634–1712, German poet, **VI:** 222, a poem in honor of Schütz

Stokowski, Leopold, 1882–1977, English conductor, **I:** 39

Stolzer, Thomas, 1480–1526, composer in Hungary, **V:** 136

Strabo, 63 BC – 23 AD Greek philosopher, **I:** 68; 76ff; 104ff; 108; 110ff; 128; 288ff; 317, on delight vs artistic beauty; 320; 323; 325, on education

Strachey, John, correspondent with Lock in 1665, **VIII:** 236

Stratonicus of Athens, 336–323 Greek harpist and teacher, **I:** 123ff; 276ff; famous early harp player

Stravinsky, Igor, 1882–1971, composer, **I:** 11

Striggio, Alessandro, 1531–1593, **IV:** 65, Giustiniani considered among the best composers of the 16th century; 85; **V:** 147; **VI:** 4, fn., 12, letter from Monteverdi regarding hiring musicians; 126

String instruments, I: 88; 184, "lutes"; **II:** 423 played on horse in thirteenth century; **IV:** 170, Cardano, string player sometimes sang while playing; 326, Lope de Vega on string

instrument construction; **VI:** 231ff, Grimmelshausen describes the itinerant fiddler; **VIII:** 7, the 24 *Violons du Roi*; 74, Bunyan strings are heavenly; 106, "begging Fiddlers"; 127, re Fiddlers Songs; 205, fn., 69 ("Enter a noyse of Fidles"); 208ff; 220, Dekker on the beer fiddler; 319, dance music in the Restoration plays was almost invariably associated with violins; 370; 405, the dance fiddler; 426, Evelyn documents the first appearance of strings in English churches; 427, description of the dance fiddler; 447, Addison , on the violin, first thinks of improvisation

Strozzi, Bernardo, sixteenth century Germany composer, **V:** 167

Stubbs, Philip, English Puritan writer of *Anatomy of the Abuses in England* (1583), **V:** 195; writing in support of Gosson; 203; 211; 239; 288, fn., 5

Student, III: 75, Machaut's ideal student described; **IV:** 108, Giraldi, the attitude of the student is critical in epic poetry; 277, Vives, duties of the student; encourages memory; "empty slate" theory; student discipline;

Suckling, Sir John, 1609–1642, English poet, **VIII:** 103; 107

Suetonius, 69–130 AD Roman historian, **I:** 364; 422; 459; 468; 475

Sufi philosophy, I: 41

Sulla, Lucius Cornelius, 138–78 BC, Roman general and statesman, **I:** 352, was a singer

Sully, Maximilien, 1560–1641, chief minister under Henry IV of France, **VII:** 1

Sumarokov, Aleksandr, VII: 264, recipient of a letter from Voltaire

Sumponyah, musical instrument mentioned in the Book of Daniel, **I:** 66

Susato, Tielman, d. 1561, trombonist and leader of the Antwerp town band, **V:** 2ff

Sweelinck, Jan, 1562–1621, organist at Amsterdam, **VI:** 126; 280, music ideas still rooted in Plato

Swift, Jonathan, 1667–1745, Irish philosopher, shared a grandfather with Dryden, dean at St. Patrick's, **VIII:** 353; 358; 366; 369; 371; 377; 379; 380; 383; 394ff, a satire on the ancient Greeks belief in the value of music to improve character; 412; 415; 423, on the founding of the *Tatler;* 445

Sylvester II, pope, tenth century, **II:** 229ff, encouraged liberal arts

Sympathetic vibrations, II: 100, sixth to eighth century

Symposium, I: 143, fn., 10

Tacitus, 56–117 AD Roman senator and historian, **I:** 460; 470ff; 501

Taillefer, jongleur under William the Conqueror, eleventh century, **II:** 237

Talbot, James, 1689–1703, English Baroque writer, **VIII:** 32

Tartaglia, Niccolo, sixteenth century Italian theorist, **IV:** 43

Tartini, Italian Baroque composer, **VII:** 157

Tasso, Torquato, 1544–1595, Italian poet, author of *Discourses on the Heroic Poem,* **IV:** 1; 10, follows church dogma distrust of emotions; 17; 19; 91ff; 103ff; 117ff; 125; 200; **VII:** 276

Taste, VI: 52, Geminiani: good taste must be learned, is a gift of nature and cannot be learned by rules; 157, Scheibe on Germans learning Taste from the Italians; 160, Heinichen on Taste; **VII:** 22ff, seventeenth century French views on Taste: Rousseau, Couperin, Rameau, Saint-Lambert, Brossard; 122ff, views of Baroque French philosophers, Brossard; 123–126, debate on French vs Italian music by Le Cerf de La Viélle and Raguenet; 257; 258 (Voltaire); **VIII:** 251, Hume was author "Of the Standard of Taste" 253, Hume's lengthy discussion on Taste; 285, Shaftesbury on the development of taste; 381, Swift; 389, Wycherley believed that hearing popular music did not affect our taste for higher music; 391ff, contemporary descriptions of a gentleman of high taste in London; 412ff, views of Restoration writers;

Taylor, Silas, Restoration composer mentioned by Pepys, **VIII:** 442

Tdradellas, VIII: 26, fn., 16, Judged by Avison as a composer of modest ability

Teacher, I: 225 (qualifications), 397, fn., 94, Cicero: teachers work after their death through their books; **II:** 104, character and behavior of; 124, fourth century Church view of role of teacher; 175ff, sixth to eighth centuries; 236, cruel, eleventh century; **III:** 21, Petrarch; **IV:** 98, Vida: students need rest; 99, portrait of a great teacher; 124, Aristoso on scholars character; 138, in Castiglione; 217; du Bellay describes; 249, Montaigne on requirements of a teacher of children; 275ff, Vives, duties of the teacher; 276, encourages competition; teacher's job is to sort out levels of ability; **V:** 19, Erasmus's concerns and ideals on; 20 on cruel teachers; why are they so casually hired?; 128, comments on the teaching of Josquin des Près by his student Adrian Coclico; 202, Ascham: most men pay more for the care of their horse than the teacher of their children; 203, Stubbs (1583) says the problem causing poor schools in England is the poor pay for teachers; 204, Peacham on poor teachers; 291, Greene on the characteristics of a good teacher, but (292) condemns the liberal arts; **VII:** 2, typical private teaching contract in seventeenth century Paris; 69, Mersenne: teachers should demonstrate for their students; **VIII:** 63, Hall attacks teachers with metaphor of a cracked bell

Tegula, Publius Licinius, c. 205 BC, Roman composer, **I:** 362

Telemann, Georg, 1681–1767, German composer, **I:** 15; **VI:** 131; 140 founds the civic collegium concerts in Leipzig, with announcement for a concert in 1736; 140ff a similar activity by Telemann in Hamburg, 154; 159

Telephanes, first century AD aulos player, **II:** 40

Téllez, Gabriel (see Molina)

Temple at Medamund, Thebes, I: 73

Temple of Dandera, I: 73

Temple, William, 1628–1699, Restoration philosopher, author of "On Ancient and Modern Learning," **VIII:** 264; 269, Voltaire: Temple closed his eyes to the wonders of his contemporaries, and opened them only to admire the ancient ignorance.

Tempo, VI: 200, Mattheson on the definition of Italian tempo words; **VII:** 26ff, on movement vs time; 180, Descartes on tempo and the emotions; **VIII:** 30, Avison on the use of the Italian terms; 48, North on the Italian terms

Terence, 195–159 BC, Roman playwright, **I:** 353; 356; 363; 366; **III:** 38; **IV:** 265; 279; 334

Terentianus, fl. 110–136, Roman writer, **II:** 191

Terpander of Antissa in Lesbos, 710–670 BC, famous lyre player of ancient Greece, **I:** 127ff; **V:** 40 (Erasmus)

Terpnos, kithara player and teacher to Nero, **I:** 459; 467

Terpsichore, Greek god of dance, **I:** 134, 209

Tertullian, second century Church philosopher, **II:** 4, on the water organ; 46ff, don't question Church authorities; 48ff, against theater; 52, attacks poets for associating emotions with gods; 58ff; 62ff, soul is older than speech; 69ff; 72

Tesselschade, Maria, 1594–1649, Dutch poet, painter and musician, **VI:** 277

Thales, 624–547 BC, Greek philosopher, **I:** 103; 156; 160

Theages, fifth century BC, Greek philosopher before Plato, **I:** 153

Theater Music, II: 92ff, fourth and fifth centuries; **V:** 316, trumpet fanfares to begin the play, as was the case in Monteverdi's *Orfeo*, as well as music between the acts; **VI:** 50, make sure the musicins are seated where they can see the faces of the actors; 52, Tossi on stage appearance; **VIII:** 155, size in the Jacobean Period; 179–189, incidental music in the Jacobean plays; 159, Wait bands, as the "Waits of Southwark" in Beaumont and Fletcher's *The Knight of the Burning Pestle*; 160ff, further examples of civic musicians used; 255, Hume on Tragedy

Theater, II: 116, fifth century description of decay in quality; 151ff, St. Augustine, on the theater; 195, decline, sixth to eighth centuries; **III:** 293, Encina on fifteenth century Spanish drama; 322, England fifteenth century; **IV:** 129, Scaliger, Julius, 1484–1558, in his *Poetics* (1561) adds to Aristotle's purpose of Tragedy, that it must also be educational; 129 performances should last not less than 3 hours, nor more than 4; 302, Cervantes on; 325, Lope de Vega, in theater emotions are supplied by the music; 333 on what is needed to write poetry; 336, Cervantes on imitation; Lope de Vega on method acting; 337 defining the good actor; **V:** 193, quoted by Gosson in 1579, Maximus Tyrius, second century AD,

suggests that the addition of instruments ruined the theater; 209ff, sixteenth century English views; 316, stage performances based on real Elizabethan practice; trumpet fanfare to begin the play and concerts after the production (see Hentzner) or before (see Philip of Stettin-Pomerania); 317, the "music room" and use of Wait bands; 318, brief ensemble performance during the play, beginning with the earliest Elizabethan play, *Gorboduc* of 1570; 318ff, music in the stage directions of the plays containing music descriptions; 350ff, Shakespeare's discussion; 350 on the forms of drama; the play is an analogy of life; 351, advice to the actor; 365; **VII:** 183ff, major discussion of seventeenth century French drama; 185, François Hédelin (1657) on the rules of ancient theater; 188ff, Corneille on the nature of Tragedy and its emotions; 190, Saint-Évremond, on the rules of ancient and modern drama; 197, on the purpose of drama; 199ff, on the audience; 205ff, 284ff, Voltaie on ancient vs modern theater; 287, on the contemporary French theater; **VIII:** 68, Bunyan classifies dramatic plays with "fools, apes, knaves and rogues" and theaters themselves with alehouses and whorehouses; 84, (Bacon); 214, The Puritan Fuller opposed to plays, but Overbury found them more necessary than schools; 220, Dekker claims some theaters in ancient Rome seated 80,000 viewers; 268, because of its central feature, action, Rymer finds sight even more important than language; 275, an extraordinary survey of the varieties of communication by the eye; 286, Shaftesbury on an interesting discussion on the development of poetry (and theater) in England; 303, Hawkins, in his general history of music (1776) provides interesting comments on the Restoration theater and its tendency toward low entertainment and the development of popular music; 304, Betterton assigns part of the failure of contemporary theater to the training of the actors themselves; 306, William Congreve, 1670–1729, perhaps the best of the Restoration writers, on the definition of comedy, "Humor shows us as *we* are"; 306, on drama's universality and being too close to human experience; 306ff, Betterton and Congreve on the educational purpose of drama; 326ff, Dryden on drama; 328 on the closing of the theaters in the Cromwell period; 383, Restoration philosophers discuss

Theater, music to announce, II: 49, trumpets and auloi; **VIII:** 370, (Swift)

Theile, Johann, 1646–1724, teacher of the Hautboisten of Friedrich I, **VI:** 147

Theioi, "the divine," a name for lyre players, **I:** 118.

Theocritus, c. 315–264 BC, Alexandrian poet, **I:** 293ff

Theodora of Constantinople, empress in eleventh century, **II:** 237

Theodore of Cyrus, d. 460, Church writer, **II:** 130

Theodoric, 454–526 AD, Roman emperor, **I:** 459; 463; **II:** 97

Theodorus of Boeotia, second century BC, famous Roman aulos player, **I:** 354

Theodosius, Roman emperor in 385 AD, **I:** 475

Theophilus, Archbishop of Alexandria, d. 412; **II:** 177, destroyed all early pagan manuscripts he could find

Theophilus, early twelfth century author of *De Diversis Artibus,* **II:** 296, on Reason, part of which is genetic; 296ff, Grosseteste on same

Theophilus, priest in 1190 in Paderborn, Germany, **II:** 271, describes post-crusades pre-Renaissance; 296

Theophrastus of Eresus, 372–287 BC, Alexandrian philosopher and student of Aristotle, **I:** 105; 284ff; **II:** 96, on music therapy

Theopompus, second century BC, Roman aulos player, **I:** 354

Theopompus, 378–320 BC, Greek historian, **II:** 16

Thepis, ancient Greek playwright and dance teacher, **I:** 171, Athenaeus

Thibault de Courville, Johann, d. 1581, French musician, **VII:** 78

Thibault, Joachim, sixteenth century French poet, **IV:** 203

Thibaut of Champagne, 1201–1253, trouvére, **II:** 379

Thirty Years War, 1618–1648, **VI:** 121

Thomas, Lord Vaux, 1510–1556, English poet, **V:** 261

Thomsen, Magnus, V: 148, extant sixteenth century trumpet choir music

Thomson, James, 1700–1748, Restoration playwright, admired by both Voltaire and Lessing, but not his countrymen, **VIII:** 312, as playwright: *Alfred,* 312; as writer: 347; 350; 351; 359ff; 361; 369; 371; 425, on French and Italian opera

Thucydides of Athens, c. 470–398 BC, historian, **I:** 141ff; **IV:** 230

Thyard, Pontus de, 1521–1605, French philosopher, **VII:** 87; 55

Tibullus, 54–18 BC, Roman Lyric Poet, **I:** 421, 423ff, 426ff, 434, 451

Timagenes, ancient philosopher, **III:** 175

Timosthenes (fl. c. 270 BC), Greek composer, **I:** 288; **V:** 40

Timotheus of Miletus, ancient Greek lyre player, **I:** 129

Tinctoris, Johannes, 1435–1511, fifteenth century theorist, **III:** 237ff, still associated music with mathematics and is threatened by contemporary musicians

Tintore, Jacopo, sixteenth century painter, **IV:** 20

Titian, 1488–1576, Italian painter, **IV:** 18; 22; 178

Titus, 79–81 AD, Roman emperor, **I:** 462

Tolstago, Petr, seventeenth century Russian visitor **VI:** 23, records his hearing the young women of the *Incurabili* sing in Venice

Tomás de Sancta Maria, sixteenth century writer on keyboard performance practice, **IV:** 288 and 288, fn., 73

Tomkins, Thomas, 1572–1656, English composer, **VIII:** 123

Tommaso de'Cavalieri, IV: 180, received poems from Michelangelo; 183

Tonality, VII: 24ff, Charpentier on emotional qualities of various tonalities; 76, Mersenne on tonality and the colors of organ pipes

Tonarion, pitch pipe for oratorical use, **I:** 365

Torquemanda, Juan, seventeenth century Spanish writer, **VI:** 92

Torri, Pietro, seventeenth century Italian composer, **VI:** 17

Tosi, Pier Francesco, 1653–1732, castrato and Italian singing teacher, **VI:** 49, on the evils of working for the court; 52, sing only the best music; 54, on singing from the heart; 55; 56ff,

in the manners of singers; 59ff, on improvisation; 65, on ornaments, 66, on begging for applause; 68, styles of church music

Tosso, Torquato, 1544–1595, **IV:** 1ff; 91, regrets the level (lack) of respect poets have

Tourneur, Cyril, 1575–1626, Jacobean playwright, **VIII:** 167, d. 1626, Jacobean playwright; *The Atheist's Tragedy;* 167; 173; 198; 206, fn., 72

Traherne, Thomas, 1634–1674, seventeenth century English poet, **VIII:** 100

Trajan, 52–41 AD, Roman emperor, **I:** 459; 463

Traversari, Ambrogio, 1386–1439, humanist, **III:** 163, praises accompanied arias; 188

Trawick, Buckner, contemporary writer, **VI:** 71

Trichet, Pierre, VII: 26, on communicating of emotions on strings

Trithemius, Johannes, abbot of Sponheim, early Renaissance German humanist, **III:** 253, "the days of building monasteries are over"

Triton, sea god, **I:** 103

Troiano, Massimo, court singer, diarist under Albert V at Munich, **V:** 147

Troilo, Antonio, seventeenth century Italian canzoni composer, **VI:** 21

Trombone, VIII: 69, Bunyan on the doleful trombones and bass instruments

Troubadour and Trouvères, II: 355ff, twelfth and thirteenth centuries; 369ff; **III:** 292, Encina, on the difference between a poet and a troubadour

Truchsess, Christoph, V: 11ff, letter to Erasmus on the conservatives toward the humanities.

Trumpet choir, V: 139, on the repertoire of the Duke of Graz; Praetorius *sonadas;* Maximilian II, 1564–1576, trumpets are named "musical" and "not musical"; 147; 148, extant repertoire by Hendrich Lübeck and Magnus Thomsen; 151 to wake up the sixteenth century drunken Bishop of Münster; 177, Praetorius on use in church; 230 of Elizabeth I; **VI:** 5, examples of court trumpet choir appearances in seventeenth century Italy, including those serving the pope; 81, on its composition and improvisation (Kircher); 127; 133ff, German Baroque, "golden age"; 133 Altenburg on the importance of the trumpet choir (1795); on the memorized concert pieces (Hentzschel); guilds; **VIII:** 444, Pepys reports he has been told by Gervasse Price, the court "Serjeant Trumpet" of the court that an Italian composer is preparing a composition of three-parts for the royal trumpets of James II

Trumpet signals, I: 69; 71; 93ff; **II:** 94; "slow notes" in battle; 195, Procopius; 283 (on ships in 12th century); 366, in *The Song of Roland* 7,000 trumpets play unison signals; in Layamon's Romance, *Brut,* 60,000 play together; **III:** 100, for servants; **IV:** 119, to control ships in Tasso, Ariosto; 322, on ship for joy; to announce the king; 344; **V:** 53, Erasmus on public fear of trumpet signals—Jesus was announced not by trumpets, but by singing; 285, to depart and to rest, in Spencer's *Faerie Queene;* 316, trumpet fanfares to begin the play, as was the case in Monteverdi's *Orfeo;* 365, in Shakespeare for introducing kings and highest royalty: 366 and 366, fn., 86; 367ff, specific forms given by Shakespeare: **Flourish,** 367: *King Henry VI: Part III; King Henry VI: Part II;* 367, fn., 92: *Richard II; Richard III; Troilus and Cressida; All's Well That Ends Well; Henry VI: Part I; Henry VI: Part II; Henry V; Titus Andronicus; Hamlet; King Lear; Macbeth; Antony and Cleopatra;*

Henry VI: Part III; **Sennet,** 369, *Coriolanus; King Henry VI: Part I;* 370, *King Henry VI: Part II; King Henry VI, Part III; Richard III; Henry VIII; King Lear,* 370, fn., 105; *Macbeth,* 370, fn., 105; *Antony and Cleopatra,* 370, fn., 105; *Richard III,* 370, fn., 105; **Tucket,** 370, *King Lear; The Merchant of Venice; Timon of Athens;* 370, fn., 109, *Troilus and Cressida;* **Alarum,** 371, *Troilus and Cressida; Macbeth; King Henry VI: Part II; Antony and Cleopatra;* 371, fn., 110; *Richard III;* 371, fn., 113, *King Henry VI: Part III,* **Retreat,** 372, *King Henry VI: Part III; King Henry VI: Part I;* 372, fn., 119, *Troilus and Cressida;* 372, fn., 119, *King Henry VI: Part I;* 372, fn., 119, *Macbeth;* 372, fn., 119, *Antony and Cleopatra,* 372, fn., 119, *Coriolanus;* **Parley,** 372, *King Henry VI, Part I; Timon of Athens;* 373, *Richard II;* 373, fn., 123, *King Henry VI: Part III;* 373, fn., 123, *King John;* 373, fn., 123, *King Henry VI, Part I;* 373, fn., 123, *Henry V;* 373, fn., 123, *Coriolanus;* 373, additional trumpet signals; **VI:** 102, Quevedo on the trumpet of the Day of Judgment; 103, Góngora on the shrill trumpet; **VI:** 114ff, in seventeenth century Spanish theater; **VII:** 315 (Voltaire); **VIII:** 75, Harrington, to accompany public announcements; 344ff, in Dryden's plays

Trumpet, I: 75, female player in ancient Egypt; 81; 89; 93, Gideon's battle; 145, fn., 14; 92, Mosses on trumpet construction; 103; 110 fn., 26; 136; 185, Cornu; 466; **II:** 49, to announce theater; 82, as metaphor; 204, Day of Judgment, eighth century; 204, sixth to eighth century riddle describing a trumpet; 279, religious trumpeter of the Great Hallelujah! of 1233; 356, played by jongleur; 366 descriptions of the sounds of various trumpet types and uses in twelfth and thirteenth century French Romances; **III:** 11, Pietro di Bartolomeo trumpeter in Treviso; 131, for nobles, processionals, fourteenth century English; in a private chamber, indoor ceremonial music; **IV:** 344, as ambassador; **VI:** 108ff, trumpet used as a metaphor in seventeenth century Spanish theater; 133, praise by Andreas Werckmeister; **VII,** 15 (Mersenne); (Kastner); 16, Ménestrier on the value of trumpets in teaching horse dancing; **VIII:** 5, regarding the use of the trumpeter as an abassador; 69, Bunyan equates the cry of the beggar with a 'shrill trumpet'; 74, Donne on the use of trumpets in the Old and New Testament; 219, Puritan view of the trumpet player; 313; in Vanbruch's *Aesop,* "The Trumpets sound a Melancholy Air"; 405, in role as ambassador

Truth in Music, I: 217; **II:** 101, fourth and fifth century; 101, fn., 8, public does not always want the Truth; 205, sixth to eighth century poem; **III:** 81, Machaut; 145, Chaucer; **IV:** 67, Mei: purpose of theory is to find Truth, but it is found in performance; 95, Tosso on poetry; 144, Time is the father of truth, Castiglione; 232, Bodin on history and Truth; 252, Montaigne: perhaps God supplied Truth to common men and not to philosophers; **VI:** 250, Leibniz: Music is a form of Truth; **VII:** 107, is perfection and beauty (La Rochefoucauld); 107, Boileau on Truth and the sublime in performance; 107ff, Boileau, on Truth and the sublime in performance; **VIII:** 67, Rev. Hall on the kinds of Truth; 327, Dryden: Time is the surest Judge of Truth

Tubal, inventor of music, Old Testament, **V:** 111; **VIII:** 190 (Genesis 4:22)

Tuberville, George, 1540–1595, English poet, **V:** 258

Tullius Sabinus, first century AD poet, **II:** 39

Tullius, King of Rome, 578–535 BC; **II:** 184

Tunstede, Simon, fourteenth century music theorist, **III:** 110ff

Tutankhamun, c. 1343–1323 BC, Egyptian ruler, **I:** 81

Turner, James, seventeenth century writer on miliary music, **VIII:** 19

Twenger, Johann, sixteenth century German artist, **V:** 150

Tyard, Pontus de, 1522–1605, French poet and philosopher, author of *Solitaire premier, ou, Prose des Muses & de la fureur Poetique* (1552) **IV:** 32, describes affect of performance on emotions; 195ff; on the impact of music; 200; **VI:** 33, on words vs emotions; **VII:** 55

Tye, Christopher, sixteenth century London composer, **V:** 228, fn., 22

Tymnus, second century poet, **II:** 7

Tyrius, Maximus, second century AD, **V:** 193, quoted by Gosson in 1579

Tyrrhenian trumpet (of the Etruscans), **I:** 343, Sophocles, Euripides, Aeschylus

Uberti, Grazioso, jurist, **VI:** 16, 1630 account of concerts throughout Rome

Udall, Nicholas, 1509–1556, Elizabethan playwright **V:** 333, *Ralph Roister Doister,* England's earliest comedy; 339

Uffenbach, J. F. A., German tourist, **VI:** 8; 11; 26, testimonial to Vivaldi

Ugolino of Orvieto, author of *Declaratio musicae disciplinae,* c. 1430–1435, **III:** 165

Ulrich von Hutten, sixteenth century German writer, **V:** 114

Ulrich von Liechtenstein, 1198–1276, German poet, **II:** 412ff, songs; 421ff

Ulysses, central character in Homer, **I:** 115; 116

Universality in Music, I: 16, 24ff, 46; **II:** 101 (Ausonius: music cannot be owned); **III:** 26, Petrarch; 200ff Leonardo da Vinci; **IV:** 108, Giraldi in poetry; 143, Castiglione; 234, Jean Bodin; 301, Cervantes on the common link among poets; **VI:** 98, Gracin on the fine line between universality and popularity; **VII:** 121, André on some form of innate rational understanding in the listener; 264 (Voltaire); **VIII:** 42, North, first English writer to address this, thought perhaps genetic; 252, (Hume); 272, Wotton believed there are certain qualities in music which are universally understood regardless of the education of the listener; 288, Shaftesbury on universality in music

Universities, II: 271, twelfth and thirteenth centuries, the Pre-Renaissance and the beginning of Humanism; universities founded; 272ff, universities students moving away from church careers in favor of skills for employment such as law; 287, Bologna and Paris, thirteenth century; 288, Oxford; **III:** 188, fifteenth century Italy; **V:** 59ff, sixteenth century criticism of German universities; 80ff, Luther criticizes the university system; 324, Marlowe's *The Massacre at Paris* comments on the secularization of the universities; **VIII:** 63, Burton: universities give degrees but never learning; 64, on Oxford and Cambridge; 65 Cowley's utopian college; Bunyan classifies professors with whores and murderers; 132, Milton's criticism

Urania, one of the ancient Greek Muses, **I:** 210

Urban II, eleventh century pope, **II:** 28, led first crusade of 1095–1099; 281

Urban VIII, pope, 1623–1644, loved music, supported singer training in Rome, **VI:** 15; 17ff

Urbanus, Gregorius, seventeenth century Italian composer, **VI:** 17

Utrecht civic band in 1489, **III:** 230, plays motets also in church

Valckenborck, Lucas, Dutch painter, sixteenth century, **V:** 4

Valdes, Francesco de, seventeenth century leader of Spanish court music, **VI:** 90

Valdivielso, El Maestro Josef, 1560–1636, Spanish playwright, **VI:** 106, as playwright, *The Bandit Queen;* 111

Valentinian, 364–375 AD, Roman emperor, **II:** 90

Valerius Marial, 38–102 AD, Roman poet, **I:** 509

Valerius Maximus, first century AD, Roman writer, **I:** 471

Valgulio, Carlo, fifteenth century writer, secretary to the papal treasurer in 1481–1485, **III:** 170, on the importance of music; 186; **IV:** 27

Valla, Giorgio, 1447–1500, music theorist, **III:** 166, learning music is necessary to learning the other liberal arts; 171, on the aesthetic qualities of individual tones

Van Alsloot, Dennis, seventeenth century Dutch painter, **VI:** 279; 281

Van Dorp, Maarten, sixteenth century humanist, **V:** 12

Van Winckle, Corneilis, sixteenth century trombonist in Ghent, **V:** 3

Vanbrugh, John, 1664–1726, Restoration playwright, and architect, **VIII:** as playwright: *A Journey to London,* 308; *The Relapse,* 311; *Aesop,* 312; *The Pilgrim,* 313; *The Provoked Wife,* 315; 316; 319, fn., 34; 424

Varchi, Benedetto, sixteenth century Italian poet, **IV:** 84; 188

Varro, Marcus, 116–26 BC, Roman poet, **I:** 351; 357ff; 362ff; 369; 381, emotions; **II:** 140; **III:** 38; **IV:** 252

Vasari, Giorgio, 1511–1574, Italian biographer of artists; **III:** 191, 206; **IV:** 14; 18, on imitation; 18ff on Nature and Art; 180, fn., 17, his *Lives* is a basic source on Michelangelo; 22

Vaspasian, 9–79 AD, Roman emperor, **I:** 467

Vaughan, Henry, 1621–1695, English poet, **VIII:** 113

Vaux, Thomas, 1510–1556, **V:** 261

Vecchi, Orazio, 1550–1605, Italian composer, **VI:** 71

Venetian Civic Wind Band, IV: 83, see also Dalla Casa

Venice, II: 276 (civic musicians playing for the Doge in fourth century)

Venneo, Stehano, sixteenth century Italian music theorist, **IV:** 43

Ventadorn, Bernart de, fl. 1150–1180, troubadour, **II:** 370, made love to patron's wife; 376; 384; 386; 388ff; 394

Venus, Greek goddess, **I:** 435

Verdi, Giuseppe, 19th century Italian composer, **I:** 39

Verdonck, Corneille, 1563–1625, Dutch artist, **V:** 1

Vergerio, Pietro, fourteenth century humanist professor at Padua; **III:** 13

Veronese, Paul, 1528–1588, Venetian based painter, **VII:** 267

Viadana, Lodovico, 1560–1627, Italian composer, **V:** 162; 172; 175; **VI:** 60, on improvisation (1602); 68; 124, Italian composer who dedicated music to Ferdinand II

Victoria, Tomás Luis de, 1548–1611 Spanish/Italian philosopher and composer, **IV:** 288, author of *Book of Hymns* and *Missaorum Libri Duo;* **VI:** 124

Vida, Marco Girolamo, 1485–1566, Italian, humanist, bishop and poet, author of *De Arte Poetica* (1517), **IV:** 96ff; 115

Vidal, Peire, troubadour, **II:** 370

Villiers, George, Duke of Buckingham, 1628–1687, **VIII:** 312; as playwright: *The Rehearsal,* 312; 317

Villon, François, 1431–1463, French poet and thief; **III:** 216; 218ff; 225

Vincentino, Nicola, sixteenth century Italian composer, **IV:** 198, regarding an Italian work for quarter-tone harpsichord

Vinci, Leonardo, 1690–1730, Italian composer, **VII:** 144

Vinci, Leonardo da, 1452–1519, Italian artist, **I:** 5; 23

Virdung, Sebastian, 1465–1530, German writer, **V:** 104, author of *Musica getutscht* (1511)

Virgil, 70–19 BC, Roman Lyric Poet, **I:** 402, 415, 419, 421, 423, 432, 449, 451, 452ff, 456ff, 499; **II:** 122; 177; 200; **III:** 6, under fire from the Church; 18; 38; **IV:** 108; **V:** 40; 86; 115; 119; **VIII:** 325; 418

Vitalis, Orderic, 1075–1143, English chronicler, **II:** 327; 329ff

Vitellozzi, Cardinal, sixteenth century, Council of Trent, **IV:** 38

Vittorio Amadeo II of Torino, 1666–1732, **VI:** 27

Vivaldi, Antonio, 1678–1741, Italian composer, **VI:** 8; 11; 23; 26, testimonial to by J. F. von Uffenbach, in 1715; 52; **VII:** 158; **VIII:** 26, fn., 16, judged by Avison as being a composer defective of in harmony and invention, music "fit for children"

Vives, Juan, 1492–1540, Spanish philosopher, author of *Introduction to Wisdom;* **IV:** 273; 274ff, Vives was an early believer in childhood education; 275 in *Tradendis Disciplinis* (1531), nothing is more beautiful than learning; environment of the school itself; duties of the teacher; 276, encourages competition; teacher's job is to sort out levels of ability; 277, duties of the student; encourages memory; 'empty slate' theory; desires an universal language; student discipline; 278, on poetry, "the characteristic of their art is music," on the subjects of poetry, dangers in love poetry; 279, dramatic literature must be heavily edited; worries that teaching science may lead to ideas contrary to the Scriptures, thus hesitant about heathen writers such as Aristotle; importance of play; education must be used for the common good; 283ff

Vivola, Alphonso dalla, **IV:** 77, sixteenth century composer in Italy

Vocal Choirs, **I:** 61; 67; 69; 71; 73; 81; 87ff, Old Testament choral music; 107; 125ff; 145; 157ff; 170; 175ff; 180; 183ff; 223, regarding education; 250, Music of the Spheres; 251, Aristotle, 297, Damomenes, conductor of a male choir; 464, satire by Juvenal; **II:** 6, Callimachus, third century Roman poet on accompanied choral music; 6, chorus lascivious dancing in sun worship; 9, dancing slaves; 91, fourth and fifth centuries fewer description of movement;

117, fifth century description of placement and conductor; 211, bishop could hear choirs of angels; 249, Aurelian believed in the choir of Angels; 439, Grocheo calls *ductia* a rapid, light song sung in chorus; **III:** 14, a 14th century minstrel trio; 176, Gaffurio says some form of old choral dance still used; **V:** 329ff, George Peele's play, *The Arraignment of Paris* includes music for a double choir

Voetius, 1589–1676, professor of theology in Utrecht, **VII:** 164

Vogt, Mauritius, Baroque German writer on the Doctrine of the Affections, **VI:** 163, fn., 36

Vogtherr, Heinrich, V: 68, on the destruction of church art in 1538

Volso, Gnaeus Manlius, 2nd century BC, Roman admiral, **I:** 366

Volsungs and Niblungs, **II:** 242, ninth - eleventh centuries, North German literature

Voltaire (François Marie Arouet), 1694–1778, French philosopher, **VII:** 243–325; 247, on the Physiology of Aesthetics; 250, on the Senses; 252, on Philosophy; 254, on the Psychology of Aesthetics; 256, on the Philosophy of Aesthetics; 260 on the Artist; 263, on General Aesthetic Principles in Art; 266, on the Aesthetics of Music; 268, on the perception of music; 268, on the current musical scene; 271, on Opera; 279 on Art Music; 280 on Church Music; 281, on Entertainment Music; 283, on the Ancient vs Modern Theater; 288ff, recommendations for the modern theater; 289, on Molière; 289, on Corneille; Voltaire as playwright: *Zaïre,* 290, 293, 294, 299; *The Tatler,* 291; *Catiline,* 291, 296; *Orestes,* 291; *Mérope,* 292, 293, 299; *The Orphan of China,* 292, 296; *Alzire,* 293; *The Prodigal,* 293, 295; *Hérode et Mariamne,* 293, 297; *Brutus,* 295; *The Prude,* 298; *Pandora,* 299; 290 criticism of acters and critics; 290, on the attitude of the court; 297 on Drama as Poetry; 301, Voltaire as Poet; 301, a short history of rhyme; 304ff, on the Lisbon earthquake of 1 November 1755; Voltaire as a writer of Fiction; *Candide,* 317ff, 320, 322, 323, 325; *Memnon the Philosopher,* 319; *The Study of Nature,* 319ff, 325; *The Chinese Catechism,* 319; *Zadig,* 319; *André Des Touches in Siam,* 321; *The Blind as Judges of Color,* 323; *The Princess of Babylon,* 323ff; *The White Bull,* 324

Vondel, Joost van den, 1587–1679, Dutch poet, **VI:** 277

Wace, Robert, twelfth century English writer; **II:** 361ff; 365ff

Waelrant, Hubert, of Antwerp, **IV:** 227, composer

Wagner, Richard, 1813–1883, German composer, **I:** 26; 27; 31ff; 36ff; 39; 43; 49; 56ff

Waits of England, V: 242, Lord Mayor's Parade; 242ff, use in the theater; 245, Thomas Morley dedicates *First Book of Consort Lessons* of 1599 to the Waits

Wallenstein, Catholic military leader, Thirty Years War, **VI:** 121

Waller, Edmund, 1606–1687, English Restoration poet, **VIII:** 95; 111; 122

Wallgrave, Dr., VIII: 421ff, a "rare lutanist," heard by Evelyn, one of the greatest masters in Europe on this charming instrument

Walls, Peter, contemporary author of *The Early Baroque Era,* **VIII:** 3

Walter of Châtillon, II: 427, singing harpist and Goliard of the thirteenth century

Walter, Bruno, 1876–1962, Austrian conductor, **I:** 39; 43

Walter, Johann, 1496–1570, **V:** 57, environment for the arts in sixteenth century Germany; 86; 89, friend and musical adviser to Luther; 94; 146

Walther von der Vogelweide, c. 1170–1230, **II:** 409, sung poetry; 412

Walton, Izaak, 1593–1683, English writer, **VIII:** 110; 211; 215

Warham, William, Archbishop of Canterbury, **V:** 28, a letter from Erasmus on the topic of fine art; 33

Water organ, II: 4ff, description by Tertullian; 90, Julian describes

Watson, Thomas, 1557–1592, sixteenth century English poet, **V:** 281

Webster, John, 1580–1625, Jacobean playwright and author of a prose work, *New Characters Drawne to the life of Severall Persons, in Severall Qualities* (1615), **VIII:** 157; *The Dutchesse of Malfy,* 165, fn., 19; 189; 199; *Appius and Virginia,* 182

Wedding music, I: 237; 362ff; 363, Terence and Poem 62 of Catullus; **II:** 7, second century, hymns and "sweet" aulos music; 100, one dies; 105; 118, fourth century church says no more music for weddings; 277, civic music guilds take over this business; **III:** 157, Chaucer; 233, with civic bands in fifteenth century Burgundy; 300; 301 regarding Enrique IV the Impotent; 321, England fifteenth century; **IV:** 88, in sixteenth century Italy; 209, Duc de Joyeuse (1581); 309, Cervantes, tuned instruments at a wedding: unearthly music; 344, in Lope de Vega, musicians playing the psalms as if their lives depended on it; **V:** 138ff, Duke Albert of Bavaria; William of Bavaria; 139, Duke Johann von Sachsen in 1500; 143ff, Ludwig III of Württemburg; Margrave Casimir of Brandenburg, d. 1527; 282, a poem by Spenser on the wedding day; 380 (Shakespeare); **VI:** 2, 1608 wedding of the duke of Parma, with solo singer described; **VII:** 13, description of a seventeenth century peasant wedding music; **VIII:** 126; 200

Weelkes, V: 247, sixteenth century popular music in England

Weingartner, Felix, 1863–1942, German conductor, **I:** 39

Weldon, Mr., Restoration composer, **VIII:** 309, named on the cover of a Masque text by Congreve

Wenck, John, German fifteenth century humanist, **III:** 255, calls Nicholas of Cusa nonsense

Werckmeister, Andreas, 1645–1706, German theorist, **VI:** 133, introduced Bach to equal tuning, praises the trumpet; 152

Wernher der Gartenaere, thirteenth century, **II:** 426

What is Music?, **II:** 168ff, St. Augustine

Whythorne, Thomas, sixteenth century English writer, **V:** 184, on the well-rounded Englishman

Widsith, eighth century Jongleur in Britain, **II:** 202

Wilderk, Philip van, 1500–1553, English court lunanist, **V:** 226; 276

Willaert, Adrian, 1490–1562, composer in Venice, **IV:** 201; **VI:** 126

William of Aquitaine, Count of Poitiers, 1071–1127, **II:** 369

William of Munich, son to Duke Albert v, **V:** 138

William of Ockham, c. 1300–1349, the most important English philosopher of the fourteenth century, **III:** 106ff, on the intellect vs the senses

William the Conqueror, eleventh century, **II:** 237

William III, 1650–1702, King of England, **VIII:** 8

Wilson, John, Jacobean composer who set poetry to music, **VIII:** 95

Wimpheling, Jakob, early Renaissance German humanist, **III:** 253; 279

Wither, George, 1588–1667, Jocabean Puritan poet, **VIII:** 93ff; 98; 100; 101; 102; 105; 106; 107; 108; 109; 112, on music to improve behavior and in his "Hymn for a Musician" he suggests some musicians have manners which might be improved by changing their reperoire; 113; 119; 121, a hymn to be sung by prisoners before their execution; 123; 124; 125; 126; 127

Wolff, Christian von, 1679–1754, German philosopher, **VI:** 237; 241ff on knowledge

Wolfram von Eschenbach, c. 1170–1220, German poet, **II:** 411, his *Parzival;* 422ff

Wolsey, Thomas, English Cardinal, 1473–1530, **V:** 2; 225, the cardinal's wind band; "mumming"; 253

Women, III: 98ff, new respect in fourteenth century literature; 263, Brant on praise of women's skill in planning; **VIII:** 58, Donne's syllogism on he speriority of intelligence in women

Wotton, Sir Henry, 1568–1639, English poet, **V:** 257

Wotton, William, 1666–1727, author of *Reflections upon Ancient and Modern Learning* (1694), **VIII:** 269

Wyatt, Thomas, 1503–1542, English poet, **V:** 261ff; 269ff; 275

Wycherley, William, 1641–1715, Resoration playwright, **VIII:** 311, as playwright: *The Gentleman Dancing-Master,* 311; 315; 319; *Love in a Wood,* 315; as poet: 361; as a writer: 378; 423

Xenacles, Alexandrian lyric poet, **I:** 296

Xenocrates, I: 325, on protecting children's ears from music

Xenodamus, sixth century BC Greek poet and leader of a music school, **I:** 131

Xenophanes, 576–480 BC, Greek philosopher, **I:** 156

Xenophantus, early Greek aulos player, **I:** 106

Xenophon of Athens, c. 434–355 BC, historian, **I:** 141ff

Xerxes, 519–466 BC, ruler of Persia, **I:** 191

Yates, Frances, VII: 78, modern writer

York Civic Wind Band, seventeenth century, **VIII:** 3

Youll, Henry, seventeenth century English composer, **VIII:** 112

Young, Edward, Rev., 1683–1765, Restoration poet, dean of Salisbury, **VIII:** 348, on the poor reputation of poets; 361; 371; 380ff; 383

Zampieri, a painter mentioned in the *Tatler* for 1710, **VIII:** 447

Zarlino, Geiseffo, 1517–1590, Italian music theorist, **IV:** 26; 44; 47ff, music must not be judged by the senses alone, still thinking of mathematics; 56ff, Zarlino hopes for the day when aesthetics is the point and not mechanical rules; 60; 62; 70ff, singing quality, improvisation; **VI:** 33, on words vs emotions; the effect of emotions on the listener

Zedler, Johann Heinrich, 1706–1751, author of *Universallexikon* (1735), **VI:** 147

Zeitz Stadtpfeifers, VI: 135 (in 1743)

Zeno, 333–261 BC, founder of the Stoic School, **I:** 283ff; 292; 374; **V:** 36, Greek philosopher quoted by Erasmus, the soul is a "self-moving harmony, and for this reason can be caught up and carried away by harmonious things"

Zeus, Greek god, **I:** 125; 267; 298; 309ff; 323; 437

Zeuxis, Greek painter mentioned by Cicero, **I:** 373

Zwingli, Huldreich, 1484–1531, Swiss reform cleric, **V:** 59, fn., 8; 63; 67; 75

ABOUT THE AUTHOR

DR. DAVID WHITWELL is a graduate ('with distinction') of the University of Michigan and the Catholic University of America, Washington, D.C. (PhD, Musicology, Distinguished Alumni Award, 2000) and has studied conducting with Eugene Ormandy and at the Akademie fur Musik, Vienna. Prior to coming to Northridge, Dr. Whitwell participated in concerts throughout the United States and Asia as Associate First Horn in the USAF Band and Orchestra in Washington, D.C., and in recitals throughout South America in cooperation with the United States State Department.

At the California State University, Northridge, which is in Los Angeles, Dr. Whitwell developed the CSUN Wind Ensemble into an ensemble of international reputation, with international tours to Europe in 1981 and 1989 and to Japan in 1984. The CSUN Wind Ensemble has made professional studio recordings for BBC (London), the Koln Westdeutscher Rundfunk (Germany), NOS National Radio (The Netherlands), Zurich Radio (Switzerland), the Television Broadcasting System (Japan) as well as for the United States State Department for broadcast on its 'Voice of America' program. The CSUN Wind Ensemble's recording with the Mirecourt Trio in 1982 was named the 'Record of the Year' by The Village Voice. Composers who have guest conducted Whitwell's ensembles include Aaron Copland, Ernest Krenek, Alan Hovhaness, Morton Gould, Karel Husa, Frank Erickson and Vaclav Nelhybel.

Dr. Whitwell has been a guest professor in 100 different universities and conservatories throughout the United States and in 23 foreign countries (most recently in China, in an elite school housed in the Forbidden City). Guest conducting experiences have included the Philadelphia Orchestra, Seattle Symphony Orchestra, the Czech Radio Orchestras of Brno and Bratislava, The National Youth Orchestra of Israel, as well as resident wind ensembles in Russia, Israel, Austria, Switzerland, Germany, England, Wales, The Netherlands, Portugal, Peru, Korea, Japan, Taiwan, Canada and the United States.

He is a past president of the College Band Directors National Association, a member of the Prasidium of the International Society for the Promotion of Band Music, and was a member of the found-

ing board of directors of the World Association for Symphonic Bands and Ensembles (WASBE). In 1964 he was made an honorary life member of Kappa Kappa Psi, a national professional music fraternity. In September, 2001, he was a delegate to the UNESCO Conference on Global Music in Tokyo. He has been knighted by sovereign organizations in France, Portugal and Scotland and has been awarded the gold medal of Kerkrade, The Netherlands, and the silver medal of Wangen, Germany, the highest honor given wind conductors in the United States, the medal of the Academy of Wind and Percussion Arts (National Band Association) and the highest honor given wind conductors in Austria, the gold medal of the Austrian Band Association. He is a member of the Hall of Fame of the California Music Educators Association.

Dr. Whitwell's publications include more than 127 articles on wind literature including publications in Music and Letters (London), the London Musical Times, the Mozart-Jahrbuch (Salzburg), and 60 books, among which is his 13-volume *History and Literature of the Wind Band and Wind Ensemble* and an 8-volume series on *Aesthetics in Music*. In addition to numerous modern editions of early wind band music his original compositions include 5 symphonies.

David Whitwell was named as one of six men who have determined the course of American bands during the second half of the 20th century, in the definitive history, *The Twentieth Century American Wind Band* (Meredith Music).

A doctoral dissertation by German Gonzales (2007, Arizona State University) is dedicated to the life and conducting career of David Whitwell through the year 1977. David Whitwell is one of nine men described by Paula A. Crider in *The Conductor's Legacy* (Chicago: GIA, 2010) as 'the legendary conductors' of the 20th century.

'I can't imagine the 2nd half of the 20th century—without David Whitwell and what he has given to all of the rest of us.' Frederick Fennell (1993)

ABOUT THE EDITOR

CRAIG DABELSTEIN began studying the piano at age seven and took up the saxophone at age twelve. Mr Dabelstein has Bachelor of Arts (Music) and Bachelor of Music degrees from the Queensland Conservatorium of Music, where he majored in the performance of classical saxophone repertoire. He also has a Graduate Diploma of Learning and Teaching and a Graduate Certificate in Editing and Publishing from the University of Southern Queensland.

He has held the principal alto and tenor saxophone chairs in the Australian Wind Orchestra and has been an augmenting member of the Queensland Philharmonic Orchestra, the Queensland Symphony Orchestra, and the Queensland Pops Orchestra. For many years he was also a member of the Queensland Saxophone Quartet.

He has been a casual conductor of the Young Conservatorium Symphonic Winds, and has previously been a saxophone teacher at the Queensland Conservatorium of Music. He is a regular conductor of the Queensland Wind Orchestra, having served as their artistic director and chief conductor from 2004 to 2009.

Craig Dabelstein is a research associate for the *Teaching Music Through Performance in Band* series of books, contributing analyses to volumes 7, 8, 1 (rev. edn), and the *Solos with Wind Band Accompaniment* volume. He served as the copyeditor and layout designer of the *Australian Clarinet and Saxophone Magazine* from 2007 to 2009 and he has written many CD and book reviews for *Music Forum* magazine. He is the editor of the second editions of the books by Dr. David Whitwell including *A Concise History of the Wind Band*, *Foundations of Music Education*, *Music Education of the Future*, *The Sousa Oral History Project*, *Wagner on Bands*, *Berlioz on Bands*, *The Art of Musical Conducting*, and the *Aesthetics of Music* series (8 volumes) and *The History and Literature of the Wind Band and Wind Ensemble* series (13 volumes). From 1994 to 2012 he was a staff member at Brisbane Girls Grammar School. He now teaches woodwinds and conducts bands at St. Joseph's College, Gregory Terrace, Brisbane, Australia.